Self-Made Man

My year disguised as a man

NORAH VINCENT

ATLANTIC BOOKS

LONDON

To my beloved wife, Lisa McNulty,
who saves my life on a daily basis.

First published in the United States of America in 2006 by Viking,
an imprint of Penguin Group (USA) Inc.

First published in Great Britain in 2006 by Atlantic Books,
an imprint of Grove Atlantic Ltd.

9 8 7 6 5 4 3 2

A CIP catalogue record for this book is available from the British Library.

1 84354 503 9

Printed in Great Britain by CPD (Wales) Ltd, Ebbw Vale

Atlantic Books
An imprint of Grove Atlantic Ltd
Ormond House
26-27 Boswell Street
London WC1N 3JZ

www.groveatlantic.co.uk

But this my masculine usurped attire . . .
Conceal me what I am, and be my aid
For such disguise as haply shall become
The form of my intent . . .
Disguise, I see, thou art a wickedness
Wherein the pregnant enemy does much.

Shakespeare, *Twelfth Night*

Were it not better,
Because that I am more than common tall,
That I did suit me all points like a man?
Lie there what hidden woman's fear there will,
We'll have a swashing and a martial outside,
As many other mannish cowards have
That do outface it with their semblances.

Shakespeare, *As You Like It*

Contents

Self-Made Man

1 | Getting Started

Seven years ago, I had my first tutorial in becoming a man.

The idea for this book came to me then, when I went out for the first time in drag. I was living in the East Village at the time, undergoing a significantly delayed adolescence, drinking and drugging a little too much, and indulging in all the sidewalk freak show opportunities that New York City has to offer.

Back then I was hanging around a lot with a drag king whom I had met through friends. She used to like to dress up and have me take pictures of her in costume. One night she dared me to dress up with her and go out on the town. I'd always wanted to try passing as a man in public, just to see if I could do it, so I agreed enthusiastically.

She had developed her own technique for creating a beard whereby you cut half-inch chunks of hair from unobtrusive parts of your own head, snipped them into smaller pieces and then more or less glopped them onto your face with spirit gum. Using a small, round freestanding mirror on her desk, she showed me how to do it in the dim, greenish light of her cramped studio apartment. It wasn't at all precise and it wouldn't have passed muster in daylight, but it was sufficient for the stage, and it would work well enough for our purposes in dark bars at night. I made myself a goatee and mustache, and a pair of exaggerated sideburns. I put on a baseball cap, loose-fitting jeans and a flannel shirt. In the full-length mirror I looked like a frat boy—sort of.

She did her thing—which was more willowy and faint, more like a young hippie guy who couldn't really grow much of a beard—and we went out like that for a few hours.

We passed, as far as I could tell, but I was too afraid to really interact with anyone, except to give one guy brief directions on the street. He thanked me as "dude" and walked on.

Mostly, though, we just walked through the Village scanning people's faces to see if anyone took a second or third look. But no one did. And that, oddly enough, was the thing that struck me the most about that evening. It was the only thing of real note that happened. But it was significant.

I had lived in that neighborhood for years, walking its streets, where men lurk outside of bodegas, on stoops and in doorways much of the day. As a woman, you couldn't walk down those streets invisibly. You were an object of desire or at least semiprurient interest to the men who waited there, even if you weren't pretty—that, or you were just another pussy to be put in its place. Either way, their eyes followed you all the way up and down the street, never wavering, asserting their dominance as a matter of course. If you were female and you lived there, you got used to being stared down because it happened every day and there wasn't anything you could do about it.

But that night in drag, we walked by those same stoops and doorways and bodegas. We walked by those same groups of men. Only this time they didn't stare. On the contrary, when they met my eyes they looked away immediately and concertedly and never looked back. It was astounding, the difference, the respect they showed me by *not* looking at me, by purposely not staring.

That was it. That was what had annoyed me so much about meeting their gaze as a woman, not the desire, if that was ever there, but the disrespect, the entitlement. It was rude, and it was meant to be rude, and seeing those guys looking away deferentially when they thought I was male, I could validate in retrospect the true hostility of their former stares.

But that wasn't quite all there was to it. There was something more than respect being communicated in their averted gaze, something subtler, less direct. It was more like a disinclination to show disrespect. For them, to look away was to decline a challenge, to adhere to a code of behavior that kept the peace among human males in certain spheres just as surely as it kept the peace and the pecking order among male animals. To look another male in the eye and hold his gaze is to invite conflict, either that or a homosexual encounter. To look away is to accept the status quo, to leave each man to his tiny sphere of influence, the small buffer of pride and poise that surrounds and keeps him.

I surmised all of this the night it happened, but in the weeks and months that followed I asked most of the men I knew whether I was right, and they agreed, adding usually that it wasn't something they thought about anymore, if they ever had. It was just something you learned or absorbed as a boy, and by the time you were a man, you did it without thinking.

After the incident had blown over, I started thinking that if after being in drag for only a few hours I had learned such an important secret about the way males and females communicate with each other, and about the unspoken codes of male experience, then couldn't I potentially observe much more about the social differences between the sexes if I passed as a man for a much longer period of time? It seemed true, but I wasn't intrepid enough yet to do something that extreme. Besides, it seemed impossible, both psychologically and practically, to pull it off. So I filed the information away in my mind for a few more years and got on with other things.

Then, in the winter of 2003, while watching a reality television show on the A&E network, the idea came back to me. In the show, two male and two female contestants set out to transform themselves into the opposite sex—not with hormones or surgeries, but purely by costume and design. The women cut their hair. The men had theirs extended. Both took voice and movement lessons to learn how to speak and behave more like the sex they were trying to become. All chose new wardrobes and names for their alter egos. Though the point of the exercise was to see who could pass in the real world most effectively, the bulk of the program focused on the transformations themselves. Neither of the men really passed, and only one of the women stayed the course. She did manage to pass fairly well, though only for a short time and in carefully controlled circumstances.

As in most reality television shows, especially the American ones, nobody involved was particularly introspective about the effect their experiences had had on them or the people around them. It was clear that the producers didn't have much interest in the deeper sociological implications of passing as the opposite sex. It was all just another version of an extreme makeover. Once the stunt was accomplished—or not—the show was over.

But for me, watching the show brought my former experience in drag to the forefront of my mind again and made me realize that passing in costume in the daylight could be possible with the right help. I knew that writing a book about passing in the world as a man would give me the chance to survey some of the unexplored territory that the show had left out, and that I had barely broached in my brief foray in drag years before.

I was determined to give the idea a try.

But first things first. Before I could build this man I was to become, I had to think of an identity for him. I needed a name. The name had to be something familiar, something I might respond to when called. Failing to answer to my name would surely give me away as an impostor. For convenience I wanted something that started with the letter N. That narrowed the options considerably, and most of them were unappealing. There was no way, for example, that I was going to be known as Norman or Norm. Nick, when paired with Norah, seemed a little too clever by half, and Neil or Nate just didn't suit me.

That's when I hit upon the name Ned, a nickname from childhood that had long since fallen out of use, but one that was, as it happened, intimately tied to the project at hand.

I got the name Ned when I was about seven. I got it partly because Norah is a hard name to nick, but mostly because nothing but a boy's name really made sense when you saw what my parents were faced with in their only daughter. Practically from birth, I was the kind of hard-core tomboy that makes you think there must be a gay gene.

How else to explain my instinctive loathing for dresses, dolls and frills of any kind when other girls delighted in such things? How else to explain the weird attachments and fetishes that came so young and against all social programming? Why, for example, did I insist on dressing like a ranch hand when I was barely out of diapers? Why did I choose to play the saxophone when every other girl chose the flute or the clarinet? Why did I covet my father's tube of VO5, and shave my brothers' GI Joes with his razors? Why was the only female doll I ever owned or liked an armor-clad Joan of Arc?

Impossible to say, really. Gender identity, it seems, is in the genes as surely as sex and sexuality are, but we don't know why the programming deviates. Maybe a crossed wire somewhere, or the hormonal equivalent. It seems as likely an explanation as any for how it is that even before she's old enough to know the meaning of desire or cultural signifiers, being born gay tends to make a girl crave helmets and hiking boots. Whatever the case, I was the happily twisted result of some gland or helix gone awry, a fate that found me playing Tarzan high in the apple tree on summer afternoons, and dressing in full-blown drag for Halloween by the time I was seven.

My mother has since said that she should have suspected something then, when I borrowed one of my father's blazers and a porkpie hat, drew a beard and mustache on my face and went out trick-or-treating with all the other fairies and witches. I was, I said, going as an old man. I slid a pillow under the blazer to make a belly and I carried a cane.

But what would she have known, when I might well have been imitating her? She was an actor, and I had spent many childhood summers scampering around backstage or lurking in her dressing room as she made up for a show. One of her most memorable parts was a dual role in which she played Shen Te and Mr. Shui Ta in Bertolt Brecht's *The Good Person of Setzuan*. Shen Te is a kind-hearted ex-prostitute who owns a tobacco shop in the Chinese province of Sichuan. Prey to swindlers and malingerers who take her for a pushover, Shen Te is facing financial ruin. To save her business, she disguises herself as a man, Mr. Shui Ta, her supposed ruthless male cousin, whom she invokes to do the dirty work of collecting debts and fending off beggars and thieves.

How could seeing my mother in this role have had anything but a profoundly inspiring effect on me, a kid already fascinated by disguise? Did women really pretend to be men in real life? What if they could, I wondered, and what could they get away with? My eyes widened at the prospect.

Thankfully, for my parents' sake, my two older brothers were normal. The oldest, Alex, the consummate gentleman, also from birth, was often silently bewildered, but always kind and accommodating. Teddy, the middle one, was not. He was a hellion, the nicknamer in the family and ruthless at his trade. He was the real impetus behind Ned.

You see, Ned had a deeper meaning, connected intimately not only with my being a tomboy, but with the problems that that particular affliction presents in and around puberty. That's the time in a tomboy's life when sexual maturity and gender identity come smack up against each other in an unpleasant way.

Having older brothers means that the girls they know and like reach puberty before you do. This was always cause for anxiety among the girls I knew, since getting your period and—the real prize—growing incipient breasts was the gate we were all waiting to pass through. It meant everything. For one, it meant that you were suddenly of interest to the other half of the species. Until then, you were just dirty knees and elbows with nothing to show for yourself but the spaces between your teeth. Until then, you were just the last one picked for kick ball, and in my case, the lousy tagalong little sister who got no respect. But those early bloomers that my older brother and his friends were always ogling, the shapely sixth graders with lip gloss and B cups, they *had* something, and it drove gangly ragamuffins like me into frowning, envious retreats. Our lack of development was a sore subject not to be broached.

But broaching the unbroachable is what infernal brothers are for.

After school one day, Teddy and his friends found me playing with my small plastic army men on the front lawn. Bored as usual, they began taunting me about my lack of physical development. The unbroachable. I cowered, hoping they'd drift off if they didn't get a rise out of me. But Teddy was inspired on this particular day. The nickname Ned was already in use by this time—they'd all been using it in their taunts, none of which was remarkable enough to remember. That is, until Teddy shouted above the fray the unforgettable and infuriating:

"Ned ass and no tits."

Unsurprisingly, this elicited howls of laughter from the group.

It was true. Ned indeed had no ass and no tits and Ned knew it and wasn't happy about it. I didn't look up at this point, but I began pulling up fistfuls of grass. Then for some unknown reason—who, after all, can fathom the adolescent stream of consciousness— Teddy began shaking his hips back and forth suggestively, the way a bimbo who had hips or an ass might, and singing the word "milkshake!" as he did so. Naturally, all of his friends found this endlessly amusing and chimed in.

At this I promptly snapped. The sight of five boys loudly and publicly lampooning my pained, pathetic prepubescence in song was simply too much for me. I stood up, went into the garage, and emerged—by then in a teeth-gritting rage—brandishing one of Teddy's ice hockey sticks. The boys found this funniest of all, which, of course, enraged me even more. I chased them around the neighborhood with the hockey stick for a good hour, with them laughing, dancing and shouting "milkshake," then running and hiding, and me stalking and screaming and swinging.

And so, Ned was born. And that, in truth, was where this book began—that is, with the Ned who had no ass and no tits.

In Ned I had my new name and a starting point for a male identity. But once I had resolved to become Ned, I still had a fair amount of work to do to make passing as a man in daylight feasible on a regular basis. The first and most important step was to find out how to make a more believable beard than the slapdash version my drag king friend had taught me years before, something that would look real at close range over the course of an entire day or evening if need be.

As it happened I was lucky in this department. I had a lot of friends in theater, many of whom proved helpful in bringing Ned to life.

I decided to consult Ryan, a makeup artist of my acquaintance, who told me about a facial hair technique he'd used in a recent show. He said he thought it might work for me on the street if used sparingly.

It was far more subtle and specialized than the glue job I'd done in the Village, though in the end far simpler.

First, Ryan suggested using wool crepe hair instead of my own or someone else's real hair. Wool crepe hair comes in long braided ropes, which you can buy from specialty makeup companies. It's offered in a whole range of colors, from platinum blond to black, so I could buy whatever shade best matched my hair and always have a ready supply at hand without having to butcher my haircut.

Ryan showed me how to unwind the braids, comb the strands of hair together, then take the ends between my thumb and index finger and cut them with a hairdressing scissor into millimeter- or smaller-size pieces. By cutting them onto a piece of white paper and spreading them evenly across it, he showed me how to avoid clumping the hair when I applied the pieces to my face. He suggested using a makeup brush to do this—a large blush brush for my chin and cheeks, and a small eye shadow brush for my upper lip.

Next he applied a lanolin and beeswax-based adhesive called stoppelpaste to the portions of my face where I wanted the hair to stick. This would work better than spirit gum for several reasons. It's invisible, whereas spirit gum tends to turn white on the skin and show through, unless you're wearing a full hairpiece, which doesn't ever look real on a woman's face in the daylight. (I tried this.) Also, stoppelpaste is gentle on the skin, and can be taken off with a moisturizing makeup remover. Spirit gum, by contrast, must be removed with a harsh acetone thinner. It also dries and stiffens quickly. Stoppelpaste doesn't. This, I imagined, would give me more freedom of movement and natural expression, an indispensable tool for making Ned believable.

At room temperature stoppelpaste is fairly dense stuff and tends not to spread easily, so Ryan suggested using a hair dryer to heat it for a few seconds before applying it. This melted it just enough to make it roll on smoothly. Doing one small patch at a time, he applied the stoppelpaste to my face, then dabbed the makeup brush in the clippings, then patted my face lightly with the brush until my whole chin and upper lip were covered in a light stubble.

Later, as I refined this process, I found that the scissors didn't produce small enough pieces. If the pieces were too long, they tended to look more like they were glued to my face rather than growing out of it. I needed to make the pieces minuscule, so that they would look almost like dots. To achieve this effect, or the closest I could come, I bought a men's electric beard trimmer and ran it across the tips of the hair, producing actual stubble-length pieces that, when applied, looked like a five o'clock shadow.

The key with the beard was not to put it on too heavily. My skin, like most women's, is not only softer to the touch, but much smoother to the eye than a man's. It's also quite pale and pink in the cheeks. Consequently, as Ned, people were always telling me that I looked a lot younger than thirty-five, even though I had a lot of gray in my hair. But if your skin goes from peaches and cream above your cheekbones to Don Johnson below you look a little like Fred Flintstone. So I had to be careful not to get carried away with the stubble and try to stay within the bounds of what a young, fairly hairless man with fine skin would believably grow.

To help square my jaw I went to the barber and asked him to cut my hair in a flat top—a haircut I usually abhor on men, but which did a lot under the circumstances to masculinize my head. Then I went to the optician and picked out two pairs of rectangular frames, again to accentuate the angles of my face. One pair was metal, for all the occasions when I'd want to look more casual, and one was tortoiseshell, for the occasions—like work or on dates—when I'd want a more stylish look.

With the beard and the flat top, the glasses helped a lot in getting me to see myself as someone else, though the transformation was psychological more than anything else, and it took time to sink in. At first, I had a lot of trouble seeing myself as anyone but myself with hair glued to my face. I'd been looking at my face all my life, and I'd had short haircuts for much of that time. The stubble didn't really change that. I was still me. But the glasses did change that, or at least they began to. Then it became a mind game that I played with myself, and soon, with everyone else as well.

In the beginning I was so worried about getting caught—not passing—that in order to ensure my disguise I wore my glasses everywhere, and often a baseball hat, along, of course, with the meticulously applied beard. But as time went on, as I became more confident in my disguise, more buried in my character, I began to project a masculine image more naturally, and the props I had used to create that image became less and less important, until sometimes I didn't need them at all.

People accept what you convey to them, if you convey it convincingly enough. Even I began to accept more willingly the image reflected in the mirror, just as the people around me eventually did.

Once I'd finished doctoring my head and face, I began concentrating on my body.

First I had to find a way to bind my breasts. This is trickier than it sounds, even when you're small breasted, especially when you're determined to have the flattest possible front. First I tried the obvious—Ace bandages. I bought two of the four-inch-wide variety and strapped them tightly around me, fixing them in place with surgical tape to make sure that they wouldn't unwind midday. This made my chest very flat, but it also made breathing painful and labored. Also, depending on how I was sitting, after a while the binding often slipped down and pushed my breasts up and together instead of out and down. Not a good look for a man.

In the end, cupless sports bras worked best. I bought them two sizes too small and in a flat-fronted style. Naked, it didn't make me a board, but with a loose shirt and some creative layering it worked fine. It was the most dependable method. It never moved. It never fell. It did, however, dig into my shoulders and back, especially as I got bigger.

And I did get bigger. That was the next step in transforming my body. Lifting weights. Lots of weights. I consulted a trainer at my local gym, telling him about the project and asking his advice about how best to masculinize my body as much as possible without using steroids. He suggested building muscle bulk in my shoulders and arms.

Building muscle bulk happens in a two-step process. First by lifting heavy weights at low repetitions, and second by eating your body weight or more in grams of protein per day.

Each day I trained a different muscle. Through the week I worked each body part to exhaustion, but only once a week, taking at least one day off on the weekends for recovery. In my off time I ate and drank as much protein as I could shove down my neck. After six months, I'd gained fifteen pounds. I was still a small guy by normal measures, but my shoulders were recognizably broader and squarer, and this alone pushed me one step closer to manhood.

To complete the physical transformation, I went in search of a prosthetic penis that I could wear for verisimilitude as much as anything else. At a sex shop in downtown Manhattan I found what I have since come to refer to as a "packable softie." This wasn't a dildo, which, at its full and constant tumescence would have proven uncomfortable for me and alarming for everyone around me. Instead, this item, which I nicknamed "Sloppy Joe," was a flaccid member designed especially for what drag kings call packing, or stuffing, your pants. It was better than a sock, and would give me, if not others, a more realistic experience of "manhood." To keep it in place I wore it inside a jockstrap, since in a pair of tighty whities it moved too far afield when I walked and became too much of a distraction.

Finally, once the basic anatomy was in place, boobs strapped in, shoulders squared, beard applied and cock tucked, I took Ned shopping for clothes, in drag, of course. I bought him preppy, safe things like rugby shirts and khakis and baggy jeans. I didn't want to splurge on a suit, but Ned needed a wardrobe for work, so I bought him three blazers, several pairs of dress slacks, four ties and five or six dress shirts. I bought a large supply of men's white crew neck undershirts, which proved to be a staple of my wardrobe, casual or dress. I wore them under everything, partly as an extra layer to hide the seams of my bra, and partly to stouten my neck, or at least distract the looker's eye from my lack of Adam's apple and my hairless chest.

I made my last stop for Ned at the Juilliard School for the Performing Arts, where I hired a voice coach to help me learn to speak more like a man. My voice is already deep, but as with so many other things, I found that when you are trying to pass in drag, all the characteristics that seem masculine in you as a woman turn out to be far less so in a man.

My tutor went over a few gender cues in our lessons, but it took being Ned for quite some time before I realized just how differently men and women talk and how much damping down I would have to do as Ned so as not to arouse suspicion.

My tutor said, "Women tend to bankrupt their own breath." She described and demonstrated the process by thrusting her chest and head forward when she spoke, and cutting off the rhythm of her breathing as she forced a stream of words from her mouth.

"Admittedly, this is a stereotype," she said, "but generally women tend to speak more quickly and to use more words, and they interrupt their breathing in order to get it all out."

I found this to be true in my own speech patterns, which jesting friends have sometimes described as torrential. I often run out of breath before I've finished my thought, and either have to gasp in the middle to make it through, or push the words out faster to finish sooner.

Since my training, I have also observed this phenomenon in action at various dinner parties or in restaurants. Women often

lean into a conversation and speak in wordy bursts, asking
heard. Men often lean back and pronounce with terse auth

Naturally, what you do with your breath affects how your
voice will sound. Using fewer words, speaking more slowly and
sustaining my breath through the words all helped me to use the
deeper notes in my register and to stay there. This meant, of
course, that I couldn't allow myself to get too excited about anything, because this would change my breathing, and my voice
would pinch up to its higher reaches. Conversely, I found that relaxing and breathing deeply before I embarked on a day as Ned
helped me to get into his voice, then his bearing and then his head.

The process of getting into Ned's head raises an obvious question,
and one that many people have asked about this book, mostly as a
means of clarifying exactly what the book is meant to be and what
they should expect to get out of it.

Am I a transsexual or a transvestite, and did I write this book
as a means of coming out as such?

The answer to both parts of that question is no.

I say this with the benefit of experimental hindsight, because
after having lived as a man on and off for a year and a half, if I
were either a transsexual or a true lifestyle transvestite, I can assure you that I would know it by now.

For one thing, I would have experienced far more satisfaction
living as Ned.

Transsexuals generally report that passing as a member of the
opposite sex is an immense and pleasurable relief. They feel that
they have finally come into their own after many years of living in
disguise.

Just the opposite was true for me.

I rarely enjoyed and never felt in any way fulfilled personally by being perceived and treated as a man. I have never, as many transsexuals assert, felt myself to be a man trapped in the wrong body. On the contrary, I identify deeply with both my femaleness and my femininity, such as it is, more so after Ned, in fact, than ever before.

As you will see, being Ned was often an uncomfortable and alienating experience, and far from finding myself in him, I usually felt kept from myself in some elemental way. While living as Ned, I had to work hard to make myself do his work, to be him. It did not come naturally at all, and once he had served his purpose, I was happy to discard him.

As for cross-dressing, this, too, was not definitive for me or particularly enjoyable. I can't deny the brief thrill I felt in getting away with the disguise, and in seeing a part of everyday life that other women don't see. Wearing a dick between my legs was an odd and mildly titillating experience for a day or two. But that frisson wore off quickly, and I found myself inhabiting a persona that wasn't mine, trying to approximate something that I am not and did not wish to be.

This is, therefore, not a confessional memoir. I am not resolving a sexual identity crisis. There is intimate territory being explored here. No question. As my childhood proclivities can attest, I have always been and remain fascinated, puzzled and even disturbed at times by gender, both as a cultural and a psychological phenomenon whose boundaries are both mysteriously fluid and rigid. Culturally speaking, I have always lived as my truest self somewhere on the boundary between masculine and feminine, and living there has made this project more immediate and meaningful to me. What's more, I did partake in my own experiment, live it and internalize its effects. Being Ned changed me and the people around me, and I have attempted to record those changes.

But to say that I conducted and recorded the results of an experiment is not to say that this book pretends to be a scientific or objective study. Not even close. Nothing I say here will have any value except as one person's observations about her own experience. What follows is just my view of things, myopic and certainly inapplicable to anything so grand as a pronouncement on gender in American society. My observations are full of my own prejudices and preconceptions, though I have tried as much as possible to qualify them accordingly. This book is a travelogue as much as anything else, and a circumscribed one at that, a six-city tour of an entire continent, a woman's-eye view of one guy's approximated life, not an authoritative guide to the whole vast and variegated terrain of manhood in America.

I wanted to taste portions of male experience and I wanted the people I met, the characters, their stories and our shared encounters to play as large a role as possible in my reportage. Yet I knew I had to impose some organizing principle on the final product.

I found that simply walking down the street as a man, while fruitful the first time or two I did it, didn't give me enough substantive material to work with in the long term. I needed, I realized, to create discrete experiences for Ned in which he would make friends, socialize, work, date and be himself around people who didn't know him, but whom he would get to know and sketch as more than acquaintances. True immersion was required, as were sustainable characters in manageable settings. I felt it would be too unwieldy to throw dozens of people at the reader in one long, confusing march of scattered themes and impressions, so instead, I chose to confine each setting and cast of characters to one chapter, and let the significant themes emerge from there.

Chapter two, for example, is about my eight-month stint on a men's bowling team. Leisure, play and friendship are the salient themes, though others do present themselves and recur in later chapters. Chapter four is about strip club culture. Sex drive and fantasy are its prevailing themes. Chapters three and six cover the more normative experiences of dating and working as a man, while chapters five and seven—which take place in a monastery and a men's movement group, respectively—represent my attempts to use the advantage of my male trappings to do what I could never do as a woman: infiltrate exclusive all-male environments and if possible learn their secrets.

I had each of these experiences in the order in which they appear—that is, I finished the season on the men's bowling team before I went to the monastery, or to work, or to the men's group meetings—so the general timeline is preserved, as well, I hope, as the sense of Ned's accumulated growth and knowledge about masculine experience.

In order to disguise the identities of those involved, I have changed the names of every character, place of business and institution, and purposely omitted all specific references to location. So while I conducted my experiment in five separate states, in three different regions of the United States, I have avoided naming those states or regions.

Finally, a word on method. It will become clear to you if it is not already that I deceived a lot of people in order to write this book. I can make only one excuse for this. Deception is part and parcel of imposture, and imposture was necessary in this experiment. It could not have been otherwise. In order to see how people would treat me as a man, I had to make them believe that I was a man, and accordingly I had to hide from them the fact that I am a woman. Doing so entailed various breaches of trust, some more serious than others. This may not sit well with some or perhaps most of you. In certain ways it did not sit well with me either, and was, as you will see, a source of considerable strain as time wore on.

I began my journey with a fairly naive idea about what to expect. I thought that passing was going to be the hardest part. But it wasn't at all. I did that far more easily than I thought I would. The difficulty lay in the consequences of passing, and that I had not even considered. As I lived snippets of a male life, one part of my brain was duly taking notes and making observations, intellectualizing the raw material of Ned's experience, but another part of my brain, the subconscious part, was taking blows to the head, and eventually those injuries caught up with me.

In that sense I can say with relative surety that in the end I paid a higher emotional price for my circumstantial deceptions than any of my subjects did. And that is, I think, penalty enough for meddling.

2 | Friendship

When I told my proudly self-confessed trailer-trash girlfriend that Ned was joining a men's bowling league, she said by way of advice, "Just remember that the difference between your people and my people is that my people bowl without irony." Translation: hide your bourgeois flag, or you'll get the smugness beaten out of you long before they find out you're a woman.

People who play in leagues for money take bowling seriously, and they don't take kindly to journalists infiltrating their hard-won social lives, especially when the interloper in question hasn't bowled more than five times in her life, and then only for a lark.

But my ineptitude and oddball status notwithstanding, bowling was the obvious choice. It's the ultimate social sport, and as such it would be a perfect way for Ned to make friends with guys as a guy. Better yet, I wouldn't have to expose any suspicious body parts or break a heavy sweat and risk smearing my beard.

Still, in practice, it wasn't as easy as it sounded. Taking that first step through the barrier between Ned the character in my head and Ned the real guy among the fellas proved to be more jarring than I could have ever imagined.

Any smartly dressed woman who has ever walked the gauntlet of construction workers on lunch break or otherwise found herself suddenly alone in unfamiliar male company with her sex on her sleeve will understand a lot of how it felt to walk into that bowling alley for the first time on men's league night. Those guys may not have known that I was a woman, but the minute I opened the door and felt the air of that place waft over me, every part of me did.

My eyes blurred in panic. I didn't see anything. I remember being aware only of a wave of noise and imagined distrust coming at me from undistinguishable faces. Probably only one or two people actually turned to look, but it felt as if every pair of eyes in the place had landed on me and stuck.

I'd felt a milder version of this before in barbershops or auto body shops. This palpable unbelonging that came of being the sole female in an all-male environment. And the feeling went right through my disguise and my nerve and told me that I wasn't fooling anyone.

This was a men's club, and men's clubs have an aura about them, a mostly forbidding aura that hangs in the air. Females tend to respond to it viscerally, as they are meant to. The unspoken signs all say NO GIRLS ALLOWED and KEEP OUT or, more idly, ENTER AT YOUR OWN RISK.

As a woman, you don't belong. You're not wanted. And every part of you knows it, and is just begging you to get up and leave.

And I nearly did leave, even though I'd only made it two steps inside the door and hadn't even been able to look up yet for fear of meeting anyone's eyes. After standing there frozen for several minutes, I had just about worked up the gumption to retreat and call off the whole thing when the league manager saw me.

"Are you Ned?" he asked, rushing up to me. "We've been waiting for you."

He was a tiny, wizened stick figure, with a five-day growth of gray stubble on his chin, a crew cut to match, a broken front tooth and a black watch cap.

I had called earlier in the week to find out about the league, and he'd told me what time to show up and which guy to ask for when I got there. I was late already, and my nervous hesitations had made me later.

"Yeah," I croaked, trying to keep my voice down and my demeanor unshaken.

"Great," he said, grabbing me by the arm. "C'mon and get yourself some shoes and a ball."

"Okay," I said, following his lead.

There was no getting out of it now.

He walked me over to the front desk and left me there with the attendant, who was helping another bowler. As I stood waiting, I was able for the first time to focus on something beyond myself and my fear of immediate detection. I looked at the rows of cubbyholes behind the desk, all with those familiar red, blue and white paneled shoes stuffed in them in pairs. Seeing them comforted me a little. They reminded me of the good times I'd always had bowling with friends as a kid, and I felt a little surge of carelessness at the prospect of making a fool out of myself. So what if I couldn't bowl? This was an experiment about people, not sport, and nobody had yet pointed and laughed. Maybe I could do this after all.

I got my shoes, took them over to a row of orange plastic bucket chairs and sat down to change. This gave me a few more minutes to take in the scene, a few more minutes to breathe and watch people's eyes to see if they followed me, or if they passed over me and moved on.

A quick scan satisfied me that nobody seemed suspicious.

So far so good.

I'd chosen well in choosing a bowling alley. It was just like every other bowling alley I'd ever seen; it felt familiar. The decor was lovingly down at heel and generic to the last detail, like something out of a mail-order kit, complete with the cheap plywood paneling and the painted slogans on the walls that said: BOWLING IS FAMILY FUN. There were the usual shabby cartoons of multicolored balls and pins flying through the air, and the posted scores of top bowlers. The lanes, too, were just as I remembered them, long and glistening with that mechanized maw scraping at the end.

And then, of course, there were the smells; cigarette smoke, varnish, machine oil, leaky toilets, old candy wrappers and accumulated public muck all commingling to produce that signature bowling alley scent that envelops you the moment you enter and clings to you long after.

As far as I could see, only one thing had really changed in the last fifteen years. Scoring wasn't done by hand anymore. Instead, everything was computerized. You just entered the names and averages of each player on the console at your table, and the computer did the rest, registering scores, calculating totals and flashing them on monitors above each lane.

As I scoped the room, I noticed the team captains all busily attending to their monitors. Meanwhile their teammates were strapping on wrist braces and dusting their palms with rosin, or taking advantage of a few last minutes of pregame practice.

I could see then that this was going to be laughable. They were all throwing curve balls that they'd been perfecting for twenty years. I couldn't even remember how to hold a bowling ball, much less wing it with any precision. And that was the least of my worries. I was in drag in a well-lighted place, surrounded by some sixty-odd guys who would have made me very nervous under normal circumstances.

I was dressed as down and dirty as Ned got in a plaid shirt, jeans and a baseball cap pulled low over the most proletarian glasses I could find. But despite my best efforts, I was still far too scrubbed and tweedy amid these genuine articles to pass for one of them. Even at my burliest, next to them I felt like a petunia strapped to a Popsicle stick.

I was surrounded by men who had cement dust in their hair and sawdust under their fingernails. They had nicotine-sallowed faces that looked like ritual masks, and their hands were as tough and scarred as falcon gloves. These were men who, as one of them told me later, had been shoveling shit their whole lives.

Looking at them I thought: it's at times like these when the term "real man" really hits home with you, and you understand in some elemental way that the male animal is definitely not a social construct.

I didn't see how this could possibly work. If I was passing, I was passing as a boy, not a man, and a candy boy at that. But if they were judging me, you wouldn't have known it from the way they greeted me.

The league manager led me toward the table where my new teammates were sitting. As we approached, they all turned to face me.

Jim, my team captain, introduced himself first. He was about five feet six, a good four inches shorter than I am, with a light-weight build, solid shoulders, but skinny legs and oddly small feet—certainly smaller than mine, which have now topped out at an alarming men's eleven and a half. This made me feel a little better. He actually came across as diminutive. He wore his baseball cap high on his head, and a football jersey that draped over his jeans almost to his knees. He had a mustache and a neat goatee. Both were slightly redder than his light brown head of hair, and effectively hid the boyish vulnerability of his mouth. He was thirty-three, but in bearing, he seemed younger. He wasn't a threat to anyone and he knew it, as did everyone who met him. But he wasn't a weak link either. He was the scrappy guy in the pickup basketball game.

As he extended his arm to shake my hand, I extended mine, too, in a sweeping motion. Our palms met with a soft *pop,* and I squeezed assertively the way I'd seen men do at parties when they gathered in someone's living room to watch a football game. From the outside, this ritual had always seemed overdone to me. Why all the macho ceremony? But from the inside it was completely different. There was something so warm and bonded in this handshake. Receiving it was a rush, an instant inclusion in a camaraderie that felt very old and practiced.

It was more affectionate than any handshake I'd ever received from a strange woman. To me, woman-to-woman introductions often seem fake and cold, full of limp gentility. I've seen a lot of women hug one another this way, too, sometimes even women who've known each other for a long time and think of themselves as being good friends. They're like two backward magnets pushed together by convention. Their arms and cheeks meet, and maybe the tops of their shoulders, but only briefly, the briefest time politeness will allow. It's done out of habit and for appearances, a hollow, even resentful, gesture bred into us and rarely felt.

This solidarity of sex was something that feminism tried to teach us, and something, it now seemed to me, that men figured out and perfected a long time ago. On some level men didn't need to learn or remind themselves that brotherhood was powerful. It was just something they seemed to know.

When this man whom I'd never met before shook my hand he gave me something real. He included me. But most of the women I'd ever shaken hands with or even hugged had held something back, as if we were in constant competition with each other, or secretly suspicious, knowing it but not knowing it, and going through the motions all the same. In my view bra burning hadn't changed that much.

Next I met Allen. His greeting echoed Jim's. It had a pronounced positive force behind it, a presumption of goodwill that seemed to mark me as a buddy from the start, no questions asked, unless or until I proved otherwise.

"Hey, man," he said. "Glad to see you."

He was about Jim's height and similarly built. He had the same goatee and mustache, too. He was older, though, and looked it. At forty-four, he was a study in substance abuse and exposure to the elements. His face was permanently flushed and pocked with open pores; a cigarette-, alcohol- and occupation-induced complexion that his weather-bleached blond hair and eyebrows emphasized by contrast.

Bob I met last. We didn't shake hands, just nodded from across the table. He was short, too, but not lean. He was forty-two and he had a serious middle-aged belly filling out his T-shirt, the unbeltable kind that made you wonder what held up his pants. He had sizable arms, but no legs or ass, the typical beer-hewn silhouette. He had a ragged salt-and-pepper mustache, and wore large glasses with no-nonsense metal frames and slightly tinted aviator lenses.

He wasn't the friendly type.

Thankfully, Jim did most of the talking that first night, and with his eyes, he included me in the conversation from the beginning.

He had known Bob and Allen for a long time. They had all been playing golf and poker together several times a month for years, and Allen was married to Bob's sister. I was a stranger out of nowhere without any shared work or home life experience to offer, and Jim's social generosity gave me an in.

He was a natural comedian and raconteur, easy to listen to and talk to; the most open of the bunch by far, and charming as hell. He told stories of the worst beatings he'd taken in his life—and it sounded like there were quite a few—as if they were parties he'd been privileged to attend. He had a robust sense of his own absurdity and a charming willingness to both assign and ridicule his own role in whatever fate he'd been privy to. Even the most rotten things he'd been handed in life, things that were in no way his fault, things like his wife's ongoing ill health—first cancer, then hepatitis, then cancer again—he took with a surprising lack of bitterness. He never fumed about anything, at least not in front of us. That, it seemed, was a private indulgence, and his only apparent public indulgences were of the physical variety—cigarettes, a few beers out of the case he always brought for the team and junk food.

We all usually ate junk food on those Monday nights, all of us except Bob, who stuck to beer, but let us send his twelve-year-old son Alex, who always tagged along on league night, next door to the 7-Eleven to buy hot dogs, candy, soda, whatever. We always tipped the kid a little for his services, a dollar here and there, or the change from our purchases.

Alex was clearly there to spend some quality time with his dad, but Bob mostly kept him at bay. If we weren't sending him next door to fetch snacks, Bob was usually fobbing him off in some other way with a few extra dollars. He'd encourage him to go and bowl a few practice frames in one of the empty lanes at the end of the alley, or play one of the video games against the back wall. Alex was immature for his age, a chatty kid, and a bit of a nudge, always full of trivia questions or rambling anecdotes about some historical fact he'd learned in school. Typical kids' stuff, but I couldn't really blame Bob for wanting to keep him occupied elsewhere. If you let Alex hang on your arm, he would, and he'd make you wish you hadn't. Besides, this was men's night out, and most of what we talked about wasn't for kids' ears.

I noticed, though, that no one ever tempered his speech when Alex was around. We swore like stevedores, and nobody seemed bothered, including me, that a twelve-year-old was within earshot. I can't say that the kid ever aroused any maternal instinct in me. I went along with the make-him-a-man attitude that seemed to prevail at the table. In that sense, Alex and I were on a par in our tutorial on manhood, just doing what was expected of us. I was never mean to him, but I participated heartily when the guys teased him. When he'd been going on for too long about Amerigo Vespucci or something else he'd picked up in social studies, either Jim or Allen would say, "Are you still talking?" and we'd all laugh. Alex always took it well, and usually just went right on talking.

I got the impression that part of Bob's way of teaching his son how to relate to other men was to throw him in with the wolves and let him find his way by trial and error. He'd learn his place in the pack by seeing what worked and what didn't. If he took harsh insults or beatings in the process, so much the better. It would toughen him up.

On this subject, Allen asked me if I'd ever heard the Johnny Cash song "A Boy Named Sue." I hadn't—a lapse that, thinking back on it now, probably should have been a tip-off that I wasn't a guy, since the joke in my circle of friends has always been that every guy in the world is a Johnny Cash fan on some level, "Ring of Fire" being the universal guy guy's anthem of troubled love.

Allen told me the story of the song about a boy whose renegade father had named him Sue. Naturally, the kid gets the shit beaten out of him throughout his childhood on account of his name. At the end of the song the kid, all grown up, meets his father in a bar and beats the shit out of him in turn for giving him a girl's name. Once beaten, the father stands up proudly and says:

Son, this world is rough
And if a man's gonna make it, he's gotta be tough
And I know I wouldn't be there to help you along.
So I give you that name and I said "Good-bye."
I knew you'd have to get tough or die.
And it's that name that helped to make you strong.

. . . Now you have just fought one helluva fight,
And I know you hate me, and you've got the right
To kill me now and I wouldn't blame you if you do.
But you ought to thank me before I die
For the gravel in your guts and the spit in your eye
Because I'm the ——— that named you Sue.

It was amazing how close Allen had come to my secret without knowing it. I'd have to remind the guys of times like this if I ever decided to tell them the truth about me. I wondered if they'd get a kick out of seeing all the signposts in retrospect, the ones I was always noticing along the way.

Being Ned, I had to get used to a different mode. The discord between my girlish ways and the male cues I had to learn, like Alex, on the fly, was often considerable in my mind. For example, our evenings together always started out slowly with a few grunted hellos that among women would have been interpreted as rude. This made my female antennae twitch a little. Were they pissed off at me about something?

But among these guys no interpretation was necessary. Everything was out and aboveboard, never more, never less than what was on anyone's mind. If they were pissed at you, you'd know it. These gruff greetings were indicative of nothing so much as fatigue and appropriate male distance. They were glad enough to see me, but not glad enough to miss me if I didn't show.

Besides, they were coming from long, wearying workdays, usually filled with hard physical labor and the slow, soul-deadening deprecation that comes of being told what to do all day by someone you'd like to strangle. They didn't have the energy for pretense. Allen was a construction worker, Bob a plumber. Jim was working in the repair department of an appliance company. For extra cash to buy Christmas presents and maybe take a week-long ski trip to Vermont on the dirt cheap, he also picked up odd jobs in construction or whatever came up, and he worked part-time in a party store.

None of them got much satisfaction from their jobs, nor did they expect any. Work was just something they did for their families and for the few spare moments it afforded them in front of the football game on Sundays, or at the bowling alley on Mondays. Jim lived in a trailer park and Allen had lived in one for much of his life, though now it was unclear where he was living. Bob never said where he lived. As always, Jim cracked jokes about his class. With his usual flip wit, he called trailer parks "galvanized ghettos," and Allen chimed in about living in a shithole full of "wiggers," or "white niggers," themselves being foremost among them.

In my presence, none of them ever used the word "nigger" in any other context, and never spoke disrespectfully of black people. In fact, contrary to popular belief, white trash males being the one minority it is still socially acceptable to vilify, none of these guys was truly racist as far as I could tell, or certainly no more than anyone else.

As usual, Jim told a funny story about this. He said that he'd been coming out of a bar late one night, and a black guy had approached him asking for money. He'd emerged from a wooded area behind the bar that was well known as one of nature's crack dens in the area. The guy said to Jim, "Hey man. Don't be afraid of me 'cause I'm black, okay. I just wondered if you had some money to spare."

"I'm not afraid of you because you're black," Jim shot back. "I'm afraid of you because you came out of the woods."

They took people at face value. If you did your job or held up your end, and treated them with the passing respect they accorded you, you were all right. If you came out of the woods, you were shady no matter what your color.

They were big football fans, so on one particular Monday I introduced a hot topic of the week to see if I could feel out their positions on race and affirmative action in professional sports. That week Rush Limbaugh had made his now infamous remark while commentating on a Philadelphia Eagles game for ESPN, suggesting that Eagles quarterback Donovan McNabb, one of a handful of black quarterbacks in the NFL, "got a lot of credit for the performance of this team that he didn't deserve."

I asked the guys right out: "Do you think McNabb deserves to be where he is?"

I thought they would meet this with a flurry of impassioned responses, but the conversation ended with a single comment from each. Yeah, he was doing a great job. Yeah, he was as good as or better than the average quarterback in the league. They were happy with his performance, on some nights very happy, and that was all that mattered. The policy debate over skin color wasn't interesting to them, or relevant. They were rock bottom utilitarians. Either a guy was good and did what he was hired to do, or he wasn't, and that alone was the basis on which you judged his worth.

The only time I heard the term "reverse discrimination" mentioned, Jim was telling a story, as he did from time to time, about his stint in the army. He'd been promoted to the position of gunner, apparently, and had occupied the post proficiently for some time, when a new superior officer, a black man, was installed in his unit. Jim found himself demoted to KP and a whole host of other shit jobs soon thereafter.

"The guy had taken everyone out of their posts and put all his black friends in them instead," Jim said. "It was blatant discrimination. So I went to the sergeant in charge, who was a black guy and very fair, and told him all about it. He consulted the evidence and told me I was right, and put me back in my position."

Everyone nodded around the table and that was that.

Exposing my own prejudices, I had expected these guys to be filled with virulent hatred for anyone who wasn't like them, taking their turn to kick the next guy down. But the only consistent dislike I ever saw in them was for comparatively wealthy clients for whom they'd done construction, plumbing or carpentry work and the like. But even here they mostly laughed at the indignities inflicted on them, and marveled, more than balked, at the odd habits and hang-ups of the upper middle class, saying only "rich people are just like that."

Bob told a funny story about a buddy of his getting a wicked case of the shits on a job and being summarily denied the use of the "old lady's toilet." There was nothing for it, so as Bob described it, the guy took a newspaper and a bucket into the back of their van and camped out. After a while the old lady, wanting to know why there'd been an unauthorized work stoppage, burst into the van, only to happen upon a very unsavory scene that sent her shrieking from the premises, denouncing the men as barbarians.

There were the occasional gay or sexist jokes, but they, too, were never mean-spirited. Ironically enough, the guys told me that I, being the worst bowler in the league by far—my average was a mere 100—was lucky I hadn't bowled with them in a previous season when anyone who averaged less than 120 incurred the label "fag," and anyone who averaged less than 100 was, by default, a girl. At the end of the season, whoever had won the booby prize had had to bowl an entire ten frames in women's panties.

They each had the usual stories about being propositioned by a gay man, or happening on a gay bar unawares, but they told them with the same disarming bemusement and self-abasement as they told the stories about the habitually mysterious ways of rich people. Gay people and their affairs didn't much interest them, and if gays were the butt of a joke now and then, so was everyone else, including, and most often, themselves.

Nothing was beyond humor, especially for Jim, but he was a sharp guy, and when he made a joke he always knew, and let you know that he knew, what he was doing with a quip. He introduced the most outrageous joke he ever told in my presence with an appropriate caveat. "Okay, this is a really sick joke," he said. "I mean really sick, but it's funny as shit. You wanna hear it?" Everyone nodded. "Okay. A child molester and a little girl are walking into the woods—" He stopped here to add, "I told you it was really sick." Then he went on. "Anyway, so the little girl says to the child molester, 'Mister, it's getting really dark out here. I'm scared,' and the child molester says, 'Yeah, well how do you think I feel? I've got to walk back alone.'"

Jim was at his funniest when it came to women and relations

between the sexes. As always, his observations were startlingly as-
tute and his anecdotal way of framing them drew you in and made
you come away rolling. Apropos of nothing, he introduced the
topic of women one night with this interjection:

"You know, if guys could just learn to go without the pussy
for a while, they'd get so much shit done. I mean, that's what box-
ers do when they're training, and it keeps 'em focused for the
fight. Go without the pussy and you get strong, man. I mean, I
haven't been laid in two months, and I'm about ready to lift up the
corner of the house."

This was the kind of thing that just came out of his mouth out
of nowhere and it used to make me wonder what he might have
done with himself if he'd gone to college instead of joining the
army at seventeen. His humor was the ticket to his brain, and you
could tell it was whirring at a higher speed than most of the brains
around him.

He often told stories about his days at school as a kid, stories
that confirmed my suspicion that he had a lot going on inside his
head that had been beaten out of him on the playground, and that
he now knew enough not to share in the wrong company. Here
again, though, he was impossibly funny.

"I was one of those quiet, psycho kids," he'd say. "I never
spoke. I just sat there in the corner. You couldn't provoke me to
fight. You could be pokin' me with a stick and I wouldn't move. I'd
just be sittin' there drawing pictures of killing your family."

Every now and then Jim would come out with a word that
somebody—either Bob or Alex—would call him on, a word like
"enable," which Alex wanted to know the meaning of, and "cor-
dial," which Jim used to describe his behavior toward someone or
another, and which Bob clearly thought was a little too big for
britches.

In Jim's defense I said that the word was only "too, too" if you were talking cocktails, which, of course, only made it worse, because it made me sound like an asshole, and blew for good whatever class cover or remote coolness I might have gained.

Jim salvaged me, though, with a courtesy laugh.

Then he went on with his riff about men and women: "I mean, take work, for example. I can work with an ugly chick. There's an ugly chick works in my office with me every day, and I'm fine. I do my thing. I can concentrate fine. But every now and then there's this hot, hot woman who comes into the office, and for the whole time she's there I'm completely fucked. Everything's out the window. I don't get shit done. All I can do is stare at her like this—"

Here he made a dumbfounded expression, mimicking himself in the office ogling the hot chick.

But all joking aside, these guys took their sexuality for what it was. They felt there was no getting around it, so they found ways to work within it, ways that sometimes entailed lying to their wives about going to the odd strip club.

One night Jim was talking about his plans for a ski trip. He wanted to find a location that had good skiing, but he also wanted some lively nightlife. "I'd like to find a place that has a good titty bar," he said.

Bob chimed in, "Yeah. Count me in on that. I'm definitely up for that."

This sparked a short discussion of titty bars and how the married man negotiated them. The ski trip would offer one of the few opportunities for the boys to be boys, since their wives weren't coming along. This had to be taken advantage of, since it was clear that at least Bob's and Jim's wives had expressly forbidden them to go to strip clubs. Besides, they agreed, no vacation would be quite as relaxing without a little skin in it. For these guys, it seemed, there were just some things a married man learned not to be honest about with his wife, his abiding love of and even need for porn and sex shows being prime examples.

As Allen told me once when I asked about the secret to marriage: "You tell women what you want them to know and let them assume the rest."

None of this talk surprised me. We were, by virtue of our name, the recognized dirty team in the league. The rest of the teams had names like Jeb's Lawn Care or Da Buds, but ours was The Tea Baggers. When I heard this the first night I nearly blew my cover, blurting like an art house idiot, "Oh, do you guys like John Waters movies?" Waters's movie *Pecker* had featured the practice of tea bagging.

"Who's he?" they all asked.

"Oh," I mumbled, "I thought that's where you got the name from."

"Nah," said Jim. "It's something I saw in a porno mag. Some guy was squatting over a girl, dangling his balls in her mouth, and the caption said 'Tea Bagging.' I thought that was fucking hilarious."

The oddest thing about all this dirty talk and hiding strip club visits from their wives was the absolute reverence with which they spoke about their wives and their marriages. To them it seemed it was necessary to lie about certain things, but in their minds this didn't threaten or damage the integrity of their partnerships. They were happy and they cherished their wives.

When Jim's wife's second cancer diagnosis came through he talked about it with us a bit, but only in clipped phrases. He'd spent the previous week drinking himself into a stupor and blowing up abandoned cars on the back lot of a friend's junkyard. You could tell that the news was devouring him, and the only way he could deal with it was to tear himself up and anything else inanimate that was handy.

"You know, man," he said to me, "she puts up with a hell of a lot with me, and I can't say I've ever been unhappy with her. How many guys can say that? I've got a good woman. She's never given me a minute's trouble."

Bob agreed. "Yeah, that's how I feel. I got nothin' bad to say about my wife either. Nothin'."

It was an odd contradiction, but one that I came across fairly often among married men who talked to Ned about their sexuality. The way they told it, it sounded as if the male sex drive and marriage were incompatible. Something had to give, and usually what gave was honesty. These guys either lied to their wives about going to strip clubs, or at the very least they lied about the ubiquity of their sexual fantasies involving other women. On nights like these, among the boys, they could be honest, and there were no judgments.

The bowling part of the evening was clearly secondary to the beer and the downtime with the boys at the table, smoking and talking shit. They cared about their game and the team's standing—more than they let on—but as Jim jokingly put it to me as a way of making me feel better for being the worst bowler any of them had ever seen, the league was really just an excuse to get away from their wives for the evening. I learned later that this wasn't true. Actually, it was a money league, and every game we lost cost us twenty dollars. This made me all the more thankful and impressed that they'd taken my poor showing with such good humor.

Still, they warmed to me more and more as my bowling improved, and I got the sense that it wasn't just about the money. It was as if there was an unspoken credo among them that there was just something you couldn't quite trust about a guy who couldn't bowl. I didn't drink or smoke either, and, though they never said so, I could tell they thought this was just downright unnatural, probably the sign of someone who had it too good in life for his own good. Beer and cigarettes were their medicine, their primrose path to an early grave, which was about the best, aside from sex and a few good times with the guys, that they could hope for in life. The idea of telling one of these guys that smoking or drinking to excess was bad for his health was too ridiculously middle class to entertain. It bespoke a supreme ignorance of what their lives were really like—Hobbesian—not to put too fine a point on it. Nasty, brutish and short. The idea that you would try to prolong your grueling, dead-end life, and do it by taking away the few pleasures you had along the way, was just insulting.

The whole business of bowling, when we got down to it, was, as you might expect, tied in to masculinity in all the predictable ways—hierarchy, strength, competition—but it was much more subtly processed and enacted than I had suspected it would be, and I wasn't outside this tug-of-war by any means. I had my own issues, old issues that were bound up with being a tomboy and competing in sports with boys my whole life.

When I appeared at the bowling alley on that first night, I was late. Practice time was just ending, so I didn't get a chance to throw before we started. These guys had been bowling all their lives. They threw with spin and they hit with precision. They must have known me for the putz I was the minute I heaved the ball with both hands. There were fifty or sixty guys in that room, almost everybody smoking, almost everybody drinking. They had names like Adolph and Mac, and to a dyke scared to death of being gay-bashed, they were just downright mean looking, all seated at their respective tables with nothing else to do but watch you, the new pencil neck that nobody knew, walk up to the foul line and make an art of the gutter ball. They must have had some pretty hearty laughs at my expense.

That's how it felt anyway, and that's probably how it went down among the other teams when my back was turned. But when I'd traipse back to my table in fuchsia-faced shame with a zero or a foul blinking on the board, they never laid me low. I always got supportive advice. "You'll get there, man," they'd say. "You should have seen me when I started." Or more helpfully: "Just shake hands with the pins, man. That's all you got to do. Just shake hands with the pins."

They were far more generous with me than they had any reason to be, and it was only after a couple of months when they got to know me a little better that they felt free enough to kid me now and then about how much I sucked. But even then it was always light and affectionate, a compliment really, a sign that they were letting me in.

"Hey, we all got strikes this round," Bob would say, "except one. Who was that, I wonder?" Then he'd smile at me while leaning back in his chair, dragging deeply on his cigarette. I'd make a big show of giving him the finger, and we'd all laugh. Bob's flinty veneer was cracking.

As I tried to be one of the guys, I could feel myself saying and doing the very things that young men do as teens when they're trying to sort out their place in the ranks. Like them, I was trying to fit in, be inconspicuous, keep from being found out. And so I imitated the modeled behaviors that said "Accept me. I'm okay. I'm one of the guys."

Half the time I was ashamed of myself for trying too hard, saying fuck or fuckin' one too many times in a sentence for effect, or swaggering just a little too wide and loose on my way to and from my turns, and probably looking as a result like I had a load in my pants.

But then I could see all of these learned behaviors in Bob and Jim and Allen, too, as well as the remnant insecurity they were meant to disguise. And that, I think, was where their generosity came from. They'd outgrown that adolescent need to challenge every comer as a way of deflecting their own misgivings. As always, Jim was the most forthcoming about his stupid flights of machismo and the Dumpsters they'd usually landed him in.

"I remember when I was in the army," he'd say, "and I was drunk off my ass as usual. And there was this huge guy playin' pool in the bar I was in. And I don't know why, but I just flicked a beer coaster at him, and it hit him right in the back of the head. And he turned around really slowly and he looked down at me and he said in this really tired way 'Do we really need to do this tonight?' And I said, 'Nah, you're right. We don't. Sorry.' So he turned around, and fuck me if I didn't just throw another one and hit him again, right in the back of the head. I don't know why I did it. No fuckin' idea. And I knew when I did it that he was gonna kick my ass, so I turned around and tried to run, and I slipped in a puddle of beer and fell on my face, and he just picked me right up and bashed the shit out of me. And the funniest thing about it was that the whole time he was punching me, he kept apologizing to me for having to do it."

This was a source of hilarity to everyone, the stupid crap you felt compelled to do as a guy finding your spot in the scheme of things, and the obligatory beatings you had to give or take to reestablish order after a breach. But only Jim really had enough perspective to admit the folly of his masculinity, and to fully appreciate the absurdity of brutish necessity in the male-on-male world. A guy whom you'd just provoked twice, and who'd warned you not to trespass, had no choice but to beat you if you crossed the line. That was just how it was among men, and Jim mocked it lovingly.

Bob was more guarded. He didn't quite have Jim's gift for self-deprecation. He didn't readily admit his mistakes or the missteps he'd made in the past. I got the sense that he couldn't afford to express regret or let on that he didn't know something. Instead, he held the world at arm's length, projecting a kind of terse authority from his barrel chest, just nodding or frowning at something you'd say, as if the answer was insufferably obvious, when, of course, at least half the time he probably didn't know the answer. The way he talked to his son Alex was essentially the way he talked to everyone. He was the guy who knew stuff, and what he didn't know wasn't worth knowing.

But when it came to something that Bob felt more confident about, he'd engage you. Not that Bob's engagements were ever long or involved, but they packed a rhetorical punch. I asked him once if his workplace was unionized, and his answer surprised me. I'd figured everyone in that room, being a bona fide member of the working class, was as staunchly pro union as the liberal intellectuals I knew in New York, but Bob didn't see it that way. Neither, apparently, did the members of one of the other teams, who had called themselves the Nonunions.

"No," he said. "My shop isn't union."

"Why not?" I asked.

"Unions are for the lazy man."

"Why's that?"

"Because they're all about seniority," he said, pausing for effect. "I'll give you an example," he went on. "One place I worked was union, and it was run on the seniority system. The guys who'd been there the longest had the most clout, which meant that when there were layoffs, they'd always have better standing. There was one guy like that there who'd been there forever, and he was a lazy fucker. He used to just hang out and read the newspaper. Never did a lick of work. Meanwhile, I worked my ass off all day long. But when it came time to let people go, I was let go and he wasn't. Now that's not fair, is it?"

"No," I agreed. "It isn't."

I tried to engage him further on the question, but as I came to understand, you'd always know when a conversation with Bob was over. He'd just revert to peering at you with condescending finality through a cloud of cigarette smoke.

A lot of the guys were like that. It would take you years to get to know them on anything more than grunting terms. They were walled-in tight.

Yet even so, under the surface there remained that distant male-on-male respect that I'd felt in the first handshakes and I continued to feel every time some guy from another team would say "Hey, man" to me when we met in the parking lot or passed on our way to or from the soda machine.

But there was one guy among the bowlers who established an odd intimacy with me early on. It was so immediate, and so physically affectionate, that I felt sure he could see through Ned. I never learned his name. I don't think he knew anything consciously. It wasn't that bald. But there was an unmistakable chemistry between us.

Obviously, I'd spent my life as a woman either flirting or butting heads or maneuvering somewhere on the sexual spectrum with nearly every man I'd ever met, and I knew how it felt when an older man took a shine to you as a woman. It was always the kind of guy who was far too decent to be creepy, the avuncular type who had turned his sexual response to you into a deep affection. He showed it by putting his arm around you cleanly, without innuendo, or patting you gently on the shoulder and smiling.

This guy was like that, old enough to have gained some kind of relief from his urges, and now he was free to just like me for being a woman. Even if he didn't quite know I was a woman, his brain seemed somehow to have sniffed me out and responded accordingly. The thing was, in this context, of all places, the way he treated me made me *feel* like a woman — a girl actually, very young and cared for — and I wondered how that could have been possible if some part of him hadn't recognized me as such. It was unmistakable, and I never felt it with any other man I came into contact with as a man.

I felt something entirely different coming from the other men who thought I was a young man. They took me under their wings. Another older bowler had done this. Taking me aside between rounds, he tried to teach me a few things to improve my game. This was male mentor stuff all the way. He treated me like a son, guiding me with firm encouragement and solid advice, an older man lending a younger man his expertise.

This was commonplace. During the course of the bowling season, which lasted nine months, a lot of men from the other teams tried to give me tips on my game. My own teammates were constantly doing this, increasingly so as the season wore on. There was a tension in the air that grew up around me as I failed to excel, a tension that I felt keenly, but that seemed unrecognizable to the guys themselves. I had good frames, sometimes even good whole games, but I still had a lot of bad ones, too, and that frustrated us all.

At about the five-month mark, Jim began giving me pained looks when I came back to the table after a bad turn.

I'd say, "Okay, I'm sorry. I know I suck."

"Look, man," he'd say, "I've told you what I think you're doing wrong, and you don't listen or you get pissed off."

"No, no," I'd protest, "I'm really trying to do what you're saying. It just isn't coming out right. What can I do?"

I threw like a girl and it bugged me as much as it bugged them. If I told them the truth at the end of the season I didn't want them to have the satisfaction of saying, "Oh, that explains everything. You bowl like a girl because you *are* a girl."

But their motivation seemed comically atavistic, as if it was just painful to watch a fellow male fail repeatedly at something as adaptive as throwing a boulder. Time was, the tribe's survival depended on it. This just seemed mandatory to them in some absurdly primal way.

As men they felt compelled to fix my ineptitude rather than be secretly happy about it and try to abet it under the table, which is what a lot of female athletes of my acquaintance would have done. I remember this from playing sports with and against women all my life. No fellow female athlete ever tried to help me with my game or give me tips. It was every woman for herself. It wasn't enough that you were successful. You wanted to see your sister fail.

Girls can be a lot nastier than boys when it comes to someone who stands in the way of what they want. They know where to hit where it'll hurt the most, and their aim is laser precise. One summer when I was a maladjusted teenager, I went to a tennis camp in New Jersey that catered largely to rich princesses and their male counterparts. Most of them couldn't really play tennis on more than a country-club level. Their parents had sent them there to get rid of them. They just stood around most of the time posing for one another, showing off their tans. But I'd had a lot of private coaching in tennis by that time, and my strokes were fairly impressive for my age. I took the tennis pretty seriously.

As for posing, I looked like I'd been raised by wolverines.

The instructors used to videotape each of us playing, so that they could go over the tapes with us and evaluate our techniques. One day, my particular class of about twenty girls was standing around the television watching the tape, and the instructor was deconstructing my serve. He'd had a lot of negative things to say about most of the other girls' serves, but when it came to mine, he raved unconditionally, playing my portion of the tape over and over again in slow motion.

At this, one of the prettiest girls in the group, no doubt exasperated by the repetition, said, loudly enough for everyone to hear: "Well, I'd rather look the way I do and serve the way I do than serve the way she does and look the way she does."

Now that's female competitiveness at its finest.

But with these guys and with other male athletes I've known it was an entirely different conflict. Their coaching reminded me of my father's, whose approach to fatherhood had always been about giving helpful, concrete advice. It was how he showed his affection for us. It was all bound up in a desire to see us do well.

These guys' attentions were like that: fatherly. And it really surprised me coming from members of opposing teams, since this was, after all, a money league. But they seemed to have a competitive stake in my doing well and in helping me to do well, as if beating a man who wasn't at his best wasn't satisfying. They wanted you to be good *and then* they wanted to beat you on their own merits. They didn't want to win against a plodder or lose to him on a handicap.

But my game never got consistently better. I'd have good frames now and then, but mostly I hovered around an average of 102 and learned to swallow it. So did the guys. They knew I was trying my best, and that was all that really mattered to them. As with everything else a little odd or off about me, they accepted my clumsiness with a shrug of the shoulders, as if to say: "That's just how some guys are. What are you gonna do?"

I guess that's what I respected about those guys the most. I was a stranger, and a nerd, but they cut me all the slack in the world, and they did it for no other reason that I could discern than that I was a good-seeming guy who deserved a chance, something life and circumstance had denied most of them.

I could never have predicted it, but part of me came to really enjoy those nights with the guys. Their company was like an anchor at the beginning of the week, something I could look forward to, an oasis where nothing would really be expected of me. Almost every interaction would be entirely predictable, and the ones that weren't were all the more precious for being rare.

When somebody opened up to me suddenly, like when Jim confided how much he loved his wife and how much it hurt him when the doctor told him that the best he could hope for was to see her alive in a year, or when Bob smiled at me playfully after teasing me over a toss, it touched me more deeply than my female friends' dime-a-dozen intimacies ever did. These were blooms in the desert, tender offerings made in the middle of all that guy talk.

I'd never made friends with guys like that before. They had intimidated me too much, and the sexual tension that always subsists in some form or another between men and women had usually gotten in the way. But making friends with them as a man let me into their world as a free agent and taught me to see and appreciate the beauty of male friendships from the inside out.

So much of what happens emotionally between men isn't spoken aloud, and so the outsider, especially the female outsider who is used to emotional life being overt and spoken (often overspoken), tends to assume that what isn't said isn't there. But it is there, and when you're inside it, it's as if you're suddenly hearing sounds that only dogs can hear.

I remember one night when I plugged into that subtext for the first time. A few lanes over, one of the guys was having a particularly hot game. I'd been oblivious to what was happening, mourning my own playing too much to watch anyone else. It was Jim's turn, and I noticed that he wasn't bowling. Instead he was sitting down in one of the laneside chairs, just waiting. Usually this happened when there was a problem with the lane: a stuck pin, or a mis-set rack. But the pins were fine. I kept watching him, wondering why he wasn't stepping up to the line.

Then I noticed that all the other bowlers had sat down as well. Nobody was taking his turn. It was as if somebody had blown a whistle, only nobody had. Nobody had said anything. Everyone had just stopped and stepped back, like in a barracks when an officer enters the room.

Then I realized that there was one guy stepping up to the lane. It was the guy who was having the great game. I looked up at the board and saw that he'd had strikes in every frame, and now he was on the tenth and final frame, in which you get three throws if you strike or spare in the first two. He'd have to throw three strikes in a row on this one to earn a perfect score, and somehow everyone in that hall had felt the moment of grace descend and had bowed out accordingly. Everyone, of course, except me.

It was a beautiful moment, totally still and reverent, a bunch of guys instinctively paying their respects to the superior athleticism of another guy.

That guy stepped up to the line and threw his three strikes, one after the other, each one met by mounting applause, then silence and stillness again, then on the final strike, an eruption, and every single guy in that room, including me, surrounded that player and moved in to shake his hand or pat him on the back. It was almost mystical, that telepathic intimacy and the communal joy that succeeded it, crystalline in its perfection. The moment said everything all at once about how tacitly attuned men are to each other, and how much of this women miss when they look from the outside in.

After it was over, and all the congratulations had died down, Jim and Bob and Allen and I all looked at each other and said things like "Man, that was incredible," or "Wow, that was something." We couldn't express it in words, but we knew what we'd just shared.

I'd been playing a part with these guys for months, being Ned, the walk-on. Of course, he had it easy in a way, because everything was on the surface. Nobody knew him and he didn't really know anybody else. He was mostly quiet—listening, recording, trying not to say the wrong thing, trying not to give himself away—and that put a barrier between him and his environment. Despite the masculine intimacy that enveloped the evening, the guys and I were really only amenable strangers warming our hands together for a while over the few things we had to say to each other: the odd fag joke or tall tale of glory days, the passing home improvement reference, and of course the ritual dissection of *Sunday Night Football* and the ongoing hockey season. Nothing mysterious really. The usual stuff that guys find convenient to say when nobody's giving anything away.

So, after having bowled with these guys every Monday night for six months, I gave something away. I just decided one night that it was time to tell them.

But how to do it? I didn't know. I was wary, uncertain about how to come clean. I couldn't anticipate how they'd react. I had visions of myself running down the middle of the town's main street with my shirt ripped off at the shoulder and a lynch mob chasing me with brickbats and bowling balls in hand.

Fortunately, that night, Jim presented me with the perfect opportunity. He asked me what I was doing after we finished, something he'd never done before, so I took a chance and asked him to have a drink with me. He was the most accessible of the bunch, and I figured getting him alone and telling him first would give me a sense of how to proceed, if at all.

We went to his favorite haunt, a biker bar not far from the trailer park where he lived. When we sat down at the bar I told him he should order a shot of whatever would relax him the most, because he was going to need it.

"I think I'm about to blow your mind," I said.

"I doubt it," he said. "Just about the only thing you could say that would blow my mind is if you told me that your girfriend was really a man and you were really a woman."

"Well," I said, stunned by his exactitude, "you're half right."

"Okay," he said slowly, peering at me skeptically. "In that case, I'll have a blackberry brandy, with a beer back."

"Actually," I said, "you might want two. I'm buying."

He downed the first and ordered another. I wasn't sure if he was spooked or just taking advantage of the freebies. Knowing him, probably the latter, not that I was the big spender or any-thing. At that bar you could get good and ripped for ten dollars.

When he'd wiped the vestiges of the second shot off his lips, I started in.

"Jim," I said, "you were right. I'm not a guy. I'm a woman."

"Shut up, asshole," he said. "C'mon, really. What did you want to tell me?"

"No. That's really it. I'm a woman. Look," I said, "I'll show you my driver's license if you don't believe me."

I pulled it out of my wallet and put it into his hand. He looked at it for a second, then said, "That doesn't even look like you."

He shoved it back into my hand. "Besides, you can fake those easy."

"I swear, Jim, it's not a fake. That's me. My name is Norah, not Ned."

"Shut up," he said again. "Why are you doing this to me? I mean, I gotta hand it to you, if this is a joke, it's a good one. You got me, but a joke's a joke."

"It's not a joke, Jim."

He shook his head and took a big gulp of his beer.

"Okay, look," I said. "I'll show you every card in my wallet, including my social security card. They all have the same name on them."

I put all the cards on the bar in a row where he could see them. He looked at them all cursorily, then said, "Are you fuckin' with me? Because if you are, this is fucked up. I mean, if I'd thought of it first I'd have done it to you, but shit, you gotta tell me."

"No," I said, "I swear to God, I'm not fucking with you. I'm a woman. My name is Norah. Look, I don't have a protruding Adam's apple, right?" I put his finger on my throat and ran it up and down.

"I'm wearing a tight sports bra to hold down my tits," I said, putting his hand on my back so he could feel the straps under my sweatshirt. "Look, if you still don't believe me, let's go in the bathroom and I'll show you."

"No thanks," he blurted, jerking away from me. "I don't wanna see that shit. Jesus, man. You're fuckin' me up. And you were my coolest guy friend, too. Damnit. This is really blowin' my mind. You better not be fuckin' with me."

It took a while to get him to concede it, even remotely, and every once in a while he'd still say, "You're not fuckin' with me, are you?" But we sat there for a good three hours talking about the book and why I was doing it, and slowly I got the sense that it was sinking in.

"I gotta say," he said finally, "that takes balls . . . or not, I guess. Wow, you're a fuckin' chick. No wonder you listen so good."

We went through the whole rigmarole of hindsight, things he'd thought were a little odd at the time, but now made sense to him. We'd have long moments of silence, and then he'd say something like, "So that's why you always wear a sweatshirt even though it's so hot in there, right? It's to cover up your tits."

"Yep," I'd say. "It sucks, too, 'cause I sweat my ass off."

We'd lapse back into silence for a while and then he'd say, "That's why your lips and your cheeks are so red. I always noticed that and thought it was weird."

That was his way of saying I had a nice complexion, I think, nicer at least than all the leatherfaces in the league, which wasn't saying much. The only guy who had a face even remotely as smooth as mine, even with the stubble, was nineteen years old.

But for the most part, it seemed I'd pulled off Ned pretty well, because there weren't that many things Jim could look back on with recognition. In the end, he just said, "That stubble is really good, man. I just thought it was exactly like what I'd have at the end of a day."

That was satisfying.

When we left the bar that night, he hugged me goodnight. It was the first evidence that he had accepted me, or at least some part of me, as a woman. He was still calling me "he," which was understandable, but I knew that he wouldn't have come within a mile of Ned physically if he hadn't seen the woman in him. Some part of the truth was getting through.

But I was still in drag, and as we hugged we both realized it.

Jim said, "Shit, you don't wanna be seen hugging another man in the parking lot outside a bar like this." He pulled away quickly. As we parted ways toward our cars he shouted over his shoulder: "Hey, man, you take care of yourself over there in Iraq, okay?"

When we reached our cars I shouted back to him, "Hey, Jim."

When he turned around I pulled up my sweatshirt and my sports bra and flashed him the telltale tits. "See. I told you so."

He winced and turned away. "Jesus, you fuckin' freak. I don't need to see that shit. You've still got your beard on." He shouted it like a slur, but I could hear the laughter in his voice.

And that was the turning point in our friendship. Everything changed after that. We went for drinks a couple of times between Mondays, once with his wife, but several times alone. When we were alone he told me a lot of things about himself. Private things, things he said he never would have told a guy, some things he said he'd never told anybody. He told me that he liked Norah much better than Ned. When I asked him why, he said because Ned was just some stiff guy, and what did he need with just another stiff in his life? He had plenty of those. But Norah, a dyke who dressed like a man and could talk to him about more than football and beer, now those he didn't have so many of. People like that didn't move in his orbit. People like him didn't move in mine. He wasn't what he'd appeared to be, either.

He was a hack writer's gift, a more complex character than I could ever have invented. But he wasn't just material for me, any more than I was just a freak show for him. The way he told it, it was like Ned and Norah became a hybrid. He still thought of me mostly as a guy, at least outwardly. But he knew that I was a woman and he reacted to me accordingly—with, that is, one rather large exception. He wasn't attracted to me.

There was no sexual tension between us. This meant that he could go out with me like one of the guys and play pool or, as he would do later, go to the titty bars with me. But all the while he was treating me like one of the guys because in a way he didn't know how to do otherwise. There was no social precedent for this. Still, he could talk to me intimately the way he never could to another man. It was the best of both worlds. Like he'd said, the best male friend he'd ever had. Of course, sometimes this meant that he didn't quite know where to put me in his subconscious mind.

He used to rib me about that.

"You know, thanks a lot," he said once. "I had a perfectly normal fantasy life until I met you. Now I'll be whackin' off or something, doing just fine with Pam Anderson or whatever, and all of a sudden there's fuckin' Ned with his tits and his beard and his bowling ball smiling at me, and I can't get rid of him. You fucked me up for life."

Then he'd smile and I knew he was perversely grateful for it if only for the entertainment value. He was a freak, too, and glad at last to know another one.

I conjured up weird pictures of him, too, though they weren't really sexual, any more than his were. I wasn't attracted to him, God knew. Still, my brain didn't quite know what to do with him, either. I could see that he was a little boy inside, a boy who'd done some bad things in his life and who'd had worse things done to him. He could put up a gruff front and he was no angel, but he was really just trying to hide his sensitivities so that he could hang on to them. He knew what they were worth and he knew that I knew, and I think he sensed that it was safe to let me see them.

I used to picture him curled up next to his wife in a small white undershirt with no underwear on, like some little kid who'd just come out of the bath, all clean and warm and needing comfort. Of course, I didn't picture him like this when I was wanking, but then, there you have the classic difference between men and women.

I guess in me he'd found a "guy" friend who could understand his foulest thoughts and impulses, the ones that he didn't want to burden his wife with, or was too ashamed to tell her, the kind of shockingly crass confessions that only guys supposedly understand but hardly ever want to reveal to each other because they're too emotionally charged. Maybe he knew I'd respond to them with recognition and sympathy not only because he thought of me as part man, but also because as a woman I'd told him my black thoughts, too.

But when I responded to him emotionally, I had to modify the temptation to mother him, because after I'd heard some of the things he told me—stories about beatings he had suffered as a child and the struggles he had had trying to come to grips with the abuse in silence—the woman in me wanted to hold him and let him cry it out. But that would have been like throwing a wool blanket over his head, exactly the wrong thing to do. He needed to know I was there and listening and feeling, but I couldn't touch him or push the contact in conciliatory words. I just had to know what key he was in and for how long. It was never more than a few moments. That's all his pride would allow.

Anyway, he'll be embarrassed when he reads this, if he ever does. He'll make a joke about it, or brush it off, but at least he'll know that in my own hobbled way I cared. I hope he'll know that he taught me a lot about how to listen to a man when he's telling you something that's hard for him to say. Maybe now I'll know how to better understand what the men in my life need from me emotionally and how to give it to them.

As always, everything with Jim was ebb and flow, serious then farcical in a blink. Whenever I'd bring up something especially sensitive with him, something that he didn't want to talk about, he'd say, "Give me some time on that."

And if I pressed him he'd say, "You know, fuckin' women. You just can't let it rest, can you. You just don't know when to shut the fuck up. See, that's why you get hit."

Then he'd smile at me and we'd both laugh. Lots of people took him seriously when he said things like that, but that was one of our connections. We had the same sense of humor. We could say a lot to each other and we'd know when it was a joke and when it wasn't. When it wasn't a joke, it was always tender or raw in a way that you could never mistake. The rest of the time it was just bullshit fun.

Besides, as far as hitting women went, I'd met Jim's wife. She could knock the sass out of him with one look. She was a cool lady, and his respect for her ran deep. With her by his side, he looked almost like a porter who was just there to carry her bags.

When it came time to consider telling the other guys about me, Jim told me he wasn't sure how they'd take it. He said he honestly didn't know if they would beat me up. He thought it might be best for him to tell them in private first. We went back and forth on it for a week or two, and then on the following Monday in the middle of the game I just said to him, "Fuck it. Let's do it."

"All right," he said, sighing, "if you really want to. I'm behind you." He looked around warily and added, "I guess."

He'd kept my secret for two weeks, two Monday nights with the guys. We'd exchanged a few meaningful smirks and whispers in that time, but otherwise he'd kept his head down, respecting my need to tell the others when I was ready.

As I had with Jim, I tried to prepare the ground with Bob and Allen. I wanted to have their full attention, to have everybody sitting at the table at once. But the flow of the game was constant, with one of us always getting up to take his next turn as soon as someone else sat down.

"Listen, you guys," I said. "I've got something important to tell you."

They looked at me with vague interest but nothing more. I turned to Jim for help and he stepped in to reinforce the urgency.

"Yeah, guys, listen up. You're gonna want to hear this, believe me."

Bob had gotten up from his chair but he sat down again when Jim spoke. He and Allen both turned to me, curious now and expectant. I had their ear, but I knew I had only a moment between frames. I couldn't think of any way to ease them into a sex change that fast. There wasn't any room for hedging or segue, no way to hand off the bombshell gingerly. This wasn't the place for a tête-à-tête, and that wasn't their style anyway. It was loud all around us, with the radio blaring and guys cackling and gabbing on all sides of us. I knew that once I'd said the words I was about to say, everything would change irrevocably. Maybe they would laugh and take it as a joke, or even think of it as a welcome surprise. Maybe they'd be shocked into silence and we'd spend the rest of the night in excruciating discomfort avoiding one another's eyes. Or maybe they'd drag me into the parking lot and work me over with the broken end of a beer bottle. I had no way of knowing. I could find no clue on their faces. I was just going to have to say it and hope for the best.

So I did. I said it plain as I could make it. "I'm not a man, you guys. I'm a woman."

And there it was. It was out. I braced for impact.

But Bob just nodded when I said it as if it was nothing out of the ordinary. He leaned back in his chair and took his typical drag on his cigarette, like an FBI interrogator whom nothing could surprise. He narrowed his eyes knowingly as if I'd just confessed to committing a crime that he'd marked me for a long time ago.

Finally, with amazing nonchalance he said, "Oh, yeah?" Then after a long pause he added, "I gotta hand it to you, that takes balls — or whatever. I never would have questioned it."

Meanwhile, Allen looked puzzled.

"Okay, yeah," he said in a leading way. "So what?"

This threw me at first. He couldn't be taking it this lightly, I thought. Then I realized that he had it all wrong. He thought I was telling a joke whose first line was "So, I'm a chick, right . . ." He was still waiting for the punch line.

"That's it, Allen," I said. "That's the joke. I'm a chick. I'm not a guy."

I could tell it wasn't quite registering, or if it was he wasn't letting it. He sensed that the mood at the table was laissez-faire—pretend it isn't there and it'll go away—so he just nodded and said, "Wow."

I filled out the rest of the story for them between frames. They already knew that I was a writer, and at some point during the season I had told them I was writing a book. Now I told them that I was writing the book about them and me, and that the drag was part of the project. They seemed to like the idea and they wanted to know what their names were going to be in the book. Jim cracked that he wanted Colin Farrell to play him in the movie.

After I'd finished, they all went on to bowl one of their shittiest games of the season. I think Bob and Allen were in shock. Maybe Jim was nervous about a pending riot. But I had one of my best games. I felt free, loose for the first time, and I was knocking them down like never before. Still, I had a bad headache all of a sudden. The tension of the buildup had taken its toll.

"Hey," I said, "does one of you guys have an Advil or something? I've got a killer headache."

"No," Bob said without a moment's hesitation, "but I think I might have a Midol."

They all laughed, and that broke the tension. Then right away they started a round of chick jokes, the usual stuff about female intuition and being on the rag and so on. They seemed relieved to know that I could take a joke. Even the lesbian thing didn't throw them.

"By the way," I said, "you know I'm a dyke, right?"

"Yeah," Bob said. "I gathered that."

Again everybody laughed. He was on what for Bob was a roll.

As they had with Jim, things changed completely after that with the guys. Everybody loosened up and opened up. Everybody liked Norah much more than Ned, even knowing that I was a dyke dressed as a man. Once I'd outed myself to them I could be a full and rounded person again, much more animated and genuine than Ned had ever been. I'd spent most of my time with them as Ned trying not to stand out or say the wrong thing. I'd done it poorly, the way desperate adolescents do, and with the same miserable results. They were glad at last to have a real person in their midst, whatever her flaws and quirks.

My supposedly subversive lifestyle just didn't matter to them, or at least it didn't appear to, and this was the part I hadn't expected at all, or given them credit for in the beginning. I'd pegged them unfairly as potential thugs, and now they were showing me up as the judgmental one.

None of that politicized stuff made a difference to them. I just kept bowling out the season with them, dressed as Ned but revealed as Norah. We didn't tell anyone else in the league, and they never found out as far as I knew. The guys went right on calling me Ned and he, just as Jim had, but they knew I was a woman in exactly the way that Jim did.

For me the label couldn't have mattered less. We were finally getting to know each other and it was the easiest time we spent together all season.

Allen got drunk one Monday night a week or two after I'd told them. He spent the whole night leaning over and babbling in my ear, mostly about mundane stuff that hardly made sense. The other guys knew what he was like when he was blasted, so they just laughed and let him go on and on as I sat there in polite misery.

At one point in his rant he leaned a little closer to me and said: "You know, none of this matters to me. It doesn't affect me.

You're cool. I don't care what you are. I really like bowling with you, man. Shit, you're cooler than Bob."

This wasn't exactly the coolest thing to say in front of Bob, since Allen was Bob's in-law, and the two had been close friends for years. Still, I knew Allen meant it as a great compliment, and I took it as one. But I also knew it was something he would never have said to Ned, not just because he didn't like Ned as much as Norah, but because he couldn't talk to a guy the way he could talk to a woman.

These guys were old pals, but I got the sense that they didn't speak intimately with each other the way my women friends and I did, or the way Jim had done with me once he'd known that I was a woman. The contrast was striking to Jim, too, which was why, when I told him about my true identity that night at the bar he said, "That's why you listen so good." When Jim talked to Bob about his wife's illness, for example, a life-changing, hugely traumatic event, he spoke almost without affect, tersely, using the only available language, the facts of the catastrophe, to imply but not convey his pain. Bob listened in the same way, nodding respectfully and with clear concern, but with a little distance and discomfort, too. He was a good friend, but he seemed as trapped as Jim by his reserve. Watching them made me tense and sad, as if their exchange was happening in a sealed jar where the air was close and stifling.

Maybe that was part of the insult in Allen's comment, too. Maybe he hadn't just meant to say that I was cool, but also that he felt closer to me in some way than he did to Bob. Their friendship had sure boundaries of touch, affection and expression, and as a woman I could break through those blocks as quickly and effortlessly as I had changed my sex. Those were the rules, it seemed. As a guy you didn't make yourself vulnerable, and you didn't burden yourself or your buds with your doubt and fear. They didn't want to hear about it, and you didn't want to reveal it. But with a woman it was easier immediately. You could speak freely and get away with it, or at least as freely as your customary reticence would allow.

It seemed that getting drunk was one of the only ways Allen could express his feelings, even to a woman. They came out a little ragged and impolitic in the process, but they were touching anyway.

He may not have said much the night of my disclosure, but he'd clearly been thinking about it since. He told me that he'd been talking with his thirteen-year-old daughter that week and she'd said to him, the way teenagers do, "Oh, that's so gay," referring to some activity or article of clothing that wasn't in fashion.

"You know," Allen said, "she's always sayin' that, but this time I stopped her, and I said: 'You oughta be careful how you use that word.'"

Jim had told me a similar story about a confrontation he'd had a few days before with a coworker who'd been talking about gay characters on network TV shows like *Will and Grace*. She'd said: "Well, I don't have a problem with gays, but why do they have to keep shoving it in my face?"

And Jim said, "Oh, okay, so you're fine with gay people so long as they stay in caves and back alleys. Is that what you're saying?"

He said he'd really pinned her to the wall for it, saying finally, "Either you have a problem with gay people or you don't. There's no 'but.'"

These guys were starting to sound like a progressive party meeting and all I'd done was laugh along with them when they'd said things like, "If you're really a chick, then how the hell do you have such big feet?" But I was grateful for their support however they showed it, and I felt more than a little ashamed of how I'd un-derestimated them.

They had taken me in, and I had deceived them. They took it astonishingly well nonetheless. I had condescended to them all along, even in my gracious surprise that they were somehow hu-man. They had made that leap on my behalf without the benefit of suppressed snobbery. I have condescended to them still in these pages throughout, congratulating myself for stooping to receive their affections and dispense my own, for presuming to under-stand them. Class is inescapable in tone, and even a pseudointel-lectual will always sound like she thinks she's earning points in liberal heaven for shaking hands with the caveman or, worse, the noble savage. The most I can say is that they were far better men than I in that, and undoubtedly far worse or just as bad in ways that I would never and could never know. They made me welcome in their midst, and by so doing, they made me feel like a bit of a shithead, like an arrogant prick know-it-all. In a sense, they made me the subject of my own report. They bowled with irony after all.

They made me look ridiculous to myself and they made me laugh about it. And for that I will always be grateful to them, be-cause anybody who does that for you is a true and great friend.

3 | Love

I thought dating was going to be the fun part, the easiest part. Certainly as a man I had romantic access to far more women than I ever did as a lesbian, and this felt like the best of all possible boons. I could partake at last in the assumption of heterosexuality and ask out any woman I liked without insulting her. Of course, I was in for a mountain of rejections, and the self-hatred that came with being the sad sack pick-up artist, the wooing barnacle that every woman is forever flicking off her sleeve.

Sadly, that's how it went for Ned most of the time at first when he tried to meet strange women in singles bars. As I would soon learn, that's how it went for most guys. It was just the way of things in the wild when you were male. You were the eager athlete, the brightly colored bird doing the dance, and she was the German judge begrudging you the nod.

To be a guy I had to get out there. I had to play the game as it was played, no matter how bad it felt. But I figured it couldn't hurt to enlist a compatriot for support, so I asked a friend, Curtis, to be my backup. He was perfect for the job. He was a handsome, well-built, gregarious type, secure and sensible enough not to take himself too seriously, or care much what a stranger might think of him. He had agreed to help me navigate the scene and work with me on my male cues, which were still in need of some fine-tuning. I was never quite sure, for example, exactly how low to pull my baseball cap over my eyes. I still talked too much with my hands, and sometimes I still applied my Chapstick with a girlish lip smack. Just the day before, while out shopping at a department store as Ned, I had rubbed the insides of my wrists together after applying cologne at the men's fragrance counter. The woman behind the counter narrowed her eyes at me and then looked away as if she'd seen something indecent.

I needed another pair of eyes to correct me on stuff like this, stuff I did without thinking. Curtis had said he would nudge me when I got out of line.

He spent our first night out together kicking me under the table.

We went to several places that night, all of them neighborhood watering holes that catered to young professionals who were either on the prowl or just out for a booze-up with friends.

At the first place, an upscale sports bar, I was ready to launch with abandon, though Curtis tried his best to dissuade me. He knew better, having come of age in a man's skin. He'd gotten his nose pushed in one too many times after charging horns-first at an aloof beauty. He didn't recommend the practice.

But I was on a tear, eager to test my new treads. So as soon as we sat down, I picked out a couple of twenty-something women sitting at a table across the room. I gave them a few lingering looks to check their interest. I caught one woman's eye and held her gaze for a second, smiling. She returned the smile and looked away. This was signal enough for me, so I stood up, made my way over to their table and asked them whether they wanted to join us for a drink.

"No, thanks," one of them said, "we're on our way out in a minute."

Simple enough, right? A brush-off. No biggie. But as I turned away and slumped back across the room toward our table, I felt like the outcast kid in the lunchroom who trips and dumps his tray on the linoleum in front of the whole school. Rejection sucked.

"Rejection is a staple for guys," said Curtis, laughing as I crumpled into my seat with a humiliated sigh. "Get used to it."

That was my first lesson in male courtship ritual. You had to take your knocks and knock again. It was that or wait for some pitying act of God that would never come. This wasn't some magic island in a beer commercial where all the ladies would light up for me if only I drank the right brew.

"Try again, man," Curtis urged. "C'mon. Don't give up so easily."

Near our table there was a group of three women at the bar, clearly friends, chatting among themselves. He pointed in their direction.

"Right there. Perfect. Go for it."

"All right. All right," I said. "Jesus, this really sucks."

"Yeah, well, welcome to my world."

I swore under my breath as I got up to go. Curtis crossed his arms and leaned back against his chair, smirking.

When I reached the bar I could see that these women were absorbed in their conversation. I was going to have to interrupt, and the female me knew that my approach, no matter how unassuming, would be perceived as a little pathetic and detestable. Small-shouldered guy sidles up to cute chicks with a canned line and a huge hole of obvious insecurity gaping in the middle of his chest. I stopped at the thought of this. I didn't want to be that guy, the nuisance guy that women always dread. I was embarrassed for myself. But then how to retreat with dignity? I was already lurking awkwardly behind them, lamely pretending to flag down the bartender.

As I leaned toward the bar with a bill in my hand, the women turned to look at me, the way you do when something unremarkable enters your peripheral vision. Their eyes took me in like a billboard on the highway, running the length of me, then moving back to the point of interest elsewhere.

Succinctly, I was put in my place, stuck there with no recourse.

I thought about what I could say that wouldn't sound cooked-up, cheap or presumptuous. I decided it was best to be honest. I'd always respected that in men who had approached me. I'd once given my number to a young businessman on the street in New York simply as a reward for having had the balls to put himself out there and ask me for my number. I'd had no intention of going out with him, which, in retrospect, I see wasn't fair. When he called I had to tell him I was a lesbian, which, like most interested men, he refused to believe was a real, sustainable state of being.

"Why'd you give me your number then?" he'd asked finally.

"Because I was proud of you," I'd said.

Now, at the bar, it was my turn to make myself proud, or at least fend off crushing defeat. I decided, however, that Curtis was going to have to do his job on this one, so I went back to our table and yanked him up.

"You're coming with me," I said, dragging him across toward the bar.

He had a self-satisfied look on his face. He was enjoying himself at my expense. He knew he was teaching me a lesson and he was relishing every second of it.

When we got to the bar, the women were as absorbed as ever

in each other, huddled together, trying to talk over the music. We entered their orbit abruptly, me still half dragging Curtis by the arm. I tried to smooth over the breach:

"Hi, ladies. [Ladies? Jesus.] I'm sorry to interrupt, but I wanted to meet you. I don't mean to be a pain in the ass about this [God, I was groveling already], but my name's Ned and this is my friend Curtis."

Curtis and I had joked that he would play my wing man at times like this, my conversational stopgap. Like typical guys, we found the *Top Gun* humor disproportionately funny in this context. It made us feel better about the downsizing we knew we were letting ourselves in for.

At first the three women looked us over like inferior produce in the supermarket. Then they smiled weakly. They were well brought up. They knew enough to cover quickly with the kind of anemic politesse that we all use on bores at cocktail parties. We were in, but I could see that their patience was thin.

I focused on the woman on the left who said she had gone to Princeton and was working in a foreign policy think tank. I decided to drop the novelist persona that I'd adopted as cover with my bowling buddies, and switch to talking about my recent job as a political columnist. I thought this would make for common ground, which in part it did, but only of the nodding variety. "Oh, you write about politics. Uh-huh."

She wasn't going to bite.

As I talked on, trying to work with her clipped responses, I found myself, as I had on my first trip to the bar, switching again to her point of view. Seeing how protected she seemed, I remembered how protective of myself I had often been in encounters with strange men. I had always made the same assumption, one that my brother Ted had ingrained in me as a young teenager: all guys who make advances to a woman only want one thing—to get in her pants.

I remember him saying, "It doesn't matter what they say. They'll say anything. Just remember. They only want one thing. *That's how guys are.*"

I took that assessment at face value, an assessment that was, I have to admit, mostly borne out by my experience in college, where I found that most young men who bothered to speak to me at parties did indeed only want one thing. To the rest of them I was invisible. Why bother, I guess they figured, if you didn't want to fuck her?

Whatever veneer a man pasted over this intention, and it wasn't usually a very artful one, I always knew or thought I knew what he was after. I had, I realized, treated most men with the same coldness that these women were showing me.

And therein lay the paradox for me. Even if (and this is an enormous "if") it could be argued that most guys who chat up strange girls in bars or on the street only want one thing, it was equally true that I wasn't most guys. I was a woman, with a woman's sensibilities. Besides, I didn't want to sleep with them. They were just another test case.

Still, it didn't feel good to be on the receiving end of their suspicion. After all, there are plenty of guys in the world, the marrying kind, I suppose, who really just want to get to know a girl, but have no other means of doing so except to strike up a conversation on the fly. So should they bear the brunt of the majority of their sex's bad behavior? And was the majority really that badly behaved?

There I was, caught square in the middle of the oldest plot in the world: he said/she said. It was the woman's job to be on the defensive, because past experience had taught her to be. It was the guy's job to be on the offensive, because he had no choice. It was that or never meet at all.

It's a wonder that men and women ever get together. Their signals, by necessity, are crossed, their behaviors at cross-purposes from the start. I was beginning to feel happier than ever to be a dyke. As a woman, it was a lot easier to meet women, because even in a dating situation there was always the common bond of womanhood, the common language of females that often makes even strange women able to chat amiably with each other, almost from the moment they meet.

I wondered if the same thing would happen here. Would these women lower their defenses if they found out I was a woman?

After another ten minutes of condescension, I realized that this was going nowhere, and that I might learn more about Ned if I let them in on the gag.

I had to repeat the phrase "I'm really a woman" four times before they got what I was saying. There was a moment of absolutely stunned silence, and then the inevitable "No way," in chorus.

Then, with startling quickness we all began chatting like hens. Their aloof facade fell away, and not, I sensed, just because of the conversational fascination of the disguise, but because they felt disarmed enough, knowing that I was a woman, to let me in. The inclusion was even physical. When I'd approached as Ned they had been sitting facing the bar. They had only bothered to turn halfway around to talk to me, their faces always in profile. Now they turned all the way around to face me, their backs to the bar.

I understood this reaction immediately. I had predicted it. But still a part of me resented their prejudices. I was still the same person I had been before, just as any given strange man is a person beneath his blazer or his baseball hat. As a woman, I was accepted. As a man I had been rejected yet again. I understood intimately the social reasons for this, but it seemed unfair all the same.

As Curtis and I said goodnight and walked away, I found myself thinking about rejection and how small it made me feel, and how small most men must feel under the weight of what women expect from them. I was an actor playing a role, but these women had gotten to me nonetheless. None of these interactions mattered. I had nothing real at stake. But still, I felt bad.

So how must men feel when it's a true encounter and everything in the game seems stacked against them? They make the move, or the women bluff them—without tipping their hands—into making the move. The guys step out (stupidly, it now seems to me) into the space between, saying something irreversible and frank—a compliment or an outright indication of interest—and most of the time the women step away, or laugh disdainfully, and the guys are left with their asses in the wind. That's the sport, and men are the suckers. Women guard the gate and men storm it. Natural selection is brutal, and women do, in the immortal words of Jim Morrison, seem wicked when you're unwanted.

"How do you handle all this fucking rejection?" I asked Curtis when we sat back down for a postmortem.

"Let me tell you a story," he said. "When I was in college, there was this guy Dean, who got laid all the time. I mean this guy had different women coming out of his room every weekend and most weeknights, and he wasn't particularly good looking. He was fat and kind of a slob. Nice guy, though, but nothing special. I couldn't figure out how he did it, so one time I just asked him. 'How do you get so many girls to go out with you?' He was a man of few words, kind of Coolidge-esque, if you know what I mean. So all he said was: 'I get rejected ninety percent of the time. But it's that ten percent.'"

That made us both cackle and pound the table.

"That's the thing about being a guy," Curtis finished. "Rejection is part of the game. It's expected."

Not only was dating one of the hardest of Ned's experiences, it was also the most fraught with deception. I was deceiving people on a lot of levels and the responsible part of me didn't particularly feel good about it. But I also felt the glee of pulling off a performance in the real world, which meant that I was lying and I was enjoying the lie at someone else's expense. I was deeply involved in a way that might get me and other people hurt.

But how hurt were any of us going to get? What, I asked myself, are one or two dates in the grand scheme of things? I decided I would out myself to anyone with whom I had more than a passing, unsuccessful, date or two—which happened with three women. With everyone else, I would just be deceitful, but brief.

To most of the women I dated, even a date or two meant a lot, especially women who had been out roaming the singles scene for years in their midthirties, trying to find a mate amid the serial daters. Almost inevitably, they were carrying the baggage of previous hurts at the hands of men, which in many cases had prejudiced them unfairly against the male sex. For them, as for so many of us, romantic hurt equaled romantic blame, and because they were exclusive heterosexuals, romantic blame was assigned more often to the sex, not the morals, of the person inflicting the pain.

Bisexuals know that hurt gets inflicted by both sexes in equal measure if not always by the same means. But for these women—who had never dated other women, and thus never been romantically hurt by them—men as a subspecies, not the particular men with whom they had been involved, were to blame for the wreck of a relationship and the psychic damage it had done to them.

It's hardly surprising, then, that in this atmosphere, as a single man dating women, I often felt attacked, judged, on the defensive. Whereas with the men I met and befriended as Ned there was a presumption of innocence—that is, you're a good guy until you prove otherwise—with women there was quite often a presumption of guilt: you're a cad like every other guy until you prove otherwise.

"Pass my test and then we'll see if you're worthy of me" was the implicit message coming across the table at me. And this from women who had demonstrably little to offer. "Be lighthearted," they said, though buoyant as lead zeppelins themselves. "Be kind," they insisted in the harshest of tones. "Don't be like the others," they implied, while having virtually condemned me as such beforehand.

The bitterest women I met were usually in their midthirties or older. They'd been through the mill a bit and they'd probably had more than their share of hellish dates or hit-and-run relationships before I came along. To hear them tell it, the pool of eligible, mature, stable, reciprocating, emotionally evolved men out there was small and polluted, and having to wade through it when what you wanted most in life was to settle down and start a family would be enough to shorten anyone's fuse.

Then again, many of the women I met weren't emotional giants either, nor were they particularly well adjusted or stable. They just considered themselves to be such. And even the ones who knew they were damaged seemed to feel entitled to expect stolidity from a man, as if, in the time-honored way of things, a man is supposed to be strong, to hold things together for his woman, to hold her up when she can't do it herself.

Ironically, one of the women who was the least well adjusted, and the least graceful at dating, turned out to be one of the most important of my relationships.

I arrived on time at my local Starbucks. I had met Sasha, as I met most of my dates, through a personals Web site on the Internet. We'd exchanged photographs and a number of e-mails. After a week or so of back and forth we'd decided to get together for coffee, a brief encounter that would presumably allow either or both of us to bolt if we felt the need. Or so I thought.

When I approached her table, Sasha was already a good way through a pile of photographs she'd obviously just picked up from the pharmacy across the street. I expected her to pocket them the minute I appeared, but instead she began showing them to me. They were of a coworker's wedding—not a friend's or a family member's wedding, mind you—but a coworker's wedding. She leafed through several rolls, pointing out her office acquaintances in their morning coats and off-the-shoulder dresses, all drunkenly propped against each other, hamming for the camera.

This, I thought, was a hostile act. Everyone knows that photographic displays are one of the most boring parts of getting to know anyone, which is why people save them for later, when you actually know some of the people pictured, or care enough about the other person to endure the torture.

I found out later that this particular woman's train-wreck experiences with the opposite sex had taught her to believe that, to men, women were just, as she put it, "meat with a pulse." In retrospect I wonder if this Photomat ritual wasn't an elaborate test, maybe her twisted way of letting me know that if I was just there to get in her knickers, I'd have to do my term in her holding cell before I'd get anywhere. Perhaps she had found this to be an effective way of weeding out the louts, but it made me want to bolt.

It was only the beginning. After we'd finished with the photos, she launched into a two-hour description of her pending divorce and the circumstances that had precipitated it, one of which was an as yet unconsummated *affaire de coeur* she was still having with a married man. She was torn up, an obsessive caught in her own pain loop. I felt sorry for her, but then her situation wasn't any worse than a lot of people's. Besides, I felt mighty resentful about having been dragooned into a therapy session on a first date.

Toward the end I decided that this woman was either the most conversationally inconsiderate person I'd ever met or the most socially impervious. Whatever the case, she was taking advantage of my good manners.

I was going to get a little of my own back before the poor slack-faced coffee minions—who were by now not so subtly hinting at last call by slamming cupboards and rustling trash bags—were forced to hustle us out the door for closing.

I was mean.

"Do you live entirely inside your head," I said finally, "or are you aware that there are other people in the world?"

She thought about this for a second without the slightest hint of having taken any offense, then answered, "Yes, I guess I do kind of live in my head."

"Why are you here?" I followed.

To this she saw me and raised me one, which I had to admire. "Because it's better than staring at the walls in my bedroom."

This I could understand and pity. I had been there.

"Are you disappointed by your life?"

Again she paused, computed this, then said, "No."

I don't remember much of the rest of it. There wasn't much. We got kicked out of the Starbucks and that was basically that. But her frank answers to my questions had made me realize that I could ask this person almost anything, and that alone was interesting. She was quite happy to converse on whatever level if it kept her engaged and kept her from stewing alone. I could learn what her impressions of Ned had been, how he'd compared with other men she'd dated, what else she was expecting from a man, and whether cheap therapy was all she was wanting from a second date with Ned, or whether Ned had scored points for being sensitive, a good listener.

"I told you all of this because I wanted to be honest with you from the beginning about where I am," she said.

Clearly she wasn't ready to start dating again. She wasn't looking for a relationship. She was looking for distraction and an ear to tell her troubles to. She didn't have enough emotional energy left to get seriously involved with Ned, which I saw as a buffer zone between us, making it possible to get to know her, as a man, without causing too much romantic hardship, if any.

I was especially interested in her because she had been involved with a married man and been hurt by the experience. This is a wounded woman's cliché if ever there was one, and she followed the pattern to the last detail. She had chosen to get involved with someone who was unavailable, yet she blamed him for refusing to leave his wife. He was the cad, the coward. She was the long-suffering party, the helpmeet waiting in the wings, the used one who deserved better. Her predicament was of her own making and entirely predictable, yet she used it to bolster her distrust of the opposite sex, and as with many of the other women I dated, Ned took that accumulated load on his shoulders from the start. He was just the next man who would hurt her.

How could it be otherwise? When a woman approaches a man armed to the teeth with ulterior wounds for which men as a species are presumptively to blame, the man in question has little choice but to fight back, and when everything he says and does is measured against the front-loaded politics of sex, he can't help but shrivel or putrefy under the scrutiny. Sadly, this alienation dynamic, while temporarily unpleasant for me (the man in these cases), worked in the long run far more to the detriment of such women, who were not only desperately unhappy, but doing everything to ensure that they would remain so. Their refusal to see men as individuals, and more importantly to see their initial encounters with them as tabulae rasae, doomed them from the start.

I would see more of Sasha—wounds, armor, honesty and all.

Meanwhile I went on a *lot* of dates. I heard a lot of clichés. But I also saw a lot of women who didn't conform to patterns in the least. One middle-aged woman with whom Ned struck up a conversation in a bar summarized one cliché in three words: "Women are enraged." The reason? According to her, a complete and utter emotional disconnect between the sexes—women wanting and desperately needing more emotional communication and attention, and men being utterly baffled by this need and unable to meet it. It sounded as if she'd been reading Deborah Tannen, who wrote in *You Just Don't Understand*: "Many men honestly do not know what women want and women honestly do not know why men find what they want so hard to comprehend and deliver."

Yet the opposite is equally true, though less often discussed publicly. A lot of the women I met didn't know, didn't understand or didn't appear to care what a lot of the men in their lives wanted, either.

Perhaps women have been guilty of hubris in this regard. We think of ourselves as emotional masters of the universe. In our world, feelings reign. We have them. We understand them. We cater to them. Men, we think, don't on all counts. But as I learned among my friends in the bowling league and elsewhere, this is absolutely untrue and absurd. Of course men have a whole range of emotions, just as women do—it's just that many of them are often silent or underground, invisible to most women's eyes and ears. Tannen was right enough on that point. Women and men communicate differently, often on entirely different planes. But just as men have failed us, we have failed them. It has been one of our great collective female shortcomings to presume that whatever we do not perceive simply isn't there, or that whatever is not communicated in our language is not intelligible speech.

Ditto for the stereotype about men monopolizing conversations. Like Sasha, many of my dates—even the more passive ones—did most of the talking. I listened to them talk literally for hours about the most minute, mind-numbing details of their personal lives; men they were still in love with, men they had divorced, roommates and coworkers they hated, childhoods they were loath to remember, yet somehow found the energy to recount ad nauseam. Listening to them was like undergoing a slow frontal lobotomy. I sat there stunned by the social ineptitude of people to whom it never seemed to occur that no one, much less a first date, would have any interest in enduring this ordeal. This was a human, not a male or female, failing.

When I wasn't listening to these long laments, I was asking these women questions about themselves, mostly to fill the silences, because they rarely asked me questions about myself or, for that matter, made much of an effort to engage in a genuine conversation quid pro quo. Perhaps the art is lost to both sexes.

Weren't people supposed to be on their best behavior on first dates? Weren't they supposed to at least pretend an interest in the other person out of politeness if nothing else? Certainly, that's what I was doing, making polite conversation. So much so that I never expected to hear from these people again. I was boring myself. That's the worst part of a bad date. It makes you feel like a toad, and you keep telling yourself, "I know I'm more fun than this, and I know that when I came into this café I wasn't in despair about the human condition."

Maybe they were just bumbling through as best they could,

knowing that they'd never contact me again. But to my surprise, many of them did contact me again—enthusiastically.

To my mind my first dates were often so bad that second dates were unthinkable, even in the name of research, except in rare cases where I thought I could learn something useful from posing a series of what, under normal circumstances, would have been considered rude questions, but when aimed at the liminally autistic proved just the ticket to a vaguely interesting conversation.

If the most disgruntled women I met and dated as Ned had ever been attuned to men's signals, by the time I met them, they were long past receiving outside information of any kind. Moreover, if the way they discussed their pasts and the way they approached me was anything to go by, they seemed incapable of seeing any new man as an individual. Worse still, they seemed to transform each new man, benign or otherwise, into the malignancy they were expecting him to be. They tended to see a wolf in every man they met, and so they made every man they met into a wolf—even when that man was a woman.

Not surprising really. The women who were hostile to me made me mad, and that made me want to be hostile to them. I can't imagine men in the same position not reacting the same way. And so the self-perpetuating cycle of unkindness and discontent would go on and on, feeding on itself. These women were mostly hostile in the first place because they felt that men's bad behavior had made them so, and the men they met behaved badly because hostility breeds contempt.

It wasn't a good recipe for finding a lasting relationship, but I could remember feeling exactly the way it seemed these women did when I was a young woman in and just out of college. I found plenty of ammunition for hating men in Women's Studies 101, much of it, like the subjugation and abuse of women historically (and even currently), undeniable. What's more, I found plenty of reinforcement for my fledgling misandry in the crass undergraduates I encountered everywhere on campus. I'd read the textbooks of radical feminism, and following their lead, I thought all males were tainted by the patriarchy. For years thereafter, every guy I met was on probation.

But there's nothing like a few years in the trenches of lesbian romance to give a girl a little perspective on the supposed inborn evils of the opposite sex. As time went on I learned that girls don't behave any better than boys under relational duress, and that centuries of subjugation haven't made women morally superior.

Sasha and I struck up an e-mail relationship after our first lousy date. Indeed, e-mail is now central to dating. I made contact with almost all the women I dated via the Internet, and we usually exchanged a number of e-mails before we met. Often the process of measuring me against previous hurts began then, as did the expectation that I prove myself to be better than the rest.

Correspondence was mandatory in most cases, even with the women I met at speed-dating events and followed up with later by e-mail. (Speed dating, for those of you who are unfamiliar with the practice, is a process by which singles can meet and have minidates with ten or more members of the opposite sex in the space of an hour. One group, usually the women, sits at tables. The men then rotate from one table to the next, spending a timed five minutes with each woman. Everyone is given a sheet of paper on which they mark a yes or a no next to the name of each person they meet, indicating whether or not they have any interest in seeing that person again. The organizers then match the yeses and provide e-mail addresses to the interested parties.)

These women wanted to be wooed by language. They weren't going to meet a strange man without measuring him first, and they weren't going to waste a meal or even a cup of coffee on a suitor who couldn't be bothered to craft a few lines beforehand. I was happy to oblige. The seductive effect of a well-written letter or, better yet, a well-chosen poem, on a strange woman's mind was often strong and sometimes hilariously so, even to the women involved, who were quite aware and ready to laugh about the effect distracting missives could have on them. One date told me, long after she'd dated Ned and learned his secret, that a coworker, reading one of Ned's e-mails over her shoulder, had said: "Shit. He's sending you poems? You'd better fuck this man."

Ned made an impression not just because he gave these women at least a pale version of the reading material they seemed to crave, but because he did it so willingly. It was rare, most of them told me, for a man to write at such length, much less to write with consideration and investment.

I found this to be true in my own experience as a woman. For a little contrast, I went on a few dates with men as a woman during the course of my time as Ned. The men I met on the Internet, and then subsequently in person, didn't require this epistolary preamble, nor did they offer it. They were eager to meet as soon as possible, usually, I found, because they wanted to see what I looked like. Their feelings or fantasies would be based on that far more than, or perhaps to the exclusion of, anything I might write to them. On dates with men I felt physically appraised in a way that I never did by women, and while this made me more sympathetic to the suspicion that women were bringing to their dates with Ned, it had the opposite effect, too. Somehow men's seeming imposition of a superficial standard of beauty felt less intrusive, less harsh, than the character appraisals of women. Sure, women noticed how Ned looked, or perhaps noted is more accurate, but it was the conversation they were after, the interaction, the proof of intangible worth beyond apishness. Writing well was the prerequisite, and that was where I saw the first pattern of judgment taking shape.

Sometimes I was surprised at how early in the correspondence this process began. By way of describing my personality to one woman, I wrote that I liked to try to dodge the mundane by shaking up the world around me, making purposeful but harmless faux pas just to see what would happen, things like breaking into a silly dance in the middle of the supermarket or saying the unexpected, vaguely socially unacceptable thing at a dinner party just to poke a hole in the chatter. To this she responded that her last boyfriend had enjoyed doing things like that and one or two times it had ended up really hurting her. She said my propensities in this regard had given her serious pause. That was the end of that correspondence.

Another woman told me in her first e-mail that she needed a confident man, but she felt there had to be a fine line drawn between being secure in himself and being arrogant. She said she drew that line with every man she met. This was a double bind I encountered often as Ned, and something that made me wonder about how reasonable women's supposed unmet emotional needs actually were.

They wanted a man to be confident. They wanted in many ways to defer to him. I could feel that on many dates, the unspoken desire to be held up and led, whether in conversation or even in physical space, and at times it made me feel quite small in my costume, like a young man must feel when he's just coming of age, and he's suddenly expected to carry the world under his arm like a football. And some women did find Ned too small physically to be attractive. They wanted someone, they said, who could pin them to the bed or, as one woman put it, "someone who can drive the bus." Ned was too willowy for that, and came up wanting.

I felt this especially keenly on one of my earliest dates, waiting for a woman at a fancy restaurant I'd chosen. I was sitting alone in one of those cavernous red leather booths that you see at old-world steak houses, and I was holding the menu, which also happened to be red and enormous, and I felt absolutely ridiculous, like the painful geek in a teen movie who's trying to score with an older woman. I felt tiny and insignificant when held up against what I imagined to be this sophisticated woman's (she was a diplomat) expectations for a Cary Grant type who would know exactly what to do and say, and whose coat would be big enough to cover her. I suddenly understood from the inside why R. Crumb draws his women so big, and his diminutive self begging at their heels or riding them around the room. I was so embarrassed I almost got up and left rather than face the look of amused disappointment on that woman's face, a look that mercifully never materialized. We had a very pleasant, uneventful meal. Still, I'd never felt so inadequate on a date as I did sometimes as miniature Ned.

Yet as much as these women wanted a take-control man, at the same time, they wanted a man who was vulnerable to them, a man who would show his colors and open his doors, someone expressive, intuitive, attuned. This I was in spades, and I always got points for it, but feeling the pressure to be that other world-bestriding colossus at the same time made me feel very sympathetic toward heterosexual men, not only because living up to Caesar is an immensely heavy burden to bear, but because trying to be a sensitive new age guy at the same time is pretty well impossible. If women are trapped by the whore/Madonna complex, men are equally trapped by this warrior/minstrel complex. What's more, while a man is expected to be modern, that is, to support feminism in all its particulars, to see and treat women as equals in every respect, he is on the other hand often still expected to be traditional at the same time, to treat a lady like a lady, to lead the way and pick up the check.

Expectation, expectation, expectation. That was the leitmotif of Ned's dating life, taking on the desirable manly persona or shrugging off its dreaded antithesis. Finding the right balance was maddening, and operating under the constant weight of so much political guilt was simply exhausting. Though, in the parlance of liberal politics, I had operated in my real life under the burden of being a doubly oppressed minority — a woman and a lesbian — and I had encountered the deprivations of that status, as a man, I operated under what I felt in these times to be the equally heavy burden of being a double majority, a white man.

One woman, whom I never did meet, but with whom I had an intense weeklong correspondence as Ned, threw Ned into the male rogue basket as soon as I tried to warn her away from getting too emotionally involved. She assumed that my problem was fear of intimacy, but in my case it was something else altogether. After only a week's worth of letters I could see that this woman was making an emotional investment in Ned, and I began to feel uncomfortable with the deception. I, too, perhaps in an all-too-girly fashion, had become emotionally involved. I had grown to like this person and wanted to know her. Still, at first, I wasn't sure that I wanted to reveal my deception to her, so I was hopelessly vague, mostly indicating that she shouldn't become emotionally invested in something romantic developing between us. In response, she promptly accused me of being a married man who was lying just to get sex on the side, something she'd encountered before. She could tell, she said, by the characteristically devious quality of my prose, that I was trying to pull the other-woman scenario over on her. At that she broke off our correspondence.

Not that I blamed her for wanting to ditch—it was a healthy response—but I was struck once again by the immediate impulse to lump me in with male cheaters, a breed whose scurvy ways are, apparently, immediately recognizable on paper even in a lesbian.

Sasha and I had our series of query-filled, confessional e-mail exchanges as well. I wasn't playing a role on the page, or even in person, except in how I dressed and in my efforts to keep my voice in the lower portions of my register. I was just me. That was the point, after all, to be a real person, myself in all possible ways, culturally a woman, but in disguise as a man. I didn't try to write or say the things I thought a man would write or say. I responded to her genuinely in every way, except about my sex.

Our time together lasted the longest, three weeks or so in all. We had only three dates during that time, but we wrote several times a day, sharing our thoughts about each other and our ideas about whatever came up. Naturally, during the course of all this, we talked about her past relationships with men, which, as she indicated at some length, had been less than satisfactory. I suggested that perhaps if men were so unsatisfying to her emotionally, she should consider dating a woman. Then, I ventured, she might find out that the fault was not in the sex. To this she sent an unnecessarily sharp reply, something on the order of having about as much interest in lesbianism as in shooting heroin.

She had, by this time (about two dates and a week and a half into our correspondence) told me that she found Ned attractive, though she also made it clear that she was emotionally engaged elsewhere and was likely to remain so for a long time. This was the reason I had allowed our exchanges to go as far as they had. On the first date she had made it clear that she was still in love with the married man, and that whatever she and I could share would be circumscribed by that entanglement. She was looking for company, maybe a little male attention on the side to shore her up through a bad time, but she wasn't really single to speak of.

Still, something had grown up between us in a short time, and I decided that it shouldn't go any further. I would tell her the truth on the third date, which we were scheduled to have at the end of that week. I was curious to see what would happen to her supposed attraction for Ned when she learned that he was a woman. Would it evaporate? And if so, would that negate in her mind, or even in reality, the fact that it had ever been there in the first place? Is an attraction real if it is attached to something illusory or something that doesn't exist? Many would and have argued that that is all love ever is, an attachment to something illusory. Lacan wrote that love is giving something you don't possess to someone who doesn't exist. Perhaps Ned was an object lesson in that principle, or at least in lust, if not love.

But what if her attraction continued? And if it did, how would she deal with the knowledge that this thing she had so eschewed, lesbianism, was happening to her? Would she lash out in disgust, or would she realize that perhaps those feelings that most of us are raised to reject and despise are not as alien and perverted as she had always deemed them to be, and that, in fact, they could come as naturally as other appetites when unfettered by convention.

We met for dinner at her house. During dinner I told her right out, in the blurted way our conversations tended to go, that there was something I wasn't telling her about myself, and that I couldn't tell her what it was. I told her that if we were going to go to bed together she would have to be willing to accept the untold thing and the physical constraints it required. She took this well. She was curious. Not frightened. She didn't need to know, she said.

We talked about other things over dessert, and circled back to the topic of going to bed together, or whatever approximated version of that I could do without divulging my secret. We talked about our letters and the subject of lesbianism came up again.

"Your response was pretty vehement," I said. "You might have just said you weren't interested. Why heroin?"

"Let me put it this way, then. I think of lesbianism like India. It's enough for me to see the special on PBS. I don't feel the need to go there."

"Makes sense," I agreed.

The conversation moved on to something else and then back again to the prospect of sex, and my visible discomfort with skirting the edge of full disclosure. I had told her as much as I would. She had asked if my secret was something physical and I had told her it was. She reached her hands across the table and took my hands in hers. Would she see that my hands were small for a man's? I wondered. If she did, she said nothing.

We decided to go into the bedroom. Once there, she lit several candles by the bed. I sat on the edge of the bed, which was low to the ground, and asked her to sit with her back to me on the floor. She did so, leaning against the mattress between my legs. I gathered her long hair in my hands and draped it over one shoulder, exposing one side of her neck. I eased down the V-neck of her sweater, exposing the shoulder, and traced her skin with my fingertips, behind the ear, along the hairline, the collarbone. I leaned down to kiss the places I'd touched. She moved in response, lolling her head to the side. She reached up behind her and placed her palm on my cheek. She would feel the stubble now for sure and know that it didn't feel like stubble should. The jig was probably up.

"Do you feel it?" I asked.

"Yes."

"How does it feel?"

"Soft," she said.

She didn't seem alarmed or surprised.

This was about as far as I was willing or able to take it—the makeup was smeared now for sure—so I took her hand away then and got up from the bed to move around in front of her, to face her on the floor.

"Do you want me to show you or tell you?" I said.

"Whichever you prefer."

It took me longer than I'd thought it would to spit it out. I was holding her hands when I finally did.

"I'm a woman."

She didn't pull her hands away.

I went on immediately to fill the space. I told her about the book project and why I was doing it. Then I waited.

She was still quiet. Then she said, "You're going to have to give me a few minutes to get used to this."

We sat in silence. Clearly, whatever physical deformity she'd been expecting hadn't been femaleness.

"I'm not a transsexual," I added by way of help. "This is makeup and my tits are strapped down. I don't actually wear glasses either." I took them off. My glasses usually had a kind of reverse Clark Kent effect. Without them people always felt I looked more like myself, whereas with them, Ned stepped out of the phone booth. The tortoiseshell plastic frames I'd chosen helped to square my face and hid my eyes, which everyone found too soft for a man's. This, and the knowledge that I was a woman, helped shift the look enough for her to see the woman underneath.

"Yes. I can see it now," she said.

She took up one of my hands, which she was still holding, and examined it.

"These aren't a man's wrists," she said, caressing them, "or a man's hands, or a man's skin."

She looked me over for a few minutes in the dim light, making out the feminine parts and nodding.

"I always thought you weren't very hairy for a man," she said. She laughed a little and said, "Well, now I can tell you that my nickname for you in the past few weeks has been My Gay Boyfriend. You set off my gaydar the first time I saw you. Your hair was too groomed and your shirt too pressed, and your shoes too nice."

A lot of women had noticed and complimented me on my hair and my shoes. For Ned's dates I groomed my hair to the last strand. The women I dated seemed to appreciate the effort quite a lot, and seemed unduly glad to find a man with a manageable bush on his head.

My shoes were just basic black leather loafers, but I wore them with black socks and jeans and a black button-down dress shirt, like some slob made over by the Fab Five on *Queer Eye for the Straight Guy.* The trendy term *metrosexual* came up a lot in my company during my dating career as Ned. But it was on this point that I was sorely disabused of one of my preconceptions about heterosexual women and what they were really looking for in men. When I started the project, I had suspected that I would find hordes of women for whom Ned would be the ideal man, the ideal man being essentially a woman, or a woman in a man's body. But I was wrong about this. It wasn't that simple. Women's desires were stubbornly kaleidoscopic and their more subtle proclivities even more uncategorizable.

Sure, you could make generalizations about men and women,

what they tended to do and want, buy and consume, but all of that was really just frosting, and it wasn't until you got down deep inside the individual that you began to see the contradictions emerge and announce themselves. The concept of either/or isn't very helpful when you're trying to understand men and women, because every time you try to boil them down to their tidy habits, their anomalies poke through and leave you with a mess you can't write up very neatly in a conclusion, except to say that both are true and neither.

Ned wasn't everybody's type by a long shot. Sure, some women—like Sasha, as it turned out—still wanted to go to bed with him once they knew he wasn't a guy. But plenty of others didn't. They were just flat out heterosexuals, tried and true. As one date, Anna, explained it to me once I'd told her I was a woman: "I was not immediately sexually attracted to Ned. I thought him good-looking and likable and the date was so very enjoyable and commanded a repeat performance, and the writing, God, the writing, was what got me off. But in the end, Ned himself did not elicit an immediate visceral sexual response from me. Ned was too slight for me, too metrosexual. I would never have guessed in a million years that you were not a boy, but I like boys that weigh two hundred pounds. And yes, I find them emotionally disappointing, especially in bed, but the physical strength, the roughness I find erotic and I do not prefer sex otherwise."

Sasha and I spent hours that night talking about the book, why I was doing it, and how fascinated she was by what she'd learned about herself. Sasha was very interested in the implications of the experiment. She was curious about her lesbian tendencies or lack thereof. She wasn't in the least frightened or threatened by the switch or her attraction to Ned and her ongoing attraction to me. She was extremely pleased to have happened upon an experience that had shaken up the norm.

Sasha and I went to bed together, and obviously Sasha had to thereby revise her hard ideas about lesbianism and her desire to "go there." Yet she did so with stunning alacrity for someone who, I'm fairly certain, was not a closeted lesbian all along, or even a genuine bisexual. In our weird stilted exchanges, we had connected mentally in some way. Maybe I'd come to admire the adventurer and even the oddball in her. Maybe she just desperately needed a good friend. There could be a thousand reasons good or bad, but I think none of them had much of anything to do with sex. And this, I'll maintain in an entirely unscientific manner, is a stubbornly female tendency.

For most women sex is an epiphenomenon, the steam that issues from the engine. And the coal is mental. It's: "Do you make me laugh? Do you make me think? Do you talk to me?" It's not: "Are you handsome? Are you rich and accomplished and well hung?" I suppose, more often than you might think, it's not even: "Are you male or female?" It's really just: "Are you there and do you get me?"

But that's the quantum paradox of sexuality right there. Because just as soon as I say that, just as soon as I say that three of the women I dated and revealed myself to, three heterosexual women, wanted to or did sleep with me once they knew that I was a woman, I remember that one of those three women, Anna, didn't sleep with me because I didn't weigh two hundred pounds.

She struggled to plumb that conundrum as hard as anyone. We went back and forth on it trying to understand the nature of the attraction we both felt, an attraction that was physical, but physical because it had first been mental.

Anna was by far the best date I had as Ned. Given what I've described thus far, that may not sound like the choicest of compliments, but I mean it as one. She was a joy, and proof that real chemistry could exist between two people from the instant they met. Of course, she was also proof that chemistry was just that, particles mixing and sparking a buzz on the brain, but it wasn't a good predictor of fit or anything else, for that matter, beyond itself. It had nothing whatsoever to do with what two people would want from each other or what would work logistically when the high wore off. You could be entirely unaware of who or what you were to each other, or even, in our case, whether you were man or woman, gay or straight, and it could still be there between you, plain and undeniable. But momentous as it sometimes felt, maybe in the end it didn't mean anything at all.

We met for dinner at a cheap Chinese place I knew. All these dates were breaking me financially, and based on past experience, I was hoping it would be a short evening. But the minute Anna sat down I was so immediately at ease with her that I wished I'd taken her to a place where the prices weren't even on the menu—the kind of place where blind daters who click get slowly soused on top-shelf martinis until they're canoodling on their bar stools and feeding each other oysters by the end of the evening.

By the end of the evening we were canoodling at the bar at a place down the street. I asked her if I could touch her hand. She nodded and smiled drowsily, faintly pityingly, faintly nurturingly—the way she might have looked at a lot of imploring men—placing her hand on the bar palm up between us. And there it was. The thing sought. The simple favor granted, and a mountainous relief contained in it.

I held it and kissed her fingers. That was all. Nothing serious. We talked mostly, and thereafter we wrote a lot of e-mails back and forth, until I finally told her the truth. And then nothing changed and everything changed. I met her again later as myself, and the thing between us was still there, but she was a little afraid of it by then, uncomfortable with it in anything but the mind, for reasons I both understood and respected. That was the beauty of the experiment. It was different for everyone.

The third straight girl who still wanted to keep seeing Ned (even after she knew that he was a woman) was the only girl I succeeded in picking up in public.

Sally worked behind the counter in an ice-cream parlor. I was there buying ice cream and while she was scooping my cookies 'n' cream, I told her that I really liked her glasses. It was true, the kind of thing I would have said as myself, but also the kind of thing that would be taken much more to heart by a straight woman when I said it as Ned.

She was affable and direct. She responded to Ned's compliment with flirtatious thanks and a story about how she'd picked her frames out of the bargain basket at the optician. I gave her my phone number on a napkin and asked her to call—probably not the manly thing to do, but I thought it was the polite thing to do. My feminine empathy knew how awkward it could be to refuse someone your number, yet how much more awkward it could be to give it to him and then have to play phone dodge for the next two weeks until he either dropped the chase or turned stalker.

She called the next day. Her voice on the phone was tentative. She'd never done this before, she said. No one had ever just asked her out on the spot. She was floating on the attention. She would be mad later, I thought, and she'd have every right to be.

Sally and I went out three times together. Three chatty dates on which we talked about nothing much at all. There wasn't much to say. She was thirty-five and still living at home. Still working in the ice-cream shop she'd worked in as a teenager. She'd been engaged, but had broken it off a year prior, or he had, or they'd let it atrophy until someone moved out, it was hard to tell. She hadn't been on a date since, but she wasn't bitter, or not so as you could tell.

She coasted over things and smiled and laughed at Ned's jokes. She didn't intimidate him. She knew enough not to. There were always girls like that. I'd known them all my life. The ones who didn't challenge a boy, or later, even a man, because he was really still a boy, and the slightest sign of backbone would chase him away. In high school that's what I learned as a girl. Make light. Hide your intelligence.

But having felt so small and intimidated with women as Ned, and that despite being a grown woman, Sally's coquettishness was a mercy to me, a small kindness and a comfort, even if it was mostly an act.

Sally liked Ned, it seemed. She flirted, not just with her laughter and attentiveness, but with her hands. She touched me often on the arm or the shoulder as we spoke. Midconversation, she reached across the table to straighten the rumpled collar on my jacket, and we kept right on talking as if it hadn't happened.

At the end of the third date I revealed myself. At first she was stunned. Still smiling and sort of laughing, wheels not turning visibly. Then she said she'd known something was off, but she hadn't been able to put her finger on it.

"Maybe some part of me knew," she said. "I don't know. You made so much eye contact. You listened so well. You weren't hairy. I'm not sure."

She said she wasn't angry, but she didn't say much of anything else. But then hours later she wrote an e-mail to say that she was, actually, "kind of" angry. She wanted to know if I'd only asked her out in order to do research for the book. I tried to soften this, but it was true. I asked her to come by my place the next day to talk. I wasn't dressed as Ned.

She showed up with a bottle of wine. She sat on the couch

sipping it, not saying anything. I asked her what she wanted. She looked at me, seemingly undeterred by the change in my appearance.

"I guess to keep seeing you," she said.

This surprised me.

"But you're not a lesbian, are you?" I asked.

"I don't know," she said. "I've never really been that fond of penises."

I tried to get her to talk more about this, but she wouldn't, except to say that she could never tell her family about any of this, at least not the lesbian part. She'd be too ashamed, she said, to ever tell anyone she might be gay.

"Maybe you're not," I said. "And if you are, you won't always feel this way."

"Yeah, I guess," she said, and got up to go.

We agreed to meet again, but we never got it together. I stopped by the shop to see her once a few weeks later, and she seemed embarrassed. She said she was seeing a guy and it was going well. I was happy for her. The last time I saw her there, while getting a cone with friends, she pretended not to see me. I wasn't surprised. She'd come around past that nice pretense to letting me know how she felt, if only by giving me the silent treatment. She had her angers aplenty, but like me and so many of the women I knew, she seemed to have trouble showing them, choosing instead to suppress them and pretend that everything was fine, to make things run smoothly while she boiled underneath.

Still, feminism had cracked that curse in some of us, giving us the right to be mad and the temperament to say it, and I met those women, too.

My worst date by far was with a woman I met for coffee in New York. We'd had very little correspondence beforehand, just meager getting-to-know-you kind of stuff. Like many of the others, it was hard to pin her down for a date, but finally she agreed. She was an attractive woman, a graduate student who had done her undergraduate work at an Ivy League school and had spent time thereafter at the Sorbonne. You could tell she was used to talking down to people, assuming they hadn't read the things she had. She was one of those polyglot Eurosnobs who'd lived in various countries around the world, and now considered herself to be above the cretinous American company she was at present obliged to keep.

She had lived in the Middle East as a child, so I started the conversation on what I thought was a topical note, asking about her thoughts on the veiling of women. I imagined, I said, that having lived in both worlds, she might have some interesting insights on the matter. She leaped on the word "interesting": "I don't know what you mean by *interesting*. Westerners don't understand the first thing about it. They think it's oppressive and backward, but what's really backward is the fact that in the year 2003 Congress can pass a law outlawing late-term abortions."

Here it was, the abortion test. This had come up on other dates. Several women went out of their way, it seemed, to stake out their ground on it, presumably as a means of testing my feminist credentials.

One woman mentioned it in passing on a date while talking about someone she knew who was against abortion.

"That's interesting," I interjected. "That's the first time I've ever heard anyone be honest about the prolife position and call it what it is."

She nodded, but a few minutes later, when she had cause to mention the prolife position again, she made a point of using the popular propagandistic term "antichoice" instead. The lines were drawn.

I didn't take the bait then, and I didn't take it with the Eurosnob either, preferring not to get into a political argument. Besides, I didn't want to interrupt this woman's hostility trajectory. I wanted to see how far it went. I wanted to see if, as with Sasha, I could find out what was behind it, get her to talk about the dynamic that was surfacing between us and why it was there. I was, after all, doing research, and if I was going to take abuse, I wanted to search it for what it could teach me.

This she didn't like any more than she had liked my use of the benign qualifier "interesting." She began critiquing my conversational style as too meta. Apparently I didn't ask the right questions. I was far too serious, something she had found to be true of other men she'd dated. She had said that she was interested in Italo Calvino, so I mentioned the concept of lightness as he defined it, asking if this was what she was looking for in people. To this she responded with what for her was probably enthusiasm, agreeing that yes, that was the quality she was looking for exactly.

Here is Calvino's partial definition:

To cut off Medusa's head without being turned to stone, Perseus supports himself on the very lightest of things, the winds and the clouds, and fixes his gaze upon what can be revealed only by indirect vision, an image caught in a mirror. I am immediately tempted to see this myth as an allegory on the poet's relationship to the world, a lesson in the method to follow when writing.

This, as it happens, is a perfect description of how our date made me feel. I may not have been quite Persean enough to suit her, but she definitely turned me to stone.

In passing, much later in the conversation, I mentioned the difference in our ages. She was thirty, I thirty-five. No sooner were the words out of my mouth than she railed: "Oh, please.

You're not going to try to tell me that a man's thirty-five is equal to a woman's thirty-five. It's more akin to a woman's twenty-three."

At that point I was, for the one and only time in my dating career as Ned, sorely tempted to strip naked and shout "Look, honey, I'm a chick, too, and a dyke to boot, so drop the Shulamith Firestone routine. I outgrew that when *I* was twenty-three, and if you ever hope to land a man who isn't already a castrato, you'd better start practicing a little more of that Calvino you're preaching."

But I just fell silent and shrugged. I deserved some abuse, even if Ned didn't. I never had a second date with the Eurosnob. Better just to fish somewhere else.

So I did. And that was when I met Anna for dinner.

For me, Ned's encounter with Anna, and the crux of my dating time as Ned, was all about that moment at the bar. The moment Anna gave Ned her hand, and the way that she treated him when she did it, with such conscious, poised magnanimity, granting access with the best possible grace. No woman I met as Ned had managed it nearly so well. It was a lot to manage.

And if you have never been sexually attracted to women, you will never quite understand the monumental power of female sexuality, except by proxy or in theory, nor will you quite know the immense advantage it gives us over men. As a lesbian, I knew something of this. But it is different between two women, more an engagement of equals, an exchange of something shared. As a man, I learned much more, and I learned it, I think, from an unexpectedly disadvantaged point of view.

The women's movement was in part about redressing feelings of powerlessness—physical powerlessness, institutional powerlessness—and the fear and rage that came of it. Rape is still a statistic women live by. And as we make our way in the world, we slink around corners, we maneuver our sexuality with salty care, loosing just enough to be desired, but not too much to be unsafe, and all the while we envy the seeming inviolability of males and dread its implacable underpinnings. We think we're working from the underside up. But if Ned's experience is anything to go by, that's not how it seems to the boys.

Dating women as a man was a lesson in female power, and it made me, of all things, into a momentary misogynist, which, I suppose was the best indicator that my experiment had worked. I saw my own sex from the other side, and I disliked women irrationally for a while because of it. I disliked their superiority, their accusatory smiles, their entitlement to choose or dash me with a fingertip, an execution so lazy, so effortless, it made the defeats and even the successes unbearably humiliating. Typical male power feels by comparison like a blunt instrument, its salvos and field strategies laughably remedial next to the damage a woman can do with a single cutting word: no.

Sex is most powerful in the mind, and to men, in the mind, women have a lot of power, not only to arouse, but to give worth, self-worth, meaning, initiation, sustenance, everything. Seeing this more clearly through my experience, I began to wonder whether the most extreme men resort to violence with women because they think that's all they have, their one pathetic advantage over all she seems to hold above them. I make no excuses for this. There are none. But as a man I felt vaguely attuned to this mind-set or its possibility. I did not inhabit it, but I thought I saw how rejection might get twisted beyond recognition in the mind of a discarded male where misogyny and ultimately rape may be a vicious attempt to take what cannot be taken because it has not been bestowed. Sometimes women seem so superior when you see them through the eyes of an ordinary man that now, looking back on that feeling as a female, the very idea of ramming your dick into a woman to avenge yourself, or claim her, suddenly seems as absurdly out of scale and ineffectual as a pygmy poking his finger at the moon.

In the sex clubs I visited and in the dating I did, I inhabited an outlook imposed on me from the outside by culture, by other women and other men, and I glimpsed this deeply disturbing connection between violence and sex and women and self-worth, the hallmarks of male powerlessness, the helpless, worshipful lust and the murderous ire that may come from the same lack, the same lackey status that can turn on an instant. Want me, it all seems to say. Love me. Desire me. Choose me. I need you. You ignore me. You disdain me. You destroy me. I hate you.

Having seen it, I am more afraid than ever of male minds, and oddly I feel more powerless than ever walking in the world among them, even though I know this isn't fair. Men are not at all the same, and Ned, like every man and no man, was not all men and never could be. Yet it seems true to say that we women have far more power than we know, and because of it, even with our fears, our parries and our wits about us, we are in even more danger than we know or dare contemplate.

But there were other reasons that my time dating as Ned made me angry with women. Of course, I fell into the same trap they did. When I was Ned, women became a subspecies to blame, just as, for these women, men had become the adversary in the wrong. I did what they did and saw how almost inescapable it was when you were opposites, even though, of course, I wasn't. The brain drops data into categories, but I was in both categories at once. I was angry because I wanted them to behave more reasonably. I was angry because I wanted myself to conclude more reasonably. Dating these women as a woman in disguise was like looking at a dozen different versions of yourself and faulting every one for its specific female faults, and knowing them to be yours as well. Wearing the costume of a man, I could slip the noose for a second and say, "That's not me," that's Women, capital W. Feminists, capital F.

I disliked these women and women in general because they—we—fall prey, as we must, to self-interest and chauvinism. I became a misogynist for a time because I expected better of women, because in the beginning I expected nothing of men. Anything they did was gravy because like a lot of women, deep down I didn't think men were capable of much. In that regard, I was every bit as bad as my dates.

Ned could feel good about himself and his buddies because he was simple and nothing much was expected of him. Now, like his bowling buddies, he could do nothing but lift on his good deeds, which sometimes amounted to little more than warm handshakes and the merest pinch of self-awareness for which he could pat himself soundly on the back. But women were supposed to fly already. And I held it harshly against them that they were as small and shitty and shortsighted as everybody else, including me. Ned saw that, and then I saw Ned seeing it, and then I saw myself. I guess that was the fascination of Ned. He was a mirror and a window and a prism all at the same time.

But the truth was that for all the anger I felt flowing in my direction, anger directed at the abstraction called men, I was most surprised to find nestled inside the confines of female heterosexuality a deep love and genuine attraction for real men. Not for women in men's bodies, as the prejudicial me had thought. Not even just for the metrosexual, though he has his audience, but for brawny, hairy, smelly, stalwart, manly men; bald men, men with bellies, men who can fix things and, yes, men who like sports and pound away in the bedroom. Men whom women loved for being men with all the qualities that testosterone and the patriarchy had given them, and whom I have come to appreciate for those very same qualities, however infuriating at times I still find them.

And I came largely to forgive women and myself for our own all too apparent shortcomings. Our emotional arrogance, our lack of perspective, our often unreasonable needs and projections and blames, our failure, like men, to manage or acknowledge the imbalance on our own side of the equation.

Dating women was the hardest thing I had to do as Ned, even when the women liked me and I liked them. I have never felt more vulnerable to total strangers, never more socially defenseless than in my clanking suit of borrowed armor.

But then, I guess maybe that's one of the secrets of manhood that no man tells if he can help it. Every man's armor is borrowed and ten sizes too big, and beneath it, he's naked and insecure and hoping you won't see.

4 | Sex

"The four Fs. That's all you need to know about women. Find 'em. Feel 'em. Fuck 'em and Forget 'em."

Phil, a thirty-three-year-old professional with a wife and two daughters, was telling me about the first and only man-to-man chat he ever had with his father. He was twelve years old at the time, and that was the only advice he ever got from anyone about how to treat a lady. I had met him as Ned for the first time at another bar a few nights before, struck up a conversation with him and asked if he could show me where the good strip clubs were in the area.

He'd agreed. So here we were at the Lizard Lounge sitting at the back of a dark room at one of those square brown Formica tables that you see in truck-stop coffee shops, the kind with the rickety bases that always have a matchbook shoved under one of their feet and a filthy plastic ashtray sliding back and forth across their tops in a rash of salt. The room was filled with tables like this, set up café style, all with their metal-frame chairs turned in the same direction, and the men in them staring rapt at the naked women dancing for them on the stage. Other naked women were wandering between the tables, working the crowd for dollar bills, a wad of which they each had strapped around one ankle.

Phil had ordered a bottle of water, as had I. They didn't serve alcohol at the Lizard Lounge, which is common in places where the girls get totally naked on stage and give the more explicit private lap dances. In the places where alcohol is served, the dancers don't usually disrobe entirely, and if lap dances are offered they're usually of the tamer variety where touching isn't allowed and nothing more than frottage happens. That is, unless you find a place that's breaking the rules, which a lot of places do to some extent or another, depending on what an individual dancer is willing to do offstage.

Phil poured his water into a glass, then dumped two packets of sugar into the water and stirred it with a straw. He gulped it as he spoke.

"My dad and I have come to places like this together," he said. "We have a lot of fun with it. He came to my bachelor party here and got a couple of lap dances."

This appalled me at first, the idea of a father and a son hanging out in strip clubs together, as if it was a rite of passage. It appalled me even more that a father would advise his son to treat women like hostile organisms who were to be made necessary and expedient use of and then discarded as soon as possible. But the more I observed about the painful compulsions of male sexuality while in the company of men as a man, and the more I understood about the deep insecurity that goes along with being a man in the company of women, the more I understood what a ham-handed charade men were often putting on in front of each other, all of it in a desperate effort to hide that insecurity and pain. My bowling pals had been as full of the same off-color jokes as Phil and his dad, full of the same know-it-all insouciance that betrayed exactly how much, not how little, women and the esteem of women actually meant to them.

We'd only been at the club for a few minutes, just long enough for Phil to spin his family anecdote, when one of the naked crowd pleasers approached me. I looked at the floor as if to decline her offer, but it wasn't an offer. This was my first time in a strip club, and I didn't know the etiquette yet. I didn't know that giving dollars to the dancers wasn't really elective. You were pretty much expected to give on demand, which is why the doorman had given me eight singles in change for my twenty.

The dancer turned her back to Phil's gummy grin as she slipped between our chairs to face me. She took my right knee between her legs, and sidled her pelvis closer to my face. I looked up, past eye level, trying not to see the hard veined hands that were already roughly parting and fingering her shaved pussy. I looked past the length of her stretched belly and her small, angry breasts, to her downturned face, which I thought would be the least offensive part of her. But I was wrong. Her face was where the squalor showed the most. She looked old for this work, but she was probably younger than she looked. She peered down at me with a weathered grimace of contempt and resignation, like a prostitute posing for a mug shot.

And who could blame her?

We were the scum in her world, and a dollar didn't merit effort. She was giving us what we wanted and she was giving it dirty. She wasn't pretending that she liked us, or wanted us, or cared what we thought. She knew what we thought.

Her face didn't matter. Probably only a woman would even bother with her face. None of the other guys I saw her approach ever looked her in the eye, and I only did it out of shame and disgust. I had thought I would find something endurable in that face, but it was a mask. Her eyes were intentionally repulsive, and I looked away.

What had I expected? She knew that no matter how raunchy things got, the men would want more of it. They would look at the gash in front of them with the mild interest of entitlement, which the men around me did. They turned their eyes sideways from the stage to look at her impassively, as if she were a commercial break or a side of fries. I shoved my dollar at her just to get rid of her, but she wouldn't take it.

"Not yet," she said.

She could tell I was a cherry and she was going to amuse herself with my discomfort. She leaned over and took my head between her hands. She pulled me into her chest, sagging one meager breast on each cheek, then bobbling them back and forth with her shoulders. Maybe she was genuinely smiling now. Finally she pulled her ankle up into my lap, digging the point of her heel into my knee, and bending open the wad of bills so that I could reach in and deposit my due.

"Now," she said.

This was my introduction to a substratum of the male sexual psyche that most women either don't know about, don't want to know about, or both. How could they? Their boyfriends and husbands weren't likely to tell them, not even about things they did when they were bachelors. There is too much shame in it. Or, more truthfully, there is too much incrimination. If a man has been to a place like this and admits it, he's already blemished in the eyes of many prospective mates, and if he admits to having enjoyed it or indulged his baser instincts in the corners of the room, he's even more tainted, which is why the men I met were never honest with the women in their lives about strip joints like these or the sexual drives they are designed to satisfy.

Phil knew these dives and their offerings intimately, and he liked playing the guide and tutor. He knew I'd never been to a place like this before, and when I asked him probing questions about it, he was full of expert bluster about what it all meant, as if, just by virtue of being who he was—a prototypical guy—he had a lock on the male mind:

"What are most guys looking for in a woman? We're not looking for a nice person. We're not looking for someone to rear our children. We're not looking for someone who's going to pitch in and be a good worker and contribute to the household. A guy is looking for a woman to fuck him. We want someone we can stick our dicks into all the time. That's ninety-five percent of looking for a woman. And there's no explaining that to anyone."

Of course, I'd spoken to enough men to know that this wasn't the whole truth by any means, and Phil knew it, too, but it was a truth of sorts. Plenty of men—most, really—want wives and families for all the right and good reasons, for love, companionship, dedication. Domesticity is not inimical to them. The very idea is absurd and disproved a thousand times a day. But to hear them tell it, a lot of men do seem to struggle with their sexuality underneath, as well as all the religious, political, matrimonial—literally mothering—forces that tell them to repress it.

Men get married, but their sexuality doesn't then magically disappear amid the bliss of family life. Hence the preponderance of married men loping off in shame and secret to the strip club.

Sometimes even respectable men with respectable lives have primal ugly stuff bracketed somewhere in their minds, kept in its place apart from the purported love that goes with the responsibilities of fatherhood and husbanding. How could it be otherwise? Much as they might have liked them to, these drives and desires didn't somehow cease to exist in respectable company. It was only society's prevailing myth, or perhaps female wish fulfillment, that had pretended otherwise. As a result, individual men and women were left to sort out the sordid reality on their own, hurting and getting hurt because sometimes it was too hard to successfully re-solve the conflict between baseline male sexuality and the civilized role of a man.

These clubs and the thoughts and feelings that produce them are the squalid subbasement of male sexuality in which a lot of men have at least one foot or toe firmly planted. No matter how high they ascend in the civilized world, no matter how tall, how dapper, how educated or savvy they stand in the stratosphere of age and accomplishment, a lot of average guys still have a nudie film loop flickering in the back of their minds. And the more edu-cated, politicized, refined they become, the more ashamed of their base proclivities they often feel.

Even the mildest, most conscientious men I spoke to about their sexualities often spoke of the satyr inside them that led them, especially when they were young and crazed by the primal drive to fuck, to do things they were ashamed of.

"In college, I remember waking up in bed with women I didn't know, and worse, didn't want to know," said Ron, an Ivy-educated, literary family man who makes his living in the world of letters, "and feeling so appalled by what my body had led me into doing. Most of these women I just dropped without ceremony, and to this day I feel quite bad about that. I treated them terribly, but I just felt insanely compelled by the urge to find some relief."

Despite not wanting to know the truth about what goes on at strip clubs, most women think they know nonetheless. Popular films show women half-clad shaking it suggestively on stage, which some of them do in the tamer clubs. But the women in these first few clubs I visited were naked and there was nothing artful about their striptease. There was no tease, just cunt, bald and raw. The women on stage were usually naked within the first minute, and they didn't hint at some dreamed-of consummation, they just auctioned their merchandise at close range.

The real money is in lap dances, which in most places are twenty dollars each. But again, these are nothing like what we see in popular movies. They aren't dances at all. They're naked or mostly naked full-contact gyrations designed not for anything so quaint as titillation, but to make the man come within the five minutes he's paid for.

As I would learn later, there was actual sex going on in some of these places. At another bar about a half hour down the road from the Lizard Lounge, a place that had a reputation for being a virtual front for prostitution, especially in the midafternoon when it was slow, I fished around a bit to see how far the girls would go. I'd been told by a former regular that the wallet was the limit there, and that the garbage can in the men's room was littered with used condoms. That wasn't true the night I was there, but I asked one of the dancers anyway whether we could do more than grind. She told me it was a no go; that the management was cracking down. A girl had been fired there that very day for blowing someone in one of the VIP rooms.

It made sense that it was in the management's best interests to discourage this kind of thing, since they risked having their establishments shut down if they turned a blind eye. It was the girls alone, apparently, who pocketed the extra money if they chose to do more than dance. But then again, if a place acquired the reputation among regulars of employing girls who went the extra mile, naturally that tended to attract more customers by word of mouth. It was a balancing act either way.

After my first encounter with a floor girl, I decided that if I was really going to get inside this world I was going to have to take a seat stageside, which would mean coming out of the protective shadows, crossing the room in front of all these men, and taking one of the coveted places up front.

Up there guys put their money in their teeth and leaned into the dancers, who took the payment between their breasts or thighs, while the guys looked up at them with awe and gratitude for their favors.

Phil was gung ho, eager for me to have the full experience, so we took our bottles of water and found two spots next to the stage.

The first girl up was billed as a *Penthouse* darling, a supposed cut above the hamburger on the floor. Hence, the emcee demanded louder applause for her. But, to my surprise, the whistles and claps were scattered. Nobody was kidding himself. This was a dive. Anybody who was dancing here wasn't prime. There was about as much electricity in that crowd as there is in the weekly bingo game at the VA—which is, frighteningly enough, sort of how I'd describe the whole ambience of the place. It looked and felt like a converted rec room. There were no windows or decorations of any sort. Just the metal frame vinyl chairs, and the rickety tables, and the low stage, and a turnstile at the front entrance where two paunchy creatures standing behind an empty glass display case took the cover charge and the twenties from the private dancers.

I was right up front, a clean-cut sore thumb, with my button-down shirt and my fresh face. I wanted Ned to be handsome, but this wasn't the place for it. I was dressed for a date, and this was a hellhole.

The *Penthouse* girl came on in a cop's dress blues and an officer's cap, visibly embarrassed by the lack of noise she was generating, even at the prospect of getting naked. She strutted around for a minute shaking her French-manicured index finger at the crowd. But since this didn't elicit much remorseful applause, she ripped her shirt and pants off by their Velcro seams, revealing the black G-string bikini underneath and a pair of knee-high black vinyl stiletto boots.

"Who wants a blow job?" the emcee called out.

The dancer motioned for a volunteer to come on stage. A skinny, young Asian guy in the front row eagerly obliged. The dancer put a beach towel down on the stage in front of her, and motioned for him to lie on it on his back. As he did so, he looked at her and us with a kind of disbelieving glee, as if to say: Is she really going to blow me right here, right now?

I felt complicit just watching and every bit as depraved as the participants. I *was* a participant whether I liked it or not. The act of watching the show had made me part of it, and as a woman—and the only woman in the room who wasn't for sale—I couldn't help putting myself in the stripper's place, imagining all those dehumanizing pairs of eyes coursing over me, and the emcee's voice dangling me in front of them as bait. I couldn't separate the stripper's act from the hopeless life that I thought had probably led her or trapped her into doing this for a living. I couldn't help measuring that life against my own, which now seemed shamefully privileged and unearned by comparison. But then, looking around the room at all the thoughtless consumption these guys were doing, taking in these women like a drug, like another faceless hit from the bottle, I felt this comparison collapse, and the supposedly monumental difference between us disappear. I knew that the circumstances of her life or of mine didn't make any difference in this place. To these guys she had no life. She was generic and rootless, just her component female parts devoid of any individuation. And so, therefore, was I. I didn't have to put myself in her place. I was in her place, just another piece of ass for the picking, had they only known it.

The Asian guy threw himself down so greedily that his sneakers bounced like a toddler's as his legs flopped apart. The dancer got on her knees above him and opened his fly. She reached in, pulled up the elastic on his underwear and peeked underneath.

She held up her thumb and forefinger in the universal sign for small dick, and the crowd laughed. She reached behind her and pulled a porn-size dildo out of a black bag. She placed it on top of the volunteer's crotch, holding it with one hand as she ran her tongue up and down its shaft and around the simulated head. This brought more life to the crowd and she worked it, taking the full length of the prop into her throat. This elicited a mild frenzy and the predictable climax. She leaned back for the money shot, and the dildo squirted its milk high into the air. She held it up to reveal a pump on its underside. Again there was laughter, and then the trick was over. The Asian guy stood up and scampered off the stage, fumbling with his Dockers.

Hurriedly the stripper put her props away and stood up, motioning for more applause, but the zenith had come and gone.

"Everybody say 'Get naked,'" instructed the emcee.

The crowd coughed the response and it fell flat around them. The girl winced again with embarrassment.

"Oh, no," said the emcee, "that's not going to be good enough. You want to see her naked? Then everybody shout 'Get naked.'"

Again, the crowd obliged weakly.

Now the emcee was embarrassed, too.

"Okay," he tried again. You could hear him groaning on her behalf. "Let's try that one more time. Do you want to see this babe naked or not?"

The cry rallied louder this time—"Get naked." But you could still feel the inertia in it, overcome only by the necessity of the transaction.

It would have to be good enough. Off came the bikini to reveal the usual preternaturally bulbous fake breasts sitting way too high and semidetached on her blanded torso.

She offered them to the crowd, one in each hand, circling the rim of the stage. She stopped in front of the guy to my left, a thickspittled computer geek in ill-fitting wire-framed specs. He stood up nervously with a few crumpled bills in his hand, took off his glasses and blinked his bloated reddened eyes blindly as he tripped a little closer to the stage. He placed his head between her nurtureless breasts for a few moments, then bumbled back to his seat, replacing his glasses with a stupid smile.

For her last act Miss Penthouse distributed a few party favors, a couple of T-shirts and a few copies of her porno videos.

"Ten bucks," said the emcee. "Ten bucks for a video. Who wants one? Who's got ten bucks for the lady?"

Several shouts and bills went into the air, and the dancer strutted back and forth, running her tongue up the spine of one of the video boxes. She stopped in front of the chosen buyer, an obvious regular who, with his greased-back hair and his soiled yellow short-sleeved button-down shirt, looked like a registered sex offender. She squatted above him, spread her legs, and slid the lubricated box back and forth between her labia, then handed it to him. He ran the moistened edge of the box under his nose like a fine cigar, inhaling with a satisfied smirk. The crowd loved that.

The dancer did the same with the rest of the videos. She flossed the full length of the T-shirts between her legs, too, and then tossed them up for grabs into the seats. They too were sniffed for traces of her scent.

But I doubted if there was any scent. These women were nothing if not dry—dry and factory smooth as the dolls they were mimicking. Thinking this reminded me of a gay man I'd known, who, when I asked him why he preferred men, said, "Because they're so nice and dry."

There was the same gay misogyny on display in these clubs. These weren't women. They were factory-authorized, snipped, treated and depilated of anything offensive. The original German Barbie was modeled on a sleazy pinup, then whittled and airbrushed into peach exactitude for middle-American consumption, and these women were in turn modeled on her, right down to the plastic shoes.

In its natural state, the vagina is not a delicate instrument. It breathes and salivates and even ejaculates, and it always has an odor. These women had no odor, even when they'd been sweating on stage and they put your face between their legs, as one of them did to me when I sat up front. They were odorless. They were freeze-dried. I wondered what they did to themselves before the show to make their parts so unripe.

When she'd given away all her T-shirts and videos, Miss Penthouse left the stage, waving and blowing kisses as she went. I took the opportunity to leave Phil to his own devices for a while and vacate my seat at the front. I told him I was going to look for a private dance, and he smiled approvingly, raising his hand in the air and making the hang loose sign with his pinky and index finger.

I headed over to the back wall where the girls on deck were lounging together, smoking and staring off into the middle-distance like waitresses on a break.

Back there, off to the side, there was an open rectangular boothlike room with ten swivel chairs inside it. The chairs were lined up against the two long walls of the rectangle, and bolted to the floor. One of the long walls was only a half wall, like a pass-through in a kitchen, so that people lurking in the back of the main room could spy on what was happening in the booth.

Most of the chairs were occupied by fully clothed men, each of whom had one of the naked girls sitting on his lap, facing him with her legs wrapped around his torso or gripping the floor for traction as she ground her crotch into his. Some of the girls were facing out, also in the straddle position, with their backsides likewise grinding against the men. In this place there seemed to be no provision against touching the girls, because the men were madly pawing and sucking the girls' breasts as they thrust against them with ecstatic upturned faces.

I was staring shamelessly, but this was, after all, what I'd come for, what the management expected. Why else the open wall? This was their best advertisement. There was a long line to get into the booth.

One of the men, a very young guy in a football jersey, probably in his early twenties if that, had swiveled his chair all the way around so that he was facing the open wall. His baseball cap was turned fashionably sideways on his head, a cool affectation that only made him look younger. He was hugging the dancer loosely around the neck, his chin resting limply on her smooth shoulder. He wasn't moving his hips. His face was slack. His eyes were open, and surprisingly gentle, and he was looking directly at me almost sweetly through a glaze of comfort, like a sleepy child being carried by his mother through the supermarket. He knew I was watching him, but he didn't turn his eyes away, and he didn't judge or threaten me for looking. He just looked back at me and rested there on her naked shoulder, soaking up whatever calm it was giving him.

I looked at him like another mother—I couldn't help it—and maybe in this strange, disjointed place he could see that. Maybe he could see that I felt sorry for him in the best possible sense, and maybe that was okay when no one else was looking. Or maybe he was just too stoned to know.

The rest of the men were doing their business mechanically, lined up side by side as unabashedly as if they were pissing at the urinals in a roadside public restroom, just satisfying an urge, doing what needed to be done.

That was, in fact, something Phil had said to me early on:

"C'mon, man, you know. For us guys getting off is a biological necessity, like going to the bathroom."

It didn't matter that the couples on either side of these guys were close enough to touch, and it didn't matter that people like me were watching. Why should it? There was nothing intimate, nothing meaningful going on. To these guys it seemed that true privacy was reserved only for their midmorning shit.

Observing this, I was frightened, standing there very much alone. As a woman teeming prototypically with all my necessary illusions, confronted with this spectacle of male factory function, I felt a despair that was salvaged only by the knowledge that I was not heterosexual. I didn't want companionship or partnership with men. But most women do and that is why they don't want to know, they can't know that maybe they are making love to someone who is really just fucking them. This is not the whole picture, of course, but it is a freeze frame, a worst case scenario, and when I saw it and thought about it and allowed it to insult me, not just as a woman, but as an emotionally needy sexual mind, I felt very small and lost in my costume. I needed, as many women do, more than a carnal connection to happen in sex, but in this of all places it was absurd to go looking for it, or to be hurt when you didn't find it. I wondered, though, if I wasn't feeling a ruder version of the clash that can happen when men and women try to reconcile their sex lives.

I stayed for a little while longer at the back of the room, noticing the crowd, which was made up mostly of younger men, and a few scruffy recluses in their fifties and sixties. As I considered the expression on their faces while they watched the dancers on the stage, I could see, at times, an odd reverence in their eyes, at others a bland disinterest. But there was no condescension in their gaze, no hatred for this low thing they felt compelled to watch. They all seemed uniformly addled by the spectacle, staring at these body parts on display, as if they hadn't seen them a thousand times before in magazines and films and settings just like these.

I wanted to know what it felt like to be inside that feeling, but the closest I was going to come was a lap dance, and even then it would be different. Still, I wanted to know how these women would treat me when they were the supposed object of my lust, and I was paying for it. I looked back at the dancers who were on break, the ones who were waiting for requests, and tried to choose one.

There was one who was truly beautiful in a natural way. She was young, probably nineteen or so. Her dirty-blond hair looked real, as did her breasts. She was wearing very little makeup. In the dark it looked like none at all. She didn't need much. Her skin was uniformly smooth, as yet unblemished.

I motioned to her to come to me and she got up from her chair, playing into the fantasy, smiling very sweetly as she took my hand and led me to the creatures standing behind the glass display case up front. She held out her hand for the money, and I gave it to her. She gave it to the two men at the register with what seemed to me to be a sad resignation. For all the shabby, commercial look and feel of the place we might as well have been at the gun counter in a sporting goods store.

After paying, I asked the girl if we could go somewhere more private than the open booth. She nodded and led me back behind a partition that was off to the side of the stage. Behind it, there were five small couches, each bounded on three sides by smaller partitions that afforded a semiprivacy. She led me to a vacant one and motioned for me to sit down. When I did she asked me to take my keys and change and anything else sharp or abrasive out of my pockets. Then she draped a silk negligee across my lap. She had taken it from a group of such garments that was hanging across the top of the partition that divided this closed section from the rest of the club. When everything was in place, she straddled my lap and sat down.

She began grinding immediately. I knew that she could feel my fake dick through my pants. She was the first woman who had. It must have seemed very odd to her that it wasn't hard, but then maybe some of the people who came here did so to remedy erectile dysfunction, or persist in it anonymously.

At first I was frozen, lying back on the couch, my arms limp at my sides, my head turned away, my eyes closed almost as a reflex. I had never done this with someone I hadn't at least taken to dinner first. The act wasn't new to me, of course, but it was detached from the necessary precursors: emotion, seduction, imagination, mental connection—the things that are, perhaps, the hallmarks of female sexuality, and the very things that these strip joints and lap dances lacked. There was no pretense of foreplay here, mental or otherwise, and for me that took everything pleasurable out of the experience.

As she kept on, I put myself somewhere else. I tried to pretend that she was someone I knew and liked and wanted to be with. But it didn't really work. I tried to grind against her, too, but it was just a forced motion, tawdry and ridiculous.

Then it ended abruptly, just as the song ended, and she asked me if I wanted to go longer—lap dances are timed and paid for by the length of a song. I thanked her and said no. She smiled and stood up, pulling me up with her to make way for another dancer and her customer, who were already nudging their way into the cubicle. As I tried to collect myself, the incoming dancer brushed me away impatiently with the back of her hand.

I had a number of lap dances as Ned, and they always felt the same. Actually I could hardly remember what they felt like, because they didn't usually feel like much of anything. To me, when they were happening, they were mostly a blank, as blank as the faces of the dancers and the dead air behind their faces. I remember being struck again and again by the emptiness in the dancers' eyes. After performing, they usually made the rounds of the bar to solicit bills from onlookers, since few people ever bothered to make their way up to the stage to slip something in their G-strings. It was during these encounters, when I tried to engage them in conversation, that I saw how vapid they were or had made themselves to survive this work. That depressed me most of all.

But as I began to understand more about the shame that arose in men from the need to visit places like this, and the undoubted shame that arose in the dancers for having to work in them, I thought I began to understand something more about the kind of woman that becomes a sex object in the eyes of men. A lot of women have asked themselves why so many men are so fond of modern porn stars and centerfolds, women who aren't real women, whose breasts are fake, whose hair is bleached into straw or perversely depilated, whose faces are painted thick, and whose bodies have been otherwise altered by surgery or diet to conform with doll-like exactitude to something that isn't found in nature. Why, I had so often wondered, didn't men want real women? Was it misogyny, a kind of collective repressed homosexuality or perhaps pedophilia that really wanted a body type that more resembled a man's or a child's, fatless and smooth?

For some, this is no doubt true, or why would magazines like *Barely Legal*, full of pre- and parapubescent girls, sell so well? Why would the fashion industry, long dominated by gay men, demand that women starve themselves until their bodies, hipless and breastless, look like the bodies of adolescent boys?

But as I made my way through strip club after strip club in search of some kind of answer, I wondered if maybe it didn't come back to shame. I knew from my own sexual fantasies that there is something appealing at least in the abstract about fucking someone who isn't there. When pure fucking and animal release is what you're thinking about—and that is what the male sex drive at its basest seems to be all about—you don't want there to be any witnesses. You don't want to be a dirty, senseless animal with someone you love or respect or are capable of loving and respecting. You'd be too ashamed for her to see that part of you in the light of day, and isn't a mind something like the light of day? A real woman is a mind, and a mind is a witness, and a witness is the last thing you need when you're ashamed. So fucking a fake, mindless hole is what you need. The faker the better.

I suppose, oddly enough, when it came to genuinely heterosexual men, all of this added up in my mind to something that might have been the opposite of misogyny, the idea being that you could only treat as an object something that resembled a real woman *as little as possible,* because only then could you bear to mistreat it and yourself enough to satisfy your instincts.

Who knows? I certainly couldn't know with any kind of surety. But I knew what it was like to fantasize about women in the cold abstract, and I knew that when you did you weren't thinking about Ava Gardner. You were thinking about some anonymous, chesty, helium-voiced cheerleader slut blowing you in the locker room during halftime.

I'd been there in my head, though as I had just learned, there is a world of difference between going there in your head and doing it for real. But now I was here, where I could partake in this world as Ned, and at least stand for a while on the receiving end of what it had to offer. When I did, I found something more than the discomfort of being a woman in a man's world. I found at least what I thought was a glimpse of the discomfort of being a man in a man's world and what that did to women as well as men, and I felt something that I hadn't expected to feel. Genuine sympathy.

Still, thus far I was just a visitor, orbiting the periphery from a safe distance, and that could tell me only so much. I knew after visiting the Lizard Lounge with Phil that I wasn't going to put myself through the added torture of spending more time in these places with someone I didn't know. Besides, Phil's family life made it hard for him to get away. So after bowling one Monday night, I asked my teammate Jim if he wanted to go to the local hole and get a beer with me. We'd gotten to know each other fairly well. Besides, he'd talked of wanting to go to a strip club on his ski vacation, so I knew he had the taste for it, as well as a dire need for distraction.

His wife had been given her second cancer diagnosis a few weeks prior, and it was clear from the little he said about it that there wasn't much hope on the horizon. It was equally clear that he had nobody to talk to about it, and the rage and pain boiling up inside him were reaching critical mass. He was having trouble sleeping, so when she went to bed, often as early as nine o'clock, instead of watching cable reruns and smoking pot until the wee hours in a desperate effort to pass out, he'd head down to the bar to try to find some comfort in that oblivious company. I convinced him to come to the titty bar with me as often as he could make it, and it became a regular thing with us for a while. We'd head down there and play pool for a few hours, he'd let out some of what was eating him, and we'd soak up the miasma of that place like it was therapy, letting it corrupt us, until chatting with naked women and ducking into cubicles to have your parts rubbed seemed almost normal.

The local was windowless, ill lit and choked with cigarette smoke. Once inside, you wouldn't know whether it was day or night. This was something all these places had in common, probably because they were usually open by midday, and well patronized much of the afternoon. I guess they figured even people who make a habit of it prefer to do their sinning in the dark.

The local had a large ovoid bar, also characteristic, with two small square stages in the center, one girl dancing on each, working the pole and sprawling on the blinking squares of light that flashed on and off beneath her.

There was a kitchen in back that served French fries, hot dogs, burgers and wings, but you weren't well advised to consume anything there that had once been alive. Next to the kitchen there was a large red and white sign that said NO BIKER COLORS. I'd seen signs like this in other places, though they usually said NO CLUB COLORS, or simply, NO COLORS. I'd asked Jim what that meant, and he'd said, "You know, gangs."

Foolishly, I'd said; "You mean Bloods and Crips, that kind of thing?"

"No," he'd laughed. "These are white people."

He meant motorcycle gangs like the Warlocks—who were reputedly much worse than the Hell's Angels—and other clubs like the Breed and the Pagans. They were rumored to be regulars at places like this, though I never saw many of them. But then, without their colors, I wouldn't necessarily have recognized them for what they were.

I do remember one guy, though, whom I wouldn't otherwise have noticed, who, thinking back on it now, was probably a gang member. He was well over six feet tall and wide as a doorway, and he had that just-try-it attitude about him that made you realize he could do just about anything he wanted and back it up with lethal force. Jim and I were sitting at the bar. Jim had gone to the bathroom and had left his coat on the back of his stool. There were several empty stools on either side of us, but this guy wanted Jim's stool. He came over, took Jim's coat and threw it on the floor. As he did so, stupidly I opened my mouth to protest that someone was sitting there. He stopped in midswipe and shot me one of those mock, raised-eyebrow looks that says, "You were saying . . . ?" but whose real intent is "Do you wanna die?"

I'd never been on the receiving end of one of those gratuitous alpha male assertions, but it's the kind of thing you don't misinterpret, except maybe when you're piss drunk. I saw my error instinctively and redirected accordingly.

"Don't worry, man," I said, raising my palm in a defensive gesture, "I wouldn't dream of it."

He nodded and took the stool. Three guys sitting farther along the bar burst out laughing, as did I. I guess not everyone reacted the way I did, though. Certainly no rival biker would. Hence, I supposed, the need for the sign at the end of the bar.

Also at the far end of the bar was a large TV mounted high on the wall. Two others were placed similarly around the room. This, too, was typical of most of these places. The multiple sets were almost always tuned to a sporting event, usually basketball, football or hockey.

Off to the side there were two pool tables and the cramped couch room, which was so small and unobtrusive that I had assumed it was a broom closet until the first time I played pool and saw one of the dancers emerge from it with a customer. Even then I was still naive enough to think that only one dance could possibly be going on in there at any given time. My first time back there, though, I found out otherwise. There could be as many as three or four couples going at it in a space the size of a bathroom.

I became a regular at the local, going on as many nights as I could over the course of several weeks, sometimes with Jim, sometimes alone. I met Gina on my first night out with Jim. I'd been to the local a couple of times before on my own but hadn't stayed long. Early on I found it hard to make myself go to these places at all, much less regularly. They depressed me so much it would take me days to recover from a single jaunt.

Jim took a shine to Gina right away because she had large breasts — he liked big tits — and because she did this thing when she danced where she'd put her tit in her mouth and bite the nipple, pulling back and forth on it with her teeth for a good fifteen seconds, and stretching her flesh like pizza dough. Jim liked that a lot.

"Ouch" was all I could think.

Gina was a tiny woman, five feet tops, and aside from her double-D breasts, she was built like a sixteen-year-old gymnast. Her ass was high and tight without a hint of cellulite, and the only signs of the life she'd lived were the clutch of stretch marks on her belly, which was otherwise as firm and juvenile as the rest of her. She claimed to be thirty-four, which may have been a lie, but she could pass for it in the dark.

She said she had three sons, two teenagers and a three-year-old. She had been dancing since the age of eighteen, the year she'd had her first child. I'd assumed that that had been her reason for starting, but she claimed not to have needed the money. She had grown up with her grandparents in a wealthy suburb, and though not rich themselves, they had been well enough off to give her what she needed. She maintained that even now she didn't do it for the money, but if that was true, and not just some line she handed us, then her life was a whole lot sadder than I'd thought.

When I asked her why she danced at the local if she didn't really need the money, she said simply: "I love men." Even if this had been true when she'd started out, which was doubtful, it certainly wouldn't have remained so in this of all places. It was a little like saying you became a coroner because you were a people person.

The more we talked, the more I was struck not by her purported love of men but by her apparent distaste for women. She talked about women's parts as if they were garbage. She found them repellant, she said, and far from finding the men she pleasured disgusting, she wondered why they didn't find her disgusting. She couldn't understand, she said, why anyone would want to get within a mile of a pussy. She went on about this for a while—too long—screwing up her face as she said, "Wet sloppy pussy, ew." It didn't surprise me that she was filled with self-loathing—everyone in this place was—but the vehemence of her expressed dislike for the female anatomy and her abiding love of men as a so-called species gave me the impression that she was working pretty hard to cover over something traumatic from the past or to repel her true feelings about the present, but then I guessed that went with the territory.

She wasn't going to let me or any other customer know what she was really thinking. Deflecting the truth was part of the biz, integral to the whole show we were putting on for each other. Nobody came here looking for reality. Obviously, everyone came to escape it. And maybe to these guys, and a lot of guys, this seemed like fantasyland. But in reality it was the exact opposite. It was as real and ugly as it got, right down to the stretch marks and the careworn sofas. It was far uglier than all but the ugliest of life out there. Walking into one of these places wasn't an escape. It was like walking into the gritty subconscious, the very place most people were trying to avoid in the first place.

"I'm hot and wet," Gina said.

She said that a lot, whenever there was a lull in the conversation.

"I'm so horny," she'd add, reminding us that the relief for her condition was only a couch away.

Then she'd segue into something neutral like the pool game Jim and I were playing, as if that were just the normal flow of conversation.

"I'd shoot at the five in the side pocket if I were you. If you put a little backspin on it, that'll give you a nice leave for the seven in the corner."

She professed to be a shark, and I didn't doubt it. She'd linger with us at the table for a few minutes calling shots and watching us miss most of them.

She was a good saleswoman, the only stripper I met who could really play the game with any conviction. Unlike the other girls, who did little to conceal their dislike for you and the whole job, Gina was pretty good at pretending she liked you. Like the consummate politician, she'd remember your name from night to night, and even wave and shout encouragement at you from the stage when you were shooting for the eight ball. She'd come over between dances and put her arm around you and chat, and make you forget for a few minutes that this was all just a transaction.

She climbed into my lap one night, wrapping her legs around my waist and her arms around my neck as I sat on a stool by the pool table.

"How ya doin', Ned?" she said, smiling.

I usually dreaded these interactions with other strippers. They'd solicit you at the bar with their tits in their hands, sometimes with semisneers on their faces, and ask you how you were, often in the most hostile and obviously uninterested way. You'd have to pretend along with them, cracking that stiff smile, and make a little small talk before you put a dollar in their cleavage. Sometimes certain strippers latched on to me, holding my hand against their breasts for a good minute while they spoke about whatever came to mind. Usually what came to mind was how long and tiring a day they'd had. They probably did it hoping for another deposit from someone who looked like a sucker, but sometimes I wondered if I could feel a little desperation in it and a faint ring of truth when they'd say, "Can I take you home with me?" or when they'd stroke my hair and say, "You're so sweet. Such a baby face. How old are you?"

It didn't matter what they said. It all made me feel bad. I didn't like being their client. I didn't like how they disliked me because of it. Most of all I didn't like how much I identified with that dislike, and how much it made me want to assure them and myself that I wasn't like the other patrons. But sometimes, when I'd been playing the role for long enough, that was hard even for me to believe. After all, I was there more often than most of them were, and just being there, for whatever reason, made me feel like I was lying to myself about not belonging.

But when Gina got in your lap, she didn't hold out or expose her body parts for tips. She'd just sit there and talk to you as if she'd known you all your life. There wasn't much to say, just pleasantries, but it didn't feel forced. It was disarming, and as distant as I was from real interest, I bought into the emotional fantasy a little, out of relief mostly. For once, someone made it easy to just talk for a minute like two people who enjoyed each other's company.

All of this was designed to get you in the back room eventually. She wasn't pound foolish. She knew that if she just worked you like a mercenary, like most of the other girls did, she'd only get a few singles out of the encounter, but if she played you like a schoolgirl crush, she'd probably score at least a twenty, maybe more, on a lap dance or two before the evening was out. And that's what usually happened. I watched her work, and I saw her disappear into the couch room far more often than the other girls, some of whom were significantly younger than she was.

The first time I watched her go back there, she went with a guy who looked like Papa Hemingway, except that he was dressed in business attire: a white button-down, navy dress trousers and wing tips. Gina liked to use the couch nearest the door. It was perpendicular to the door, and it jutted out a little past the door frame. Because the black curtain across the door extended only three-quarters of the way down, you could see or surmise a lot of what was happening behind it. I could see Gina's legs. She was kneeling between Papa Hemingway's wing tips, her tiny bare feet curled under her on the floor. As she did her thing, her feet curled and uncurled rhythmically in time with Papa Hemingway's right foot, which was tapping softly on the floor, as if to a slow beat. She'd kicked off her shoes at the door. One of them had fallen on its side. Next to them was a pile of cash, Gina's take. The picture of all this, the corner of the couch, the shoes artfully kicked off, the cash on the floor, Gina on her knees and Papa's wing tips astride her, would have made the perfect advertisement for this place in all its sordid glory, or something you would have seen in *Playboy* as a cartoon, with a caption above it saying: "I'll be home soon, honey."

A big biker guy in leather and denim with a Charles Manson beard and a lot of piercings in his face sat just outside the couch room, taking the money as the girls came and went, and peeking behind the black curtain periodically to make sure everything was copacetic.

I would have said he did it for titillation, too, but from the bored expression on his face I got the feeling that once you'd been in one of these places for a while the sight of tits and ass and simulated coitus didn't do much for you anymore. It was like porn or violence in films. Seeing all this day in and day out, you'd become so inured to everything these places were selling — nudity and beer and two-bit orgasm — that you'd have to keep upping the ante to feel anything at all.

Fantasy is a necessary veil, and when you rip it away, the opposite of what you think will happen, happens. Gratification kills desire. And constant gratification kills it permanently until even naked, willing women seem made of cardboard.

At some point all of this ceased to be about desire, if it was ever really about desire in the first place, and became about something else: loneliness, or inner pain, or doing time or penance for some long ago hurt that had never healed but somehow found companionable misalliance here with all the other misfits and detritus. I don't think anybody in that place was really capable of normal arousal anymore. They were dead inside and you could see it. They were in pain and sitting with it, looking for it, maybe even getting off on it, because when pleasure is used up, pain is all that's left. It's the only thing that lasts longer.

This place wasn't just where men came to be beasts. It was also where women came to exercise some vestige of sexual power in the most unvarnished way possible. My pussy for your dollars. I say when, I say how, I say how much and I get paid for it. There was tremendous manipulation built into the rules under which these places operated. The provision against touching the girls could be bent or broken at will by each individual girl, and enforced by guys hired for the purpose, guys like the pierced biker at the couch-room door. This was an age-old whore-john-pimp dynamic, but more played at than truly enacted, and always in a controlled setting. It was a grotesque parody of what women and men did in real life, the mating dance with all the civilized pretense stripped away.

It was an unpleasant scene. There was a lot of anger in those rooms, and animus was always simmering beneath the surface. With the exception of the frat boy types who came in packs, and then only to the higher profile places, most of the men at the local came alone and sat alone nursing a beer or a whiskey. Everything about them said: "Don't bother me." They just slouched there watching the stage, leaking bad vibes like slow radiation. Even the girls often failed to wring a smile out of those glowering types, which explained why so many of them had given up trying long ago, and now came across like disgruntled cashiers at the all-night grocery. That's about as much enthusiasm as anyone had for the process: cash in, cash out; beer in, piss out; leave me alone. Like I said, this wasn't fantasyland.

The only time Jim and I ever struck up a conversation with another patron at the local, the guy started bellyaching right away about how the titty bar was just an expensive cock tease. He pointed to the pile of singles lying in front of him on the bar, telling us how it had dwindled from twenty to a few measly bills in a mere half hour. Jim commiserated in jest, pointing at our own diminished stack and suggesting that yeah, maybe getting a mail-order bride was a better idea.

"Not really," the guy said. "I read about a guy in the paper the other day who got himself one of those, and one day he came home from work and found her fucking the neighbor, so he took her outside into the street right then and there and bashed her head in."

The way he told it, it sounded like the moral of the story was that live-in whores are more trouble than they're worth. Not exactly a surprising or minority opinion in that crowd, but jarring enough to put you off a propensity for chitchat.

After a few weeks of going to the local on a regular basis, I got to the point where I just couldn't make myself go anymore. It was too much—all the accumulated pain of the despicable patrons who had nowhere else tolerable to go, and the injured dancers who could hardly contain their despair, and the surly bartenders who made shit tips. It all just fell down on you and piled up around you like the ashen, boozy smell of the place, until you just didn't want to do that to yourself anymore.

Toward the end of our time together, while we were having a drink at a regular bar that he liked to frequent, Jim confessed that he was beginning to feel the same way.

"Yeah," he said. "I'm kinda through with those places for a while. They give me bad dreams."

He'd told me a few weeks before about a particularly vivid and disturbing dream he'd had about going back into the couch room with Gina only to find that there were no couches back there at all. Instead there were only bathroom stalls with no doors and dirty old toilets in them. He dreamt that she was blowing him on one of the toilets. He said he woke up feeling really disgusted and disgusting.

All I could think was, how appropriate. Unlike most of those purgatorial scumbags, he knew this place for what it was, and that, for all his flaws, was why I liked him.

I'd been inside a part of the male world that most women and even a lot of men never see, and I'd seen it as just another one of the boys. In those places male sexuality felt like something you weren't supposed to feel but did, like something heavy you were carrying around and had nowhere to unload except in the lap of some damaged stranger, and then only for five minutes. Five minutes of mutual abuse that didn't make you feel any better.

One thing was certain, though. Everybody got his hands dirty and, politically speaking, nobody really came out ahead. It wasn't nearly so simple as men objectifying women and staying clean or empowered in the process. Nobody won, and when it came down to it, nobody was more or less victimized than anyone else. The girls got money. The men got an approximation of sex and flirtation. But in the end everyone was equally debased by the experience. Everyone, no matter what his or her circumstances, had made the choice to be there, and chances were that choice was made in the context of a lifetime's worth of emotional wreckage that had been done to their lives by people of both sexes long before they stepped through that door.

Whenever I think about my experiences in these places now,

"Well, wait a second," I said. "What if you're looking for something a little deeper and more nuanced?"

This was a woman's answer, or as close to one as I was going to come with these guys. The real woman's answer is always the professor—even for dykes he was the only palatable choice—but Ned wasn't exactly going to say that in this crowd.

"Mrs. Howell doesn't count," said Father Sebastian.

"Oh, come on, why not?"

"She just doesn't."

"Well, then, I don't think I can choose on those terms. What about you? Which one would you choose?"

"The girl next door."

What else did I expect him to say? He was the boy next door. A clean-cut, squared-off, very nice man.

I turned to Father Diego, who was sitting next to Father Sebastian.

"Okay, what about you? Glamour girl or girl next door?"

"For me the glamour girl was the girl next door," he said sighing theatrically, "and I still remember her name: Caroline Dalfur."

They may have been monks living under vows of chastity, but they were still pretty typical guys. And of course that is exactly why I chose them.

Given the alternatives, a monastery was the least terrifying venue I could think of in which to observe men living together in close quarters without women, and the only one I was likely to infiltrate successfully as Ned.

The other obvious choices were prison or the military, both of which would have required physical examinations, extensive background checks, and in the former case, the commission of a crime. Besides, I didn't fancy being anally raped and beaten senseless on a daily basis in a men's prison, or running myself ragged under a drill sergeant.

I needed to go someplace where I wouldn't have to disrobe, where I could have mental and physical privacy when I needed it. My sanity and my cover would depend on it.

That left religious orders. I considered infiltrating an orthodox Jewish community, but I knew that it would be virtually impossible for me to pass as a fellow Jew among observant Jews, since I knew very little about their religious practice or cultural traditions. I did, however, know enough about Catholic practice to pass there.

I had been raised an observant Catholic and had once taken my religion very seriously. As a child and adolescent I had been devoted to the masculine intellectual tradition of the church and its emphasis on reason in the service of faith. In college I read selections from the works of Duns Scotus and Aquinas, Anselm, Boethius, Ockham and Augustine, and had taken to heart the writings of Thomas Merton and C. S. Lewis on the subjects of Christian mysticism and theology. This tradition had deep roots in me, though in my conscious mind I had eschewed it all as nonsense long ago, or thought I had.

But once a Catholic, always a Catholic. And, well, if you were my kind of Catholic, forget it. Boethius just doesn't let go. So a Catholic monastery seemed like a natural fit. There I could live, work and pray among a small group of men who had chosen to spend their lives together, and thereby perhaps find out something about male socialization and interaction in an all-male environment.

Best of all, I thought, I might find the answer to another pressing question that my earlier experiences had raised for me. I had been to the sex clubs. I had gotten as close as I could get to the grittiest, basest and arguably the most all-consuming drive of the male animal. I had seen and experienced some of what it could do to a man. Now I wanted to go to the other end of the known universe. I wanted to know what happens when you take sex away. I wanted to know what celibacy does to a man. And I thought the answer to that question might be found in a monastery.

All of that is why I did something as crazy as hop a flight to somewhere I couldn't even locate on a map, to live among people I didn't know and who didn't know me, and all I could think about was where the hell I was going to hide my tampon applicators when I got my period.

But for all my fears, Ned slipped into the place with remarkably little effort. I had exchanged a few letters with the vocation director. We had had one long conversation on the phone. I had offered a character reference or two, and had expressed my desire to make an extended retreat. They were looking to expand their ranks among younger men who had talents to offer, they had plenty of space for guests and they were in pretty constant need of revenue (retreatants at this monastery were charged a daily fee for room and board), so they seemed happy enough to indulge my interest, whatever the outcome.

For my purposes, the place was perfect. At any given time there were around thirty monks living in the abbey, give or take those who were away periodically on church business or ministering to the faithful in local parishes. It was a relatively small, manageable group in which to mingle and observe.

Mingling and observing meant falling into step with the abbey's strict prayer and work schedule, which took some getting used to. Each day was punctuated by ringing bells. Sadly, these weren't serene pastoral bells tolling gently through the halls and hills. They were electric bells, those shrill, hammering alarmlike mechanisms they once used in public high schools to mark the beginning and end of each period. They were posted at regular intervals on the walls throughout the monastery. One of them was right outside my door. Its ring was so jarring that the first time it woke me up at the brutal hour of five-thirty a.m. I was in the hall before I knew where I was.

The first morning prayer, vigils, was at six a.m. It usually lasted until six-thirty. Then there was breakfast, which was a silent meal, followed by the second morning prayer session, lauds, at seven-fifteen. By eight o'clock you were ready to begin the work of the day, which proceeded until the midday prayer at noon. Lunch followed. Lunch was the only informal meal of the day, so conversation was allowed. After lunch the work of the day resumed until nearly five p.m. Daily mass was at five, followed by dinner. Dinner was usually a formal, silent meal during which one of the monks read aloud. After dinner came a short recreation period and then the final group prayer of the day, vespers, at six-forty-five.

All of this was set out in detail in a schedule on the desk in my room, along with a couple of devotional books, a brief history of the monastery and a set of rules and guidelines for visitors.

My room was furnished sparsely like all the other rooms, with a twin mattress on a metal spring frame, a sink with mirror, a wooden desk and chair, a bookshelf, a reading chair and a closet. It was on the fourth floor of the cloister, the floor usually reserved for novices. But there weren't any novices these days, nor had there been for several years. There were a lot of empty rooms on the floor, with rolled mattresses on the cots and nothing but lonely crucifixes on the bare walls.

Though he wasn't a novice, a monk named Brother Vergil was one of the few other people living on that floor. His room was a couple of doors down from mine and we shared a bathroom. He was living up there because he had not yet taken his final or solemn vows. He was a special case. He had been a novice at the abbey in his early twenties, and had taken his preliminary (also called simple) vows after completing the novitiate. But at the end of the normal three- to four-year trial period between simple and solemn vows, he had decided to leave the community and make a go of it in the outside world. He had gone back to school and gotten a degree in biology, worked as a lab assistant for a while, and then when the research grants dried up, he'd ended up selling insurance and cars for a living. He'd had love affairs and, as he told it, gotten his heart soundly broken. He'd acquired things: stereos, cars, gadgets, a three-bedroom house, you name it. But then in 2001 he'd decided to come back to the monastery and had taken simple vows for the second time. He was the only monk I met who had left the monastery and come back, and he was one of the very few monks I met who had come to the life as a mature man, having experienced all that the outside world had to offer.

His second three-year trial was almost over by the time I met him. He was on the verge of taking solemn vows. Thereafter, he'd be moving downstairs, having earned his place in the stable of the vetted brotherhood.

I struck up my first true friendship at the abbey with Brother Vergil, a relationship that would in the end teach me more about the limits of male friendships, and the delicate balance of camaraderie and self-reliance that seems to prevail in all male quarters, than anything I'd experienced on a night out with my bowling buddies.

Vergil was a delight, a lifeline to me in the beginning. He wasn't one of the brooding introverts I'd expected to find in the cloister. Quite the opposite. He was a goyish Albert Brooks. He had the same antic face and impish eyes, a closely clipped, silver-stubbled head and an endearing doughy body with a tumescent paunch under his belt. There was a self-effacing sarcasm and sparkling intelligence in his remarks that made me want guys like him to land in purgatory just so that doubters like me would have someone to eat lunch with. Of course, there was a lot more to

Vergil than his wit, as I would soon learn, but at first this bitter-sweet clown was a godsend.

I was delightfully surprised, for example, when, during Mass on my second day, I banged my elbow hard on my armrest mid-hymn, and as I sat there, massaging my funny bone in obvious pain, Vergil leaned over and whispered: "Oak is awfully unforgiving, isn't it?"

A friendly monk with a sense of humor? Could this be?

Vergil knew whereof he joked. Woodwork was one of his trades. He was the resident carpenter for the abbey, and his major task, when he wasn't occupied with more pressing jobs, was to build coffins for the other monks. On my first few days at the monastery I went out to the shop to assist Vergil. Per his sense of humor, Vergil made the coffins in three sizes: tall, short and short and fat. The sizes were a smirking nod to some of the monks' nicknames, one of which was Father Richard the Tall. The moniker was used to distinguish him from the other more portly Father Richard in the monastery who was known as Father Richard the Fat.

I spent hours talking with Vergil those first few days in the shop, as he taught me how to use the electric level and sander to match and smooth the edges of the coffin. Our friendship took off as we discovered our common interests and shared them.

We found that we had the same sense of humor and love of language. We expressed our political opinions and often agreed. We quoted Monty Python back and forth to each other. He read aloud from his collected works of Gilbert and Sullivan. I read aloud from my collected poems of W. H. Auden.

We talked philosophy and theology. I asked him about his vows, looking for and finding thoughtful answers to my questions about monastic life. Vergil's was a natural intellect. He didn't appear to be particularly well read outside his prescribed fields (biology, Catholic theology and his avocation, musical comedy), but he had an innate gift for logical reasoning and an insatiable curiosity, both of which were contagious.

I told him I sang opera arias to the cows in the pasture after supper and he beamed with amused excitement as he asked: "Oh, you sing?" He had a precise, clear voice and took his singing very seriously in church. Many of the other monks were hard of hearing and turned off their hearing aids during services in order to withstand the blast of the organ. Most of the rest pretty well recrucified the Lord each day in song.

Vergil seemed glad to have another appreciable voice to keep him company. He often led us in the invitatory and other hymns, and sang the solo parts in the responsorial psalms, tuning himself quietly on a pitch pipe that he kept for that purpose in the cubby of his pew.

As I was to discover, the obsessive pitch pipe tuning was one of his many anal-retentive tics, most of which I found vastly entertaining, especially because they were one of the few things about which he had no sense of humor whatsoever.

He liked things just so. Details had to be correct. Mistakes displeased him. He wanted his pitch right and his part sung perfectly. He longed for a Gregorian precision in his brothers' singing, and he winced at their sour notes. He ironed and starched his handkerchiefs and tailored his own habits, some of which he'd made by hand from scratch.

This was classic Vergil. He was in control, or liked to think he was. That was an important part of his self-image, indispensable to his sanity and sense of place in the world. He thrived on the predictable rituals of monastic life. He enjoyed order, and he seemed to need it.

I became part of that scheme.

Vergil used to call me to him in church like a dog. Depending on the day and who did or didn't show up for prayers, I'd sometimes sit a seat or two away from him in our row. Once the service had started and he'd seen that the seats between us were going to remain empty, without looking up from his hymnal, he'd motion me to his side with a curt hand gesture that meant "come." And like a trained subservient, I did come. I'd flip my book open to the right page and he'd point his index finger, again without looking at me, at the right place in the prayer. This was pro forma. I was the pupil, he the master, and in this respect our relationship had a satisfying sharpness to it, clean and by the numbers.

I lost myself a little in this ritual, or Ned did. I can't be sure which or to what extent. I know that Norah flew into her friendship with Vergil—someone who seemed to present a full complement of emotional, intellectual and spiritual stimulation. And flight is not the wrong word. Women often do fly into new friendships with abandon, touching all the points of contact like bells on a tree. Men don't. Especially with other men. And that is where Vergil and I clashed, though I say this with the benefit of hindsight.

In the moment, I simply enjoyed the care that Vergil took with me in services, even if it was his command and my following, because as much as he did it with all his martial affect, he also did it with unfailing kindness and a genuine desire to include me. Standing beside him, close enough to smell his breath, which always smelled of Listerine or Altoids, mixing my voice with his, I smiled to myself out of sheer affection. But among men, especially among men who live together under vows of chastity, where the fear of sexual desire is ubiquitous and powerful, and the boundaries of intimacy strictly drawn at a barge pole's distance, girlish crushes and even pseudo-Platonic exuberances are definitely not okay.

"You're falling in love with him," said Father Jerome.

"Oh, I am not," I said. "It's not like that."

"Yes, you are," he said, "and it is."

Father Jerome spoke with the voice of experience. He claimed he'd seen this many times before. From the moment I'd met Father Jerome and heard his stereotypically lilting voice, I'd assumed he was gay—by orientation, not in practice—and out to himself, if not by dint of the obvious, out to everyone else as well. That was one of the reasons I'd befriended him.

He was fifty, but looked ten years younger. He was a little on the plump side, with a rounded, acne-scarred face. He had a blindingly white smile with large perfect teeth, which he told me he'd had bleached by his dentist. He was a transfer from a parish somewhere up north, homeless at present, and shacking up at the abbey, perhaps hoping to stay for the duration if they voted him in after a trial period. He had been there for only a week when I arrived, so he didn't know the place much better than I did. He certainly wasn't an insider.

I hopped a ride with him to town on my third day, hoping to be mostly honest about myself with at least one person in the abbey, someone who I thought might have some perspective on the place. I could let my guard down with him, I thought. He was loose and easy. He had the generic gay sense of humor, catty hilarity. We understood each other in that. So much so, that I'd felt comfortable enough to mention it.

"I like you, Father Jerome," I said.

"Why's that?" he asked.

"Oh, I don't know, you make me laugh."

"No. Be honest," he urged. "Why?"

He was fishing.

"Oh," I hesitated. "I don't think I can be quite that honest, can I?"

"Sure you can. Nothing you could say would bother me."

"Hmm. Are you sure?" He seemed to know what I was going

to say and was encouraging me to say it. It was the kind of dance I'd done with gay people before. You sense you're in the presence of another gay person, but you don't always want to be the first one to say it, in case you're wrong or in case they're not out even to themselves.

"Of course," he said. "Tell me."

"Okay," I said, taking the leap. "Because you're such a queen."

He looked surprised.

"What's a queen?" he said.

"Oh, come on," I balked. "You don't know what a queen is?"

"No. What is it?"

I was caught here. No escape in sight. "Well, you know," I said slowly, "an effeminate gay man."

I pronounced the words "effeminate" and "gay" haltingly, trying to soften the blow. Could he possibly not know he was gay? Or was it just the terminology he hadn't heard before?

"You think I'm effeminate?" he squeaked in horror.

"Uh, yeah, kind of."

"You mean like in *The Birdcage*?"

"Well," I answered, "that was a little exaggerated. I'd say Robin Williams more than Nathan Lane. Lane was a screaming queen. I'd say you're just a queen."

"Stop saying that," he snapped. "I hate that word."

"I'm sorry," I said. "I've insulted you. Forget I said anything, really. I thought you knew."

"No. No," he recovered. "You haven't insulted me."

There was a heavy silence, then he blurted suddenly, "So you think I'm gay?"

"I know you're gay," I said. "Or let's just say I'd bet odds on it."

"But *how* do you know?"

"Well," I said gingerly, "here's another term for you. 'Gaydar.' Have you heard of that?"

"No."

"Well, it sort of means it takes one to know one."

"So *you're* gay. You've been with men." His interest was really piqued now.

"Uh, yeah," I said, scrambling. "I've been with men. And women, too. More women than men."

He leapt on this. He asked me more about it. What it was like, what did I do sexually with men and why. He spouted the usual abomination line from Leviticus, and added that he thought gay sex was disgusting. He'd been horrified by what he'd seen of it. Yet he was clearly fascinated by it. He'd researched it thoroughly on the Internet, he said, finding the most appalling Web sites. He'd even watched a few episodes of Showtime's gay dramatic series *Queer as Folk,* all purely in rubbernecking horror, you understand, not out of prurient interest.

I asked him about his sexual history, too.

He told me that he was a virgin. He'd entered the religious life at twenty and effectively killed his sexuality there. I didn't know whether to believe that or not, though the few other monks to whom I spoke openly about their sexuality had said something similar. The majority of them had joined the order very young, in their late teens or early twenties, and some, perhaps most, had done so without having had any sexual experiences at all. A couple of them, including Father Jerome, spoke of the inevitable wet dreams and involuntary erections that accompanied puberty, but they did so sketchily and bemusedly, as of something experienced long, long ago and now barely recalled. One of them said simply, "I'm not interested in sex." He looked very uncomfortable when he said it. The very idea of bodies commingling made him squirm in his seat, as if it were calling up a bad memory.

Vergil, by contrast, had been characteristically funny on the subject, saying: "There's suppression and then there's repression. Let's see now. I'm trying to remember, which one is the bad one? Oh, yes. Repression. That's when you say, 'I don't have a penis.' That doesn't work. Then there's suppression, which is when you say, 'Down, boy!'"

Not everyone had such a clear perspective on the matter, but then, unlike Vergil, many of them hadn't lived much of a separate life outside the cloister.

Either way it must have taken superhuman effort or pathological powers of denial for these men to counteract such a strong biological drive. At least Vergil had had the good sense to see that arriving at a chaste existence in this manner, by preemptive force, wasn't likely to work. He'd gone out into the world and, as he'd said, "had a really good time," and at the end of it all, when he'd reached the bottom of the fun, he'd realized that pure sex wasn't what he wanted. He'd seen that, like the world's counterparts to poverty and obedience—material possessions and limitless freedoms—lust had left him feeling empty and insatiable.

Wanton sex wasn't some eschewed evil for him. It was more like a dish once devoured, found wanting and now passed over, not without occasional pangs, but with a kind of earned laxity. Still, Vergil had serious issues with control, and as Ned would learn, that was still part of the sexual and emotional package and probably always would be, partly because Vergil was just Vergil, but mainly because Vergil had chosen to rejoin a community of men that was all about control, self and otherwise. That's what chastity and obedience meant in the abbey. Nobody there was practicing nonattachment. They were doing it the Western way, discipline, stone cold.

Father Jerome was a classic example. On our trip to town I had come around to telling him about my friendship with Vergil, and that's when, like an old pro, he'd said, "You're falling in love with him." But how did he know? How could he really know if he wasn't recognizing in me feelings he'd had himself?

"I don't know," I'd conceded at last. "Maybe I am."

I honestly didn't know. Feelings got strange in that place, isolated from the neat perspectives of the outside world. I suppose if Ned had really been a boy, any moderately observant person would have been right to assume that he was as gay as a parade and having impure thoughts about Brother Vergil. In comportment, I wasn't bothering to be very butch. I was being me, though purposely less demonstrative than I would have been as myself.

Still, even toned down, as a man, my hallmark female behaviors, my emotive temperament and even my word choice read as gay, or at the very least odd. Jerome, eager to dispel conjecture about his own sexuality, was quick to jump on these cues and stomp them with all the force of his own self-hatred.

In his presence I made the mistake once of referring to one of the other monks as cute—the kind of thing that women say all the time about sweet elderly gentleman like the one to whom I was referring. He was in his nineties, and succumbing to Alzheimer's. Every time you saw him he'd put his hand on your arm, smile at you in the most beatific way and say, "Bless you." I found it very touching. Though uninventive, "cute" was the word that came to mind over lunch that day, and puppy mush-mush the tone that came with it. But as soon as the offending remark was out of my mouth, Father Jerome pounced on it, sneering.

"He's not cute. You don't call other men cute."

I made similar mistakes in front of the other monks. One night at dinner I goofed hugely when I told Father Richard the Tall that he looked very good for his age. He did. I couldn't believe he was eighty. As soon as the remark came out of my mouth, everyone at the table stopped eating mid-forkful and looked at me as if I had three heads. Father Richard the Tall said a very suspicious, squint-eyed "thank you," and looked away, clearly embarrassed.

But the implication from other quarters was clear: "What the hell's wrong with you, kid? Don't you know that properly socialized males don't behave that way with each other?"

Naturally, I didn't, and I was going to get a bigger lesson in that sooner than I knew. I was going to have to learn, as I suspect most boys do by the time they reach puberty, not to be such a Nancy. This was something I had observed, though not yet thoroughly experienced.

I had seen the same thing happening with Bob's son Alex at the bowling alley. By all accounts Alex was a sissy, a mama's boy who needed toughening up. Everybody kicked him around a bit emotionally for that purpose, pushing him off with a sharp remark when he came to us in tears over losing his ball in the alley machinery, or getting gypped out of a game by the desk clerk.

"Don't be such a baby," Bob would say. "Jesus. Go and get your money back. Or do I have to do it for you?"

In the same spirit, Jim had once had Alex put his hand on the table and hold it there as long as he could while he thwacked his knuckles repeatedly with a plastic ruler. Alex endured it as long as he could, grimacing, but determined not to fail the test. It was all done in jest, and Jim didn't seriously hurt Alex, nor did he intend to. The ruler wasn't that rigid. But the spirit of the thing was there, and the message clear. Thicken your skin, boy.

And so it was for Ned, though the process was far less overt.

It wasn't just the sexual tension of Ned's presumed gayness, and his awkwardly expressed attachment to Vergil, but his seeming ignorance of masculine boundaries.

To some of them I think it became clear fairly quickly that I was the weak man in the platoon, the guy you'd have to break in basic before he got to the front lines and put everyone's life in danger. I didn't understand this dynamic at first. I certainly hadn't expected it in of all places a monastery.

And, of course, it was entirely different than anything you'd find in the military. It wasn't as if the monks burst into my room in the middle of the night, tied me to my bunk and beat me with bars of soap twisted in pillowcases, or made me do push-ups in mud pits in the pouring rain until I promised not to talk about my feelings.

But I got a fairly clear sense by the end of the first week that I was a threat to their fragile ecosystem of terse masculine rapport.

I wasn't surprised when I got sour looks and disapproving shakes of the head from Father Jerome or from people like Father Cyril. Cyril was the prior of the monastery, which meant, as he lost no time in informing me the first time we met, that he was the second in command after the abbot. At sixty-eight, he exuded the jaundiced outlook of an unhappy man who knew there was no remedy for his unmet aspirations. He was too old to change or grow or do the things he'd left undone, and he took out his insecurities on anybody he thought inferior in intellect or station to himself.

If I'd been a serious contender for a spot in the novitiate, Father Cyril would surely have done his best to snuff my candle. I expected that of him. He didn't want anyone in his chosen small arena coloring outside the lines or challenging his authority. Besides, it was his job to enforce the hierarchy of the abbey, which was its organizing principle.

As a newcomer, you either fit or you foundered. You either learned your place or you left. There could be no place for an upstart in a world where obedience was a vow, and learning to be like the others was a mark of fidelity. Jerome had obviously internalized that message long ago and was a knot of denial and mishap as a result.

In that place I could see how a person could be broken down.

It began happening to me. And once that was accomplished, once you had accepted the terms of the monastic rule and sufficiently humbled yourself before God and the order, Cyril's ounce of authority, which in the outside world was on par with a manager's power at a McDonald's, would suddenly mean a hell of a lot more. In this way it was no different than the military. Submit. Become like the others, a pure predictable machine, ordered and in hand, and never, ever show weakness or need.

But I was used to showing those things—a free woman's privilege.

I was clueless young Ned, at the bottom of the heap, seeking instruction, guidance, open arms. I got lost in the politics, and the pack mentality of the abbey, and I was amazed at how quickly it happened. Ned fell right into character. Ned did fall in love a little bit with Brother Vergil right away, just the way novices and postulants do and aren't supposed to, and his crush had to be corrected, because that was the obligation of his superiors, cut it off at first sign. In intimate groups of men, Freudian impulses are expected to arise and with help and guidance resolve themselves. It's part of the process in monasteries, too, part of what the novitiate is for, getting up all the buried stuff, all the daddy issues, the brother issues, the fag issues, and dispensing with them early, before they become entrenched and before the community has wasted too much time and too many resources on a maladaptive cub.

Still, I was pretty sure that what I felt for Vergil wasn't sexual, or even romantic, though the twisted mentality of that place, always on the lookout for forbidden desires, had made me wonder. The feelings were very real whatever their motive, and utterly unexpected. They were what drew me into the emotional vortex of the abbey and the fullest possible experience of being a young man at expressive loose ends in an all-male environment designed to rid young men of their messes.

Experiencing this strange and foreign treatment firsthand, I developed new sympathy for boys and young men, and I felt sadness for the damage done to them in those rites of passage we all condone and inflict to make them into men. I remembered my brothers' plights with this same process, seeing them as young boys weeping at home with my mother, telling her of the petty cruelties perpetrated against them by other boys and men at school and summer camp. In those days they were every bit as vulnerable as I was, and still able to show it. What's more, they could still ask for and find comfort and sympathy for their pain. But now, like so many other men, if my brothers show emotion at all, they show only anger, because that's all they've been allowed. I have not seen them cry for a very long time. Perhaps they can't anymore.

I know as much was true of at least one of the more candid monks, who, when I asked him how many times in his life he'd shed tears, said that he could count the number of times on the fingers of one hand.

"I'm a very rational person," he said ruefully. "I'm not given to outbursts. It's part of my Germanic male upbringing." He said he was just beginning the process of unlearning this with his own spiritual adviser, who, significantly enough, was a woman. But it was going slowly, and he had much to overcome. Almost all of the other monks had similar issues, he implied, but most of them weren't even close to addressing them.

In such an environment it should have come as no surprise when my first amicable week with Vergil turned inexplicably sour on a dime.

He stopped inviting me to the shop. He began ignoring me at services, and emanated an unmistakable hostility when forced into close proximity with me. At lunch he sat as far away from me as possible and if we spoke at all in passing, he was curt and superior.

It was an unmistakable snubbing that caught me completely off guard, and threw Ned into juvenile pangs of self-doubt.

Father Jerome had noticed Vergil's defection, too.

But then he was looking for it. Kicks and wounds fit right into his schema. He claimed to know the ways of monasteries. He knew, he said, all about crushes and unnatural attachments, and the hierarchies of weakness and hurt, betrayal and emotional control, that festered under the ritual surface of cloistered life.

"He's doing you a favor by cutting you off now," he said. But this was said in the context of so many other paranoid ideas and nasty undercurrents that I didn't know whether or not to take him seriously. He sounded deeply stung most of the time, as I'm sure I did.

He'd say things like, "Don't ever trust anyone here. They'll betray you. Believe me."

He was already paranoid about the ramifications of our "gay" conversation. Every time we saw each other he'd say, "You haven't told anyone anything we said the other day, have you?"

I assured him that I hadn't, which was true, but this didn't seem to assuage his doubts or deflect his constant circumspection. He was afraid of being exposed to the group and his fear turned him vindictive.

He assumed an I-told-you-so tone when he raised the subject of Vergil's new and sudden coldness toward me.

"Boy, he just can't stand to be near you, can he?" he said with relish.

"So I'm not just imagining it?" I asked.

"Nope, he definitely doesn't want anything to do with you."

That was a dig. He wasn't just rubbing my face in his predictions, he was also having a go at me for being gay. Ever since the gay chat, he had been sliding jabs into our casual banter, the odd homophobic remark designed to needle me—like quoting a recent newspaper article in which a prominent member of the Catholic leadership had said that marrying a person of the same sex was like marrying your pet. He laughed heartily as he told me about it.

"I fell on the floor when I read that. It was so funny."

"You're an idiot," I said, visibly angry. "And so is the person who said that."

As I turned away, I noticed that Brother Felix, whom I didn't yet know by anything but name, was suppressing a laugh as he got up from his chair two seats down from Father Jerome.

I had noticed Brother Felix before but hadn't spoken to him directly. He, like many of the other monks, had glasses, a belly and a bald spot in the middle of his thinning hair. At fifty years of age, he was one of what I would come to think of as the midgeneration, or bridge, monks. He was significantly older than Brother Vergil but quite a bit younger than the octogenarian monks like Richard the Tall. He was post–Vatican II, but not so post that he'd entirely escaped the pull of the old ways. Yet he was still young enough to understand and identify with the younger generation. For me, this unique position in the abbey hierarchy would make him the key to understanding Ned's emotional plight at the abbey and contextualizing it within the framework of the fraught masculinity at work there. He would prove a far more reliable source than Jerome, though not an entirely contradictory one.

But those revelations came much later. At first, I misunderstood Felix utterly. At first, he was just another purveyor and consumer of the usual homophobic jokes that abound in almost all exclusively male environments, the monastery being no exception.

We met formally over a game of mah-jongg in the rec room. I'd never played the game before, but on his invitation, I'd joined a foursome that included him, Vergil and Jerome. I had a bit of trouble getting my pungs and chows straight, and I made a number of mistakes up front. Felix was in a cranky mood that night, and this wasn't the best of circumstances under which to make his acquaintance. As I got to know him better, though, and earned his respect, I found that these moods were fairly rare, and usually directed at people he took for fools. I was, in my ignorance of the game, displaying the marks of a fool. I had to be corrected on a number of my moves, and his corrections were startlingly sharp.

"*No.* You can't pick up from the discard pile unless you have a pung or a chow to show."

"Okay. Okay. Sorry. Relax, Brother. Relax," I said.

"Please," he added, between gritted teeth.

As we played on I got distracted by the television, which was playing in the background. Usually, at this hour, a gaggle of the older monks gathered round the tube to watch the news. One particular segment on the American obesity epidemic had caught my attention. The camera was focused on a man's enormous wobbling midsection as he waddled down the street. I couldn't look away. I was still staring when my turn came up.

"Hello?" said Felix in a crescendo of irritation. "Your turn."

"Oh, sorry," I said. "I was just mesmerized by that man's belly."

"I beg your pardon," he said.

Jerome looked down at his pieces. Vergil burst out laughing.

I squirmed immediately, regressing in an instant, trying to cover myself like a teenager caught in a flub.

"What?" I clamored. "The guy was enormously fat. That's all."

But it didn't matter what I said. I wasn't being entirely honest with them anyway, so I could hardly complain that they were having a little joke at my expense. Besides, these jokes were part of their badinage and I couldn't blow my cover by deflecting it with a dirtier innuendo, as I might have done in the outside world.

Essentially, this was harmless boys' stuff, being the first to make the fag joke and laugh the loudest—the trope of every male-bonding ritual. In this, they were hardly different from my bowling buddies, though naively I had expected them to be. Still, their remarks had a testing edge to them that I had never felt with Jim, Bob and Allen. I sensed, the way you do when you hear an old married couple sniping at each other, that there was a lot being said without being said.

Mingling behavior in the rec room taught me a lot about the monks' ways with each other, their interpersonal skills or lack thereof. Watching and listening for only a short time, I could see how rigid and inept most of them were at relating to each other, and why by contrast I stuck out so sorely. By the way they tripped over each other and backed away, you'd almost have thought they were virtual strangers, not people who'd been living together, some of them for as many as thirty or more years.

Tuesday nights were supposed to be social nights. The abbot had ruled that on that one night out of the week the monks would sit in a circle and try to talk to each other. It had to be mandated or it wouldn't happen. It was supposed to foster greater closeness or openness among the monks, something they'd been trying to work on for some time at the abbey in various ways.

Apparently they'd once tried instituting a hugging program. This, too, they'd had to enforce in a formal way to make it happen at all. Some of the monks, especially the older ones, who'd had ingrained in them an aversion to any physical contact with other men, just couldn't do it spontaneously. Vergil and Felix had each told me about this incident. It was obviously a big event in the history of the abbey, one that Vergil had scoffed at, but Felix had better understood. Felix had told me about the semiabsurdity of it, how some of the hugs felt natural, or almost natural, but hugging some of his fellow monks, he said, was like hugging a board. The exercise hadn't lasted. The discomfort with enforcing affection had been too great, or perhaps, as Vergil seemed to suggest, some monks' repugnance for new age role-play techniques had swamped the spirit of the thing and sunk it before it took hold. Clearly each man had his own struggles with intimacy—all of the monks did—and these attempts to address those struggles were always prickly, though necessary in a community where men were trying to live in a spirit of love with each other.

From what I could tell, it wasn't just that, as Christians, they felt they had to express greater affection for each other, or even that, as housemates, they had to learn to mingle rather than simply coexist. It was that their needs, whether they could admit it or not, were poking through the formal web of this living arrangement. Their needs for affection and touch and companionship and compassion were making themselves felt. For some of them it was only in the harrowing run-up to death, for others, it was in the trough of late middle age, and for some it was happening out of sheer constitutional sensitivity refusing at long last to be put down.

But they were socialized men and they didn't know how to talk to each other about much of anything at all let alone their feelings. And who could blame them? That, in our culture, has traditionally been the feminine role and it has not yet been entirely bred out of us. Women are still often the communicators, the interlocutors between men and themselves, men and their children and even men and each other. Observing the monks I couldn't help thinking that without the connective tissue, without the feminizing influence, these guys were like bumper cars trying to merge.

Those Tuesday night gatherings were painful to watch. We'd all sit around in our chairs in a circle. There would be long silences, and then little pathetic attempts to fill the silences with talk that sputtered and rarely flew.

Then someone would pick up a magazine and start leafing through it. Someone else would pick up the abbey's copy of *The*

Best of Calvin and Hobbes and do the same. I, and one or two of the monks would gravitate to the *New York Times Sunday Crossword Omnibus* that was usually lying open on one of the tables. Eventually people would peel off and leave the room or stand by the door to the patio and pretend to be fascinated by the impending weather pattern shaping up outside the window. Finally the abbot would give up, or the bell would ring for vespers.

Father Richard the Fat was the monk with whom I most often did the crossword. He was the novice master, which meant that, like Vergil and me, he resided on the mostly empty fourth floor. True to his nickname, he was indeed round, Santa-like, with a white beard and mustache and a jolly, breathy laugh that would crinkle his nose and show his gums and baby corn teeth. He always had a generous spray of dandruff on the front of his habit. It made me think affectionately of a crack Jim had once made about a fellow bowler: "He doesn't need Head and Shoulders. He needs Neck and Chest."

With Father Fat, doing the crossword was a form of intimacy, and a lesson in intellectual humility. It was a way into his mind, which was where he lived. I found it very fulfilling, sitting next to him, both of us leaning over the puzzle, laughing about the things we'd gotten right or wrong or the too, too coy clues and their esoteric answers. With him that was a brave start for anyone, and I considered it a victory. After all, it wasn't as if you were going to walk up to him, put your arm around him and say, so Father, tell me about your childhood. His interpersonal style was very subtle and hands off.

Vergil had a lot of affection and respect for Father Fat. He told me once, in his usual tone of sardonic remove, that Father Fat dealt with the novices the way he dealt with his plants, of which he had dozens all over the fourth floor. The plants were tangled, untamed, prehensile-looking creatures that you felt sure were going to reach out and grab you as you passed. There wasn't a single flower among them. They were manly plants, all sturdy, rubbery greens that even a black thumb would have been hard pressed to kill.

Novices had, it seemed, to be as sturdy as that foliage to make it on Father Fat's watch. The way Vergil told it, if you were a novice and Father Fat saw that you weren't doing well where you were, he'd move you to a spot where you'd get more light or shade. If he saw that you needed watering or pruning, he'd do that. But he wasn't going to stand over you or check on you every day. He'd let you take your course, and make a slight adjustment periodically, if necessary, but that was about it.

That was his intellectual style, too. He was brilliant, a mathematician by training, but an obvious polymath, well versed enough in pretty much anything to do a crossword like he was just filling out a form. But he didn't feel the need to beat you over the head with his brainpower. What he knew, he'd converted into a quiet wisdom. He never interrupted or overwhelmed. He never tried to convince. He offered. He suggested, and his suggestions were so profoundly right, so purely expressed, that they made you feel by comparison like a donkey who'd been temporarily granted the power of speech.

He was a benign, almost avuncular presence when you got to know him, but a formidable one, never to be trifled with by the likes of Cyril or Jerome. I had the impulse to hug him, but out of sheer respect, I didn't dare.

Still, as much as the monks disdained it, and as flat as it fell, the hugging idea wasn't altogether without merit. Actually, it was just what the doctor might have ordered. This revelation came to me while talking the first time with Father Henry.

Father Henry was dying of prostate cancer. He'd had all the chemo and radiation his body could tolerate, and the doctors had told him that there was nothing else they could do for him. He was very sick, but he could still get around. He still went every Friday to one of the local maternity wards to participate in a cuddling program for premature infants. He and the other volunteers would each hold one of the infants for several hours, stroking, and snuggling, and talking to them in an effort to increase their chances of survival.

When Father Henry was explaining all of this to me in the rec room one night, I said: "Wow. That's amazing. Maybe I could join you sometime. I could really use some cuddling right about now."

Vergil shot Felix a look. I felt suddenly exposed, embarrassed once again in a way that I would never have allowed anyone to make me feel in another context. I might have protested, had I not been a young man surrounded by other men who, I could tell by their shared looks, were now deeply suspicious that I was gay and needy and undisciplined in suppressing those tendencies.

I, in turn, was duly becoming the young guy who would be shamed into eschewing emotional admissions. The weight of my brothers' disapproval would assure it, or mangle me in the process.

This I hadn't expected. I hadn't thought that I could really become Ned so fully as to feel embarrassed by the conjectures of monks, or to smart under the sting of their disapproval. Yet it was precisely that experience, the immediacy of it, that led me to see and understand the dynamic of fraternal acceptance and rejection that underlay the community and defined the emotional well-being of its members.

Feeling it at work in myself, I began to see it at work in the others, too, though in them it was much more skillfully disguised than it would ever be in me.

Even with years of practiced stoicism behind him, hardened

Vergil hadn't quite been able to hide from inferior Ned how much he needed the approval of his peers. One day toward the end of my stay, he received the news that he was to be allowed to take solemn vows. He came to my room electrified with pride. He'd been distant for days, but now he wanted me to share in his joy. Not the joy of his impending profession, but, as he emphasized, the joy of his inclusion. He had been voted in by his brothers. They had accepted him as one of their own. These men, with whom he had lived for three years, had deemed him worthy enough to spend the rest of his life with them. The vows he was taking were in a certain symbolic sense collective nuptial vows, not so much to God, but to this band of brothers who lived together in sickness and in health and buried each other south of the church.

This I felt sure was closely connected to these men's decisions not only to take the vow of chastity, but to enter the monastic way of life instead of becoming diocesan priests. It was an entirely legitimate way for men to marry other men—to cultivate the lifelong company of their own sex—and this held true for both hetero- and homosexuals. It was the one thing all the monks appeared to share in common, a deep desire for fraternal and paternal approval and support, an almost inconsolable need for a bonded male family.

Homosexuals found it convenient presumably because they could thereby avoid committing the grave sin of sodomy—in theory, at least—while at the same time enjoying all-male domestic arrangements and avoiding the dreaded expectations of "normal" heterosexual existence—intimacy with a woman.

Heterosexuals, too, saw the appeal of marrying other men. Several of the monks with whom I spoke about chastity gave me the impression that women weren't creatures they could handle on any level. These guys weren't gay. They just didn't want the emotional demands and constant struggles of navigating the opposite sex. They were Henry Higgins types, confirmed old bachelors. They wanted to be among their own kind, to be understood and left mostly alone to go about their business without a hectoring wife bearing down on them. But, and this was crucial, they didn't want to be lonely. One monk told me, "I tried that [living alone] and it didn't work." Life in the abbey was a little like life in a college dorm, and for a certain personality type it could offer the perfect solution to sexual alienation and loneliness. It was, in many ways, a much easier life than the alternatives. A lot less stressful. A lot less involved, especially if you were the kind of man who didn't want to cook or clean up after himself, and who thought of women as a separate, intolerable species.

But therein also lay the rub. Living among the guys at the abbey had its downside, too. The nurturing influence that women could provide, the communicative skills they could lend and foster were lost to these men, and much to their emotional detriment. Most of them were hurting inside, needing each other's consolation, but utterly unable to communicate those pains and needs, much less to offer consolation in return.

Father Claude was a perfect example of this sad dynamic at work. At eighty-two, he was the second oldest monk in the monastery. Emotionally speaking, he was old school. You weren't going to get him to talk about his feelings. Or at least that's what I thought at first, and I got the impression that that's what the other monks had thought for a long time. Probably with good reason. Claude had been the novice master at one time, and Vergil had told me that he was tough in that role. Emotionally tough. That is to say, not a hugger. Vergil said that when he was a novice, back when he first came to the monastery, one time while they were walking together, Vergil put an affectionate hand on Claude's shoulder, the way you do when you're talking animatedly with someone you like. Vergil said, "You've never seen anybody pull away so fast and furiously."

I first met Father Claude in the woodworking shop on one of those days early on, when I was helping Vergil with the coffins. Claude tended the vegetable garden and the beehives, which were both located in a small clearing about fifty yards from the shop.

He used to come into the shop now and then for a break and a chat. He'd stand there wiping away the sweat on his forehead with a handkerchief, his face and hands covered with liver spots, his baggy work clothes hanging off his slight frame, his blue eyes rheumy with old age. He and Vergil had an affectionate, bantering rapport that consisted on Vergil's end mostly of references to Claude's extreme old age and questionable compos mentis, and on Claude's end mostly of snide remarks about Vergil's youthful sass and ineptitude. The game endeared both of them to me.

After one of Claude's visits, Vergil said: "He can be a little silly sometimes. We have a joke about him. We say, when Father Claude goes senile, how will we know?"

It was one of Vergil's sweet jests, full of awkward, untranslatable love.

I made a point of visiting Claude after that. With great pride, he showed me his garden and his hives. He said he had probably been stung hundreds of times in his life, either gathering honey or transferring hives, but he said it never bothered him. He just loved bees. He could talk about them for hours, tell you anything you wanted to know. The other monks called the bees his six-legged friends, and I suppose talking about them was Claude's version of talking about the weather, a neutral banter that made him comfortable.

But as I spent more and more time with Father Claude, asking him questions and walking with him in the garden, he began to open up. He did have things to say if you probed him. Maybe it was old age, the mellowing that happens to some people. Maybe it was my feminine approach, even if he didn't recognize it as such. Whatever it was, he told me things about his childhood, gave me images that I'll never forget. And in the end, he said the most intimate, heartbreaking thing that anyone there ever said to me.

One night in the rec room I asked him if he'd ever regretted becoming a priest. I think this took him by surprise because almost as a reflex he said no, not in a defensive way, but in a puzzled way, as if he'd never really considered it. But then the next day he found me in the refectory at the end of lunch and he leaned over and said, "You know, I've been thinking about what you asked me yesterday and I remembered something a fellow priest once said to me. He said, 'You know, sometimes I wish we were novices again.' And I asked him, 'Why's that? Because it was such a wonderful time?' And he said, 'No. Because then I could quit.'"

Father Claude chuckled at the memory and squeezed my arm. I laughed and took him by the shoulders and said fondly, "Father Claude, I really like you so much. You give me hope."

"Oh, thank you," he said, tilting his head down slightly toward the floor. "I wish my brothers felt that way."

I couldn't believe he had said this. It was supposed to be the kind of thing Father Claude would never say or feel.

"Don't they?" I asked.

Pursing his lips together in a rueful, pained half frown, he said, "They don't seem to."

Even staid Father Claude, the once commanding novice master who wouldn't suffer a friendly touch on the shoulder, a man who had chosen to spend his entire adult life in this very same cloister, even he was without fellowship in the end, without the sense that his confreres esteemed him.

This made me wonder how esteem was truly won and lost between the brothers. I knew from Vergil that being accepted into the community was an enormous affirmation. Presumably, it had been so for all the monks. But I also knew from Vergil, and had gathered from other comments Felix had made, that there was at least one monk among them who had lost the respect of his brothers. No one was indiscreet enough to name him at first, but as my stay extended, and Ned's own troubles with the esteem mill ground on, I found out who it was and why the other monks thought less of him.

The subject first arose one day in the shop. Vergil mentioned that one of the other monks, Brother Crispin, was suffering from depression and taking medication for it.

"He's depressed because he feels that the rest of us don't respect him," he'd said. "And he's right, we don't. Yet he keeps doing the very things that lost him our respect in the first place."

The implication was that if Crispin just got off his ass, he'd gain their respect and—poof—no more depression.

Felix, I found, shared Vergil's dislike for Crispin. "Some people," he interjected, during a conversation we were having about life at the abbey, "would rather take Prozac than deal with their problems."

We were taking a drive together that afternoon. I didn't have access to a car, so in an effort to spend some private time with him and to get to know him better, I asked him to take me out for the day, and he agreed. It was then that I learned how wrong I was about him. How I'd misjudged him. Despite his remark about Crispin, he wasn't at bottom the brusque, cutting bully I'd taken him for. On the contrary, he was very kind and open with me.

We talked about emotional life at the monastery and he

admitted that there were serious problems with intimacy in the community. Most of the monks, he said, were incapable of talking about their feelings with each other, or for that matter discussing anything more than sports and the weather. They were typical guys in that respect.

"It's possible," he said, "in a monastic setting like this to go twenty years or more without speaking to someone and not know why."

But, he emphasized, there were a lot of forces militating against good communication skills. Aside from all the emotionally repressive socialization that men of their generation traditionally underwent, the older monks had had the added burden of being trained from seminary on not to socialize with each other. Getting them to loosen up now would mean contravening everything they knew.

He told me that in the old pre–Vatican II days the novice monks were forbidden to spend time alone with each other. They were forbidden to go anywhere in groups of less than three. Partly the idea behind these rules had been to foster a sense of community, but the more pressing concern had been to remove the temptation of inappropriate intimacy between the brothers. Inappropriate intimacy wasn't entirely a euphemism for gay sex. The monks were supposed to avoid deep friendships or platonic attachments of any kind with anyone of either sex, lest these attachments come between them and God or create competing loyalties within the group. But as Felix put it, sexual tension was a pressing and ubiquitous near occasion of sin nonetheless, and the rules existed largely to keep the men out of temptation's way.

He spoke of a growing generational divide between the older and younger monks. Moreover, he said that a number of the young novices they'd had in recent years had found it as difficult as I had to integrate themselves into the community, and for similar reasons—the emotional remove of so many of its members, the institutionalized stifling of harmless intimacies, spontaneous affections and even, dare one say it, joy. As Felix spoke, I remembered Father Fat telling me about one failed novice who had been caught keeping a kitten concealed in his room, a serious no-no. For my part, it had struck me right away as a noticeable lack that the monastery harbored no pets of any kind, even outdoor ones, which the grounds could surely have accommodated. I asked about it and was told that it was a matter of policy, and one that now didn't seem at all incongruous with the somewhat stunted emotional life of the abbey.

Felix got a little defensive then.

"You might be tempted to think that we don't even like each other, but there's a lot about this community that an outsider doesn't see, a lot that goes on beneath the surface that makes us a community."

I knew this was true, partly because I had learned so much already about the silent quality of male friendships, but also because I had heard other monks speak about these hidden intimacies. They spoke of knowing other monks by the sound of their footsteps in the hallways, or knowing that Felix himself always sneezed in groups of four. Even in my short time at the abbey, I had learned to recognize Vergil's shuffling, slippered gait as he passed my door on the way to and from the bathroom. I could see how there might be a million tiny intimacies like that between these men, great kindnesses given in passing. But they could not entirely replace what wasn't there.

Felix admitted as much. As he told it, he had once been more open to and even attempted more direct emotional contact with his confreres, but he said he'd gotten hurt and had since shut himself down.

As I asked him questions about himself and as he spoke and

revealed more of his private thoughts to me, and saw that I was open to receiving them, I could see his doctored imperious persona falling away. I could feel his loneliness, his need for intimacy so long suppressed, pushing out like the palms of someone's hands against the window of a sinking car. He was still alive in there, intact behind the dejection and neglect.

That's why I knew that when he said, "Some people would rather take Prozac than deal with their problems," he was really saying, "Does Crispin think he's the only one here who's in pain?"

It was also just the old masculine reflex, the same one that Vergil had had. To them, Crispin was weak and he was using a pill to do what he should have been resolute enough to do for himself. But there was, I thought, also a touch of envy in their judgments. He had had the courage to cry out.

I was curious to know how Brother Crispin saw all of this, so finally I decided to go and see him. I hadn't spoken more than a couple of words to him since I'd been at the abbey. He was very quiet, the kind of person who disappears in a group. I simply hadn't noticed him much. Now I knew why, and I felt bad about it.

He was seriously overweight, by a good seventy-five pounds or so. In the almost ashamed, self-deprecating way he seemed to inhabit his flesh, you could see the magnitude of his isolation and unhappiness written all over him. His black hair was shaped in the old bowl cut monk style minus the tonsure. The bangs were blunt and high over his forehead. He was pasty and his face was defenselessly young. Despite his forty-one years, you could still almost see the eighth grader in him.

Whatever anger Crispin felt had turned inward, as it so often does in depressives, and he presented a meek, defeated front, his shoulders sagging down and in as if to shield the solar plexus, his

gait lumbering and slow. He worked in the library, literally barri-
caded in by the books. They were piled all around him, though I
doubted he had the energy or focus to read them. I knew I didn't
when I was depressed.

Getting him to talk was work, but we finally came around to
the topic of his depression and he said he'd been on Prozac but
had switched to Zoloft. I asked him when the depression had
started. He said that a few years back, during one of the periodic
gatherings in which the monks discuss community business, he'd
lost it. He said he just stood up and screamed at everybody, finally
unleashing years of suppressed discontent.

It was hard to tell from what he said whether that scene had
precipitated a genuine breakdown in him, or whether the monks
simply deemed that kind of public display of uncontrolled emotion
psychotic under any circumstances. In any case, Crispin said that
after the incident he'd "gone away" for a while. Again it was hard
to know whether he went to an actual mental ward in a hospital or
to a special monastic retreat facility, and whether he'd gone of his
own accord or whether he'd been sent. I got the impression he'd
been sent, but Crispin was reluctant to say more and I didn't want
to push him on the question.

I could see my own story in Crispin's. Just being in that place
for a few weeks I'd already begun to feel that if I'd really been a
young man considering this life or if I'd been young enough not to
know better, and had joined in a fit of visionary zeal, I'd have been
heeled and reduced just as surely as Crispin had been.

And again it struck me that Crispin's fate was not linked primarily to monasticism, but rather to the all-male environment in
which he lived, the only difference being one of degree. Far, far
worse would have happened to him in prison or the military,
where the weakest are always weeded out or trampled by the
strong. But the instinct was the same. He was at the bottom of the

pile, the fat kid on the playground, the hated projection of every-body's hidden weaknesses, the shivering manifestation of failed masculinity on display. He was a grown man, like Ned, who hadn't had the pink properly pounded out of him.

My time with Crispin had left me feeling sad and anxious to leave the abbey. I, too, had started getting depressed amid all the pain I'd uncovered. But I didn't want things to resolve themselves in this way. I didn't want to leave with nothing but a mound of bad feelings in tow. Yet I only had a couple of days left.

I needed to change the tenor of my encounters. I needed someone to talk to, someone outside the fray. Father Fat came to mind immediately.

But outside the rec room it was hard to command Father Fat's attention. He was very busy during the day, as most of the monks were, and if you were going to take up his time, it had bet-ter be a cosmic matter. That meant, more or less, confessing your sins. So I decided to confess my sins. It was odd to think of the confessional as being a place where you could get to know a man better, but Brother Felix knew Father Fat a lot better than I did, and he had suggested it.

"Doing crosswords is one way to get to know Father Richard," he'd said. "Another is by asking him to be your confessor."

Besides, I'd been looking for a confessor among the monks. The burden of having lied to get into the monastery, and of having continually deceived these people on a matter that would be a grievous offense to them if they knew about it, had been weighing on my mind for my entire stay. I felt guilty and I wanted to come clean.

Two days before my departure, I arranged to meet Father Fat in my room midmorning after lauds. Right on time he knocked on my door. I asked him where we should go, and he said, "There are two chairs. Let's do it right here."

So we did. He sat in my reading chair and I sat in my desk chair and we started.

"Forgive me, Father, for I have sinned," I said. "It's been longer than I can remember since my last confession."

That was the only formal thing I said during the whole confession. The rest was just talk, which was exactly what I'd been hoping for. It began with me expressing regret for the ill will I bore some of the monks. Then I touched on some of the points of Catholic theology that had always bothered me. He interjected things now and then, but mostly he just listened.

Then I began to ask him about himself, his background, why he became a monk. With characteristic economy, he said: "Somewhere between becoming a policeman and becoming a cowboy I became a priest." It was probably the most honest answer anyone there had given me. Though Father Claude hadn't said it in so many words, I gathered that he'd joined for a similar reason. It was a form of civil service to a certain generation, like being a soldier. If you weren't cut out for one, you did the other.

But there was far more to it than that for someone as complex as Father Fat. He had gotten his degree at the local college where he and many of the monks now taught, and he said that when he was a student there he had been very impressed by the monks he met.

"I thought that if they got to be the kind of people they were by living that life," he said, "then I wanted to give it a try."

And if ever there was an advertisement for the life, Father Fat was it. He was an exemplary man. Not by any stretch perfect. But exemplary. Deeply good. Deeply kind. Solemn, humble, generous.

I asked him about the hugging thing and the difficulty so many of the monks had in showing affection for each other. I was curious about where he fell on that spectrum. He told me about his friendship with Father Henry, which had been a long and devoted one. He said that he went to visit Father Henry in his rooms or in the hospital quite often these days. They would talk for an hour or two and then they would always hug long and hard at the end of it.

"I'm helping my friend to die," he said.

We just sat with his last remark for a while. Father Fat had looked me right in the eye when he'd said it, to see if I could take it, if I'd look away or be embarrassed. I held his gaze and nodded, and we kept looking at each other for several long moments. Finally, we broke the contact and he brought us back around to my confession.

"Okay, but all of that's not what we're here for, right?"

"No," I said. "There's something else I need to tell you. But I'm worried about telling you."

"I think maybe I know what it is, and it's okay."

"Oh, you do? That's interesting. What?"

"You're gay."

This made me laugh. Hard. Even *he* thought Ned was gay. I knew he hadn't given the time of day to Father Jerome, and I knew he didn't really concern himself about the sinfulness of anyone's sexuality. That was clear. But I was curious about where he'd gotten the idea.

"Well, yes," I said, "I'm gay, but not in the way you think, and that's not the thing I have to tell you. But, I'm curious, what made you think it?"

"Well, your mannerisms are pretty effeminate."

This was rich. As a woman, no one had ever accused me of being effeminate. Here was another of Ned's tricks. Dress as a man, and thereby emphasize the woman. Reveal the truth under the rubric of a lie.

Father Fat went on, "Okay, if it's not that you're gay, what is it?"

"This is really bad," I said, "and I'm afraid you're going to feel compelled to break the seal of the confessional when I tell you. How do you feel about the seal, by the way? I mean, if I told you I was a murderer—which is not what I'm going to tell you, but if I did—would you feel compelled to go to the law, or to tell your brothers?"

"No," he said.

Still, I was going to put him in a sticky position. But I had to hope he'd keep the confidence, even though he would have been well within his rights to tell *me* not to keep it, to compel me morally to disclose my wrongdoing. I knew that myself.

"Okay," I said, finally. "Here goes. I'm not a man. I'm a woman."

He'd been smiling his tolerant, jolly smile, and it froze on his face. Dead silence.

"I'm not a transsexual or anything," I went on. "I'm a full biological woman, and a lesbian, by the way. I came here in disguise to study and write about this community of cloistered men. It's part of a larger study I'm doing about men and women and how they are treated differently in the world."

He began nodding slowly, the smile fading, but still there as a form of shock. Then very slowly he said, "Like Margaret Mead."

"Yeah, sort of."

There was another silence. Then I asked, "Are you angry?"

"Well, it does give one the feeling of being used."

"Yes," I said, "I know, and I'm sorry. Do you think you can forgive me?"

"Yes, I forgive you," he said without hesitation.

"The thing is," I said, "I've had real experiences here. I

haven't just been an observer. And while some of them have been painful, I've undergone some spiritual change as well, and I've connected with people and myself in certain ways that I won't soon forget."

He nodded. Then he started to laugh.

"What?" I said.

"I was just thinking that I wish you'd put me in your will or something so that I could tell this story—'There was this one time . . .'"

"Well, maybe I can release you to talk about it," I said. "We'll see how it goes."

He gave me absolution and he said by way of penance that I should go and sit in the church and think.

As we were finishing, I said, "Knowing I'm a woman changes everything, doesn't it?"

"Yes," he said.

"See, now I can hug you, right? I couldn't have really done that before, could I?"

"Yes," he said, "and no, you couldn't have."

For Father Fat, hugging a dying old friend like Father Henry was one thing. Hugging a young would-be novice was quite another. But hugging a woman friend, a foundling daughter who couldn't help thinking of you as a lost grandfather, that was something else altogether.

We both stood up and came together. I put my arms around his neck and my head on his shoulder. He squeezed me tightly with great affection.

"Thank you," I said as he walked out of the room.

He smiled again. After he'd shut the door, I smiled, too, when I looked down and saw that I had dandruff all over the front of my black sweatshirt.

Later that morning I did my penance. I went to the church

and thought. I thought about whether or not to tell Vergil and the others about my true identity. I wondered if they, too, could forgive me.

I had reached the end of my run, or one end. Had I stayed longer there would have been many more emotional disasters and reforms, because that was the designated course, a very old paradigm, and the essence of what our culture has come to think of as masculine tutelage applied roughly to the moral soul: break a man down to build him up stronger. Find the fault in yourself and heal it.

I was, after all, the one among them who had committed the greatest transgression, and in forgiving Ned so readily and completely, not only had Father Fat shown me the clarity of mind and heart that emotional self-discipline at its best could give to any man or woman able to stand up to it, he had shown me the rigors of insight that Ned had yet to find in himself.

After my confession with Father Fat I knew I needed to talk to Vergil, so on my second-to-last night I arranged to meet him for some private time together. We decided to take a walk around the grounds. It took a fair amount of preliminary chatter before we got down to the real subject. Vergil was uncomfortable with what he sensed was coming, but by this time I wasn't hiding anything anymore, and finally I just cut through.

"So," I said, "what happened between us a while back? One day we were friends, and the next it was as if you hardly knew me. Did I do something to make you angry? Did I disappoint you in some way?"

He deflected calmly.

"No, not at all. I don't know what you mean."

"Oh, come on, Vergil, you do, too. I didn't imagine this. Something changed radically after the first week, and I'd like to know why."

We went back and forth on this for a few minutes, with

Vergil claiming to have been busy and preoccupied with his coming profession and a whole host of other things unrelated to me. They were plausible explanations, but there was more to tell and Vergil was too honest at heart to hide this very well, even in his disclaimers.

Then in frustration I said, "Look, just tell me the truth, even if it hurts my feelings. I'd really like to know. I promise, if you're thinking what I think you're thinking about me, you're wrong."

Vergil didn't reply, so I went further and said the obvious. "I know everybody here thinks I'm gay. But I need you to know something, and you're just going to have to take my word for it. I'm not sexually attracted to you."

He interrupted here. "See, the fact that you would even feel the need to say that—that that would even enter your mind . . ."

"I know, I know. You think, like everybody else, that I'm in denial. The more I protest, the truer it must be. But you're just wrong. Believe me."

I could tell he wasn't really buying it, but he didn't press me, so I said, "Never mind that for now. Tell me what it was that bothered you about me."

"Oh, all right," he said, relenting at last. He sighed. "You were too clingy. You were like this thing I just couldn't get off me." He pronounced the last four words slowly with emphasis, shaking his right hand in a flicking downward motion, as if it were covered in muck.

"I could see it happening," he went on. "I recognized the signs."

As Jerome had said, Vergil had felt me developing an affection for him, had assumed it to be homosexual in nature and had taken steps to squelch it.

"So I was right," I said. "You did back away purposely."

"Yes," he conceded. "But look," he added, "I think you've had a good influence on this community. You've brought emotional awareness and the possibility of change. You're not a follower. We need that."

Coming from Vergil this was a great compliment indeed, and it confirmed for me what I hoped had been the case—that however much of an intrusion I had been in their lives, and however poorly I might have handled myself at times among them, I had touched these men in some way. After he said this, I felt momentarily overwhelmed by a sense of healing and possibility, a sense that for all their stoic showing, these men were warm at the center, and breathing—crippled, perhaps, but not nearly dead, and by no means without some hidden ability to affect me, and for the better.

I knew then that the time was right to tell Vergil the truth about me.

"Vergil," I said trepidatiously. "I've got a confession to make."

"Okay," he said with complete composure. "What is it?"

"There's something about me that I haven't told you."

"Oh?"

"Yeah. Something important."

We walked a little farther in silence, and then I turned to him. At this point, since I was on the verge of leaving anyway, I wasn't wearing my beard anymore. I hadn't been wearing it for several days. To me it should have seemed obvious that something wasn't quite right. But this was the test of perception that continually arose with Ned. People saw in him what I had conditioned them to see. When I removed the beard, they saw nothing but a shaved boy. But I wanted to press Vergil on the point. He was perceptive and I wanted him to see. Could wanting to reveal myself reveal me as surely as wanting to disguise myself had disguised me? Did the suggestion work both ways?

"Do you have any idea what it is?" I asked.

He thought for a minute, then ventured something he'd obviously been thinking for a while.

"You're not Catholic," he said.

This was typical Vergil. He would see heresy in a microbe before he'd see the transvestite staring him in the face. He was hard-core about his doctrine, though being his sardonic self he couldn't refrain from making a crack or two on the subject now and then. I remembered how once while we were looking through the monastery bookshelves together for some appropriate reading for Ned, and had come across the work of So-and-So, S.J., he had reshelved it immediately, saying, "No, that won't do."

"Why not?" I'd said.

"I have serious doubts about whether Jesuits are even Catholic," he said.

I loved him for that. He was a crank and he knew it.

I'd given enough of my unbelief away in theological argument over the last three weeks that Vergil's question didn't surprise me in the least.

"No," I said. "I'm Catholic, all right, or I was, though you're right that I'm not anymore, or at least I'm not insofar as you can ever cease to be Catholic."

Vergil glared at me over this last remark, as if I'd poked him with a stick, which of course I had. This was part of our game, when it was on, part of what had bonded us to each other all along.

"Guess again," I said.

"Hmm. Let's see. You're an escapee from a mental institution."

"Nope. Not technically, though being a New Yorker surely counts."

The monks had all been tickled by the fact that I made my

home in a neighborhood called Hell's Kitchen. To them, the freak show of New York City was about as far from their home as you could get. To me it was and it wasn't.

At this point, I stopped Vergil on the path, stood facing him and said, "Look at me. It's right in front of you. Can't you see it?"

"What?" He looked into my face. "I see a guy with graying hair."

"No, that's not it," I said. "Look closer." I took off my glasses.

"I don't know," he said, perusing me again. "What is it?"

He was blank. Puzzled.

We both turned and kept walking. I tried one last thing.

"I'm not what I appear to be."

This sank in as we rounded the corner of the footpath by the carpentry shop and began the last stretch back to the cloister. Suddenly he turned to me, the moment of revelation having come at last with full force.

"You're a woman."

"Yes," I said with relief.

By now we were in front of the abbey. A discovery of this magnitude was going to require at least one more loop around the grounds. We kept walking. Vergil was quietly registering this information. I was watching his face. He was stealing looks at my chest.

"I do have them," I said, catching him midglance. "They're just under a tight sports bra. I'm not a transsexual. I'm a woman in disguise."

This seemed to answer the first question in his mind. I went on with the rest of the explanation.

"I'm also a lesbian," I said, "which, you will now understand, is why Ned couldn't possibly be gay and why I never wanted to sleep with you. You see?"

He nodded. He seemed both disappointed and relieved. I had expected the relief, but not the disappointment. There was something more to this.

I told him about the book. He wasn't pleased at first, for all the reasons you might expect, feeling betrayed and lied to and used. His orthodox strain kicked in, as expected, but not in the punitive way I had thought it might. I had broken the seal of the cloister, and that, he reminded me, was a fairly serious breach of canon law. He suggested I go to confession on the matter. I told him that I already had, with Father Fat, and that my decision to tell him was part of my penance.

Vergil accepted this on some level as right and proper, but to my great surprise his reaction then turned personal, something I hadn't really seen in Vergil before.

"Why me?" he asked. Why had I chosen him, singled him out for special attention?

This was a question that only my female dates had ever asked me before.

"Because I was there?" he asked, hurt, it seemed, just as the others had been, to think that my interest in him hadn't been genuine.

"Well, yes, and no," I answered truthfully, as I had answered all the others. "That's why I chose to speak to you initially — because you were there. But the feelings I developed later were real. I couldn't have faked those. No way. This may sound like a con to you, but it's not. Very real and profound things can happen — and for me have happened — under the cover of a falsehood. That has been the whole point of this experiment. The truths I've learned and experienced would not have revealed themselves otherwise."

He agreed, it seemed, though he said nothing. He was calm, his head inclined in conference. I went on.

"Vergil," I said, "I care a lot. That's why I'm telling you all of this. And I'm truly sorry for the lie. I hope you can forgive me."

We talked on, going over the particulars, and to his credit, Vergil made it very easy for me. He was receptive, understanding, immediately forgiving, just as Father Fat had been. He showed every aspect of his best and wisest self though he had every reason not to, and I was both admiring and grateful.

"Now I can tell you," I said finally. "This is a really hard place to be a woman."

"Well, it's supposed to be," he laughed. And so did I, though I did so with an underlying sense of puzzlement. I have thought often of that comment in retrospect, and, whether this is fair or not, it does, in a sense, confirm a lot of what I'd felt about the defeminizing of Ned—and Crispin, too—in that environment. It was an odd answer on the face of it. In theory, living together amicably as men didn't necessitate creating an atmosphere that was hostile to women or even to femininity. But that is what the monks had done, and according to Vergil, they had done so by design. Ned's hazing hadn't been imaginary, and this consolidated masculinity that reigned so heavily in the monastery wasn't, it seemed, just the natural result of men living together without women. It was the result of men actively working to squelch any creeping womanly tendencies in themselves and their brothers.

But why? Why this need for such a macho atmosphere? Granted, this was workhorse machismo of a particularly tight-lipped, straight-backed and, as Felix had said, Germanic variety. It wasn't rugby and beer. But it was machismo all the same in its need to obviate its opposite. And that seemed entirely superfluous in a world where the soul was ostensibly God's instrument.

So why? Why the cultural misogyny? The answer, when it came to me, was not at all mysterious. A cliché, in fact. Felix himself had said it. They took refuge in machismo because they feared inappropriate intimacies between men. A feminized man is a gay man, or so the stereotype goes. A feminized man is a weak man, and a weak man who allows intimacies is prey to the assertions of chaos and his libido.

It seemed painfully obvious in my own particular case. The jokes, the paranoia, the shutting out.

The thought that Vergil might be gay had crossed my mind before, but I hadn't been at all sure about my instincts on the matter, not nearly as sure as I had been about Jerome. But now Vergil and I were confessing to each other, so I decided to take the risk that he might be honest if only I asked him the right way. I remembered him talking about his time away from the monastery, about how he'd said he'd had "a really good time," as if he'd done his sinning all at once at a big party. But he had been carefully non–sex specific about it. I remembered another cryptic remark he had made at the time that now made a lot more sense to me: "We are all God's creatures and love is love and sex is sex and they are not the same thing."

In other words: Lord, make me straight but not now.

I decided I had to ask, but I didn't want to make him use the word gay. He was uncomfortable with it, I sensed. This wasn't an interrogation. So I just asked him, as if in passing, if the people he'd had relationships with during his time away from the monastery had been men.

The lines were open between us now. Maybe knowing I was a woman had taken away some of his fears, enough to know that I wasn't a threat to him anymore. His physical attraction, if it had been there, would presumably have died with my disclosure, the temptation removed.

He didn't resist the admission. He nodded his assent.

"So you've never slept with a woman?" I asked, more boldly.

He looked at me archly. "Not that I know of."

Vergil was a comic to the last and, like Father Fat, in his lack of umbrage he was a credit to his order. When it counted most, when he was sorely deceived, he was true to his commandments: to love, to forgive and not to judge.

He was also a soft touch. He'd let me off easy and I was grateful.

I'm sure that part of him was relieved, too, and that made it easier for him to greet my news so forgivingly. When Ned became a woman the gay problem disappeared and with it the transgressive masculinity he embodied, as well as the inappropriate intimacy he had provoked. In this context a woman must have felt like a gift, especially since I was leaving anyway. A female was far more acceptable than a fag. She could be held at bay, her needs and emotive untidiness satisfactorily explained, then set aside. But in a man those qualities were far more troubling. They could get inside, infiltrate, threaten and, worst of all, seduce. The odd man out was dangerous, like the slightest touch at a pressure point that could bring the whole edifice down. It was a crisis they were well rid of.

Vergil and I parted on newly intimate terms, awake to another potential in ourselves and each other. He assured me that I had a brother in him if I needed one, and I knew that he meant it. A brother to a sister. Easy. Normal. Good.

We promised to write.

Aside from Vergil and Father Fat, Felix was the only other person I wanted to visit before I left. I wanted to tell him about me and I wanted to apologize. I saw him in the rec room and told him that I was leaving the next morning. I thanked him for our time together. Before I could say anything about my true identity, he threw his arms around me and hugged me tightly, very tightly, squeezing me with intense gratitude and immediacy. It was obvious from the way he gave it, that this was a hug he had been longing to give — but hadn't given — for a very long time, because there had been no one willing or able to receive it. In that hug I could feel all that was locked up in Felix and by proxy in Claude and Vergil and in so many other men I had yet to meet outside the abbey.

When we pulled apart I told him that I had something to tell him. I sat him down and abruptly spilled the news. He sat for a second, looking at me with a shock that he was, out of politeness, trying desperately to disguise. I could tell he was uncomfortable. But I could also tell that our friendship was undamaged. The bond that we had established was sexless, and what Felix said next confirmed this.

"Well, this doesn't really change anything, does it?"

He said this more as a statement than a question and I agreed. It didn't. And this made him the only person in my entire career as Ned who didn't change his attitude toward me when he learned that I was a woman. We hugged again to say good-bye, and the hug was the same hug. He hadn't needed to know that I was a woman in order to give it to me the first time, and he didn't change its aspect when he gave it to me the second time, knowing full well that I *was* a woman. It was a small, but to me remarkable, moment and the perfect parting gift.

I left the abbey the next morning feeling renewed and positive about the real affections I had shared there.

Thinking back on it now, I don't pretend that the abbey was a normal place to go looking for male experience, the kind of place you'd expect to find prototypical guy-guys milling around in their element — a sports bar, say, or a bowling alley. The vast majority of American men never come within miles of a monastery, nor do they willingly relinquish their sex lives, autoerotic or otherwise. But as I said at the outset of this chapter, that is part of why I went there, to see what happens to men when they are out of their element, when they are without the company of women.

And what I found there should not, I suppose, have surprised me. But it did. In all its reductive simplicity, it did. Most American men may not be monks, but the monks I knew were certainly American men, or to modify an old adage, I found that you can take the man out of his element but you cannot very often take the element out of the man. At the abbey I expected to find a breed concerned primarily with spiritual matters, a place where one's style or quality of manhood was irrelevant, where the artificial socialized boundaries that stymied male intimacy in the outside world would have long since fallen away, and where locker room fears of homosexuality would be so far beneath the radar as to be inconceivable. But instead I found a community steeped in commonplace masculine angst.

I found masculinity distilled, unmitigated by feminine influences, and therefore observable in a concentrated state. These men were suffering together in silence under a hurt they could barely acknowledge, let alone address. The cause of their distress and dysfunction mostly eluded them, yet to an outsider it was perfectly clear. Or at least it was to an outsider like me who had lived a woman's life, and then had been subjected to their treatment as a boy. I lived in the cloister among them, as one of them, yet I remained myself, and from that peculiar point of view I could see them both from the inside and the outside at once. The contrast was stark.

I felt firsthand the loss of the emotional freedoms that I had enjoyed in my life as a woman, and not just the loss, but the active squelching of those freedoms in the name of masculine order, reserve and isolation, as well as homophobia. I could see that the abbey was indeed a very hard place to be a woman, and I could see, as Vergil had said, that it was intended to be. But as Ned I could see that it was also a very hard place to be an emotional man, and in that sense it was not so unlike the outside world after all.

This is not to say that I did not also find peace, deep love and elevation of the soul in that place. I did. It was unmistakably present to anyone willing to receive it, and if my experience had been as one-sided as the likes of Father Jerome could have made it, I would not have become as emotionally embroiled as I did. Vergil and Felix and Claude and Henry and Father Fat, among others, were profound human beings who gave me the great gift of genuine contact. They struggled, of course, with masculine as well as everyday human troubles, but they burned very brightly at their cores. They were good people concerned about the well-being of their fellow creatures, trying to contribute what they could to the spiritual awakening of those around them.

I came to care deeply about them and since leaving I have corresponded with several of them as myself. I am told that the general reaction in the community to the news that I was a woman was mostly amusement and some embarrassment. But when it came down to it, I was a minute disturbance, a short episode in a very long stay. I was there for no time at all. They were there for life.

I miss the monks often. I miss taking long walks around the grounds with them and alone, looking for the elusive great horned owls, who reputedly made their nests at the top of the cloister tower. I often heard them hooting at dusk, and I spent many evenings after vespers following their calls, hoping to see them at perch, but never succeeding. On my last night there, I went in search of Father Claude's beehives instead.

Out at the back of the orchard, in a low branch of one of the pecan trees, I saw an abandoned wasps' nest. I was only about seven feet away at most as I peered at it in the dimming light, wondering if Father Claude had seen this. But as my eyes focused I realized that I was not looking at a hive or a nest at all. It was the body of a very large owl. He was napping, his eyes closed, his body swaying ever so slightly as the branch creaked in the evening breeze. I must have stood there for a good minute, amazed. Then sleepily he opened his eyes and saw me standing there, way too close for comfort. A look of actual surprise registered on his face, and then a vague annoyance. He stared back at me for a few seconds, pondering, it almost seemed, how a clodhopping human had managed to sneak up on him. Then disdainfully he spread his massive wings and flew away.

6 | Work

"Attitude Red Bull." That's what the ad said and it said it all. I was looking through the want ads in the local paper trying to find a place where Ned could get what a writer friend of mine so appropriately called the *Glengarry Glen Ross* experience—that is, a balls-to-the-wall sales job in a testosterone-saturated environment where people emasculated each other by saying things like, "My watch cost more than your car."

I felt sure such places still existed—I knew they did—especially on Wall Street, but a thirty-five-year-old dilettante with a moldering degree in philosophy wasn't going to get past the mailroom at Goldman Sachs when firms like that were recruiting credentialed undergraduates. I had to think smaller and, alas, shadier.

So I was looking for entry-level jobs that required no experience and no pedigree. That's when I fell down the rabbit hole and found myself in the land of the Red Bull. In that Sunday's career supplement, I had circled all the ads for which Ned could possibly qualify, or at least passably interview, and except for a few oddballs, like a nudist colony looking for an assistant ("will train" it said), and a dog in need of a chauffeur, they were all remarkably similar. They wanted steam-spewing go-getters who were "high-powered" and "hungry for success," champing at the bit to trample the competition. Positive attitude a must. No experience required. They promised "FUN!" and, for those with the right stuff, prompt advancement.

Entry-level management trainees wanted in what appeared to be fast-track corporate environments. This was Ned's ticket to the office bullpen, quick and dirty. I called all three ads first thing Monday morning and got appointments for later that day or early the next. "No business casual," they said. "Wear a suit." Even better, I thought. Ned could finally wear his jackets and ties, full male regalia for the first time.

I drank a Red Bull that next morning to get in the mood. It gave me a headache and turned my pee green, but not a lot else. Maybe the mojo didn't mix well with estrogen. Clearly, I was no bull.

But then, of course, bulls are known for their balls. Bulls essentially are their balls. The terms are interchangeable, which is why flabby literati and other blowhards with masculine insufficiencies run with the bulls in Pamplona. It takes balls to run with the bulls, or gives them, as the case may be. This is also why an energy soft drink called Red Bull is made for boys, or would-be boys, and really means blue balls, just as surely as the popular behemoth SUV called the Hummer is made for pinpricks and means blow job. So, when an ad says "Attitude Red Bull," you can be fairly sure the paradigm is male and you're going to get the *Glengarry Glen Ross* experience, no matter what you or your coworkers have or don't have between your legs.

And so it was. Ned tied one of his four tasteful, patterned Perry Ellis ties in a Windsor knot with a dimple, matched it to his sage green shirt, his gunmetal gray trousers, his ever so faintly mottled earth-toned blazer and his black dress loafers polished to a plaque shine, and appeared on time for his interviews, résumé in hand.

His résumé was my résumé, a little toned down and fudged here and there—impressive enough to get me in the door, but not so impressive as to make my application seem suspicious. As it turned out, there were no worries on either count. My education got me to the front of the queue with a nod, and nobody questioned my story about wanting to try a new career at thirty-five simply for the challenge of it. But then these places were interviewing just about anybody, and they were interviewing constantly. Most of them had standing ads in the paper every Sunday. This alone should have told me something about their turnover. So should a chance encounter in the restroom.

At one of these places, all of which rented tiny suites in office parks, I arrived early for the interview, so I went to the john to check my beard and adjust my tie. A guy from another office on that floor followed me in, pretending to wash his coffee mug. I pretended to wash my hands.

"Hey," he said. "What do you guys do in there, anyway?"

"I don't know yet," I said. "I'm here to find out. Why do you ask?"

"Well, I just see a lot of people coming and going out of there all the time."

"You think maybe it's a prostitution front?" I ventured.

He didn't crack a smile.

"No."

But it might as well have been. And it was in a way, but I had yet to find that out. At this point I was just happy to have a chance to try out my duds in an office and enjoy the rush they were giving me.

I was walking taller in my dress clothes. I felt entitled to respect, to command it and get it in a way that Ned never had in slob clothes. The blazer neatly covered any chest or shoulder worries I had, filling me out square and flat in all the right places, allowing me to act with near perfect confidence in my disguise. A suit is an impenetrable signifier of maleness every bit as blinding as the current signifiers of attractiveness in women: blond hair, heavy makeup, emaciated bodies and big tits. A woman can be downright ugly on close inspection, and every desirable part of her can be fake, the product of bleach, silicone and surgery, but if she's sporting the right signifiers, she's hot. She is her disguise, not a person but a type. A suit, I found, does very much the same thing for a man. You see it, not him, and you bow to it.

I, in turn, responded to these shifts in expectation. For the first time in my journey as Ned I felt male privilege descend on me like an insulating cape, and all the male behaviors I had until then been so consciously trying to produce for my role, came to me suddenly without effort.

My voice moistened instinctively, loosening me into the pose of someone who doesn't need to speak up to be heard. I spoke more slowly, and with what seemed to me to be an absurd authority, especially in my interviews, where bluster was expected of me. I met that expectation with embarrassing ease. I leaned back in my chair and crossed my legs wide, ankle over knee, resting my arms on the arms of the chair or letting them fall by my sides. My hands felt heavier somehow, more knowing, swinging as I walked, lazy with self-importance.

Nobody ever thought *this* Ned was gay.

My manner changed, too. I stopped obsessively saying sorry, please and thank you in restaurants, gas stations and shops the way I always seem to do as a woman. Instead, I just asked for what I wanted, right out, no apology, no squirm. Just "give it to me now the way I want it." And the oddest part was that somehow, even without these words of courtesy, I didn't do it rudely, and no one ever interpreted it that way. It was like partaking in a common understanding that that's just how guys are. That's how they talk. They're direct, terse. No need to explain. We understand.

To the gas station attendant I'd say, "Give me a pack of that gum, too," as she cashed out my order. To the waitress at the steak house where I ate a business lunch with one of my male coworkers I said, "Get us two filets." Even my "thanks"—never "thank-yous"—were brusque when I said them, but they managed to sound magnanimous, as if I were gracing a servant who was beneath my deference.

As a woman, I so often speak in qualifiers. "You know, I think we're going to try the steaks. Are they good here?" I try to establish a connection with the servers, an implied apology for their job and my orders in everything I say. "I hate to bother you, but could we have some more water when you have a chance?" The thank-yous are ubiquitous and the tone of voice more pleading than perfunctory. To the gas station attendant I'd have said, "Oh, you know what? Could I have a pack of that gum, too?" And if it came too late in the ring-up I'd append an extra "sorry" to the request.

Ned got away with a lot, and people liked him for his balls when he showed them. But I feel sure he sometimes benefited from a subtle dose of Norah on the inside, a mitigating slide or soft touch, like a knuckleball, that distinguished him from the boys around him. He had a strange mix, as one pair of female coworkers put it, of cockiness and humility that they found very charming. "I don't think I've ever encountered that before," one of them said. "But I like it." Women saw something in him that was less repellant than the juggernaut come-ons and trash talk of the other men in the office. Their eyes softened on him and pleaded with him humbly as if he was the new guard on prison row and they hadn't seen a male human being in a very long time.

I went to a lot of interviews and in them I honed my arrogant behaviors in response to the cues I was getting from my interviewers, all of which were very different than any cues I'd ever gotten as a female interviewee.

As a female I'd been interviewed and hired by (and hence had bosses of) both sexes. The men were almost always stiff and formal, well trained not to say or do anything that might be interpreted as offensive. They were like that as bosses, too. All business. Equal opportunity to the hilt and not a shred of innuendo. Of course, later, after I'd worked in a place for a while, some male bosses, usually the top dogs and those for whom I did not work directly, flirted with me harmlessly in their corner offices when I brought them papers to sign. I would play along with just enough youthful indiscretion to let them know that I knew my place, but I'd return the compliment with enough sass to keep them at bay. It was an easy game. Never serious and never anything I couldn't handle.

Often I had a much harder time with my female bosses. In the interviews these women were all smiles, full of the fakest girl talk you can imagine. "Oh, we have this in common. . . . Oh, we'll have such fun."

And I was just as bad, making nice and smoothing over, as we women are socialized to do and often feel obliged to persist in doing, at least on the surface, even in competitive or hierarchical environments. Meanwhile, they were exactly the right age to be thinking, "All the old knives that have rusted in my back, I drive in yours, *ma semblable, ma soeur*!"

And boy, we stabbed. They did and I did. We fought the kind

of underhanded bitch fights that sororities are famous for. They were insecure in their power, and I wouldn't quite stand down to it, and the ameliorations of meaningless flirtation couldn't smooth the works.

But in Ned's interviews, people didn't expect him to make nice. They expected him to brag about himself, to be smugly charming and steadfast, and so I did and I was. I got away with a lot, and I was able to be a far better actor than I really am. Confidence is everything, and in his interviews Ned was nothing if not a shit storm of confidence.

Most of these interviews, especially the ones for the Red Bull jobs, required you to fill out an application rehashing most of what was on your résumé. To that was attached a questionnaire designed to determine your attitudinal fitness for the position. Almost invariably one of the questions was: on a scale from one to ten how would you rate your people skills? These were sales jobs, after all, managerial sales jobs eventually, and your ability to manipulate people would be the key to your success both in the field and in the office. I always gave myself an eight and a half for my people skills, and when asked what I meant by that I could always back it up with some crap about being a chameleon.

"I can talk to anyone," I'd say.

Yeah, right. The truth is I hate people. I especially hate people who use phrases like "people skills." And when I do talk to people it's usually to crazy people on the street in New York, because I can be rude to them without them noticing. But Ned was a con artist, and he hid my contempt. His female interviewers flirted with him, exercising the subtle control of their positions, but enjoying the subtext of traditional male domination all the same. His male interviewers gave him the full-on man-to-man treatment. "Hey, buddy, how ya doin'?" We speak the same language.

In one interview with a male interviewer and another male

applicant, the interviewer said, "Well, you know how it is with most television advertising. When the commercials come on you reach for your remote and change the channel, unless, of course, it's Cindy Crawford, right?"

Har. Har. Boys being boys. But this was just a precursor to what I'd find on the job when we boys were bonding full tilt. Guys in this environment expected you to swear and make sexist jokes. Women didn't, of course. But even when I said things that were inappropriate, somehow even they managed to work themselves to my advantage. In answering a question about my people skills with a female interviewer I said, "Well, you know, I talk to everybody. Maybe it's something I picked up in New York. You know how it is there [she was a New York transplant], you can just talk to people spontaneously in the check-out line or whatever and they don't look at you like 'What the fuck is up with you?'"

"Well, Ned," she said, laughing coquettishly, fanning her face, "I must admit, the New Yorker in me is even blushing. I've never heard anyone say 'fuck' in an interview before. It's kind of refreshing actually."

I was sure I'd tanked that job, but that evening I got the call-back for it. In fact, Ned was offered every job for which he applied, a half dozen in all. Not that this was much of an accomplishment since the Red Bull job interviews were basically cattle calls. But for a person with a serial killer's people skills, a Schopenhauerian outlook on life and a bottomless loathing for salespeople of every kind, Ned pulled off the performance of a lifetime.

People bought his act. They thought he had the right stuff, the kind of stuff they could enslave and perfect in their image and send out into the world to make them more money. They thought—as one coworker who was tight with the bosses later told me—that Ned had upper management written all over him.

The interviewers were always the same: slick, young, whistling voids of painted-on work ethic, all of them going word for word by the company script.

"Ned," they always said, "this is a real departure for you. What got you interested in this position?"

"Well," I'd say, "I rose to the top of my field in three years and I get bored very easily. If I conquer something I just want to go on to the next thing."

The fact that this came out of my mouth, and no one laughed in my face, is a testament to how far trash talk can get you in image projection, especially when you're male. If I'd said this as a woman, especially the way I said it as Ned, that is, with my dick in my teeth, I can pretty well guarantee that the scrotum of the little boss man who happened to be interviewing me that day would have tightened in terror, crippling his sperm's motility for weeks. Clearly Dano, the gatekeeper and BMOC at Clutch Advertising, the guy with the superenlarged still of the black besuited gangsters from *Reservoir Dogs* hanging over his desk, was looking for certain answers. When Ned said his wildly exaggerated piece, he was the man. He was Dano's kind of guy.

"Wow," Dano said. "Okay, so give me two or three qualities that best describe you, Ned."

Duh.

"Confident. Competent. Ambitious."

"Great," he said writing these down on my résumé and circling them. "And what are you looking for in your next position?"

Duh again. "A challenge," I said.

Bing. Right answer.

These were my stock responses, and they were always greeted with the same approving nods.

The Red Bull jobs all ran on the same formula. If you passed the first interview, you'd go on to the second. This was an all-day observational period during which you tagged along with one of the sales people in the field, watching him work, telling him more about yourself, and getting a feel for the business. If you survived the second interview, you passed on to the third, which was essentially the job offer with a lot of ego-pumping preamble attached to it.

When you went on these second interviews you realized very quickly why the Red Bull offices were so small and sparsely furnished. Usually they had a reception area, one office with a desk and two chairs, one small conference room, and another small, unfurnished room plastered with motivational posters that said things like WALK IT. TALK IT. DRESS IT. and BE THE BEST. EXPECT THE BEST. in large black letters.

Nobody but the top one or two people was ever there during the day. They were the managers, and they were constantly conducting interviews. People quit or were fired at such an astounding rate that the managers were forced to renew the stock every week just to keep their rosters filled.

Other than being a whorish in-'n'-out parlor for conducting interviews, the office was just a place for the salespeople to dump their stuff and powwow at the beginning and end of each eleven-hour day, which they did eagerly and with relish. Psyching yourself up at the beginning of the day, and congratulating yourself profusely for what you'd accomplished at the end of it, was central to the Red Bull attitude. It was the only thing that kept anybody going through the grueling, demoralizing hours in the field.

The bulk of the eleven-hour days were spent walking door-to-door selling things, whether it was phone service or entertainment books or VIP cards. The entertainment books were filled with coupons for local businesses, and the salespeople sold those by going from house-to-house in the residential areas that surrounded the advertised businesses. The VIP cards offered similar incentives to residents and businesspeople. For the cost of the card (say, seventy-five dollars), a local spa might offer the VIP card holder three "free" visits to its facility.

That was it. That was the job. Go door-to-door in the hot sun, the pouring rain or drifts of snow, hour after hour, making the same pitch at least fifty times a day to people who were mostly hostile to solicitors. If you didn't sell, you didn't eat. You worked on 100 percent commission, and the bosses who sat on their asses in the office got a handsome cut of everything you sold.

Dano thought he had a live one in me. Educated, articulate, brash and ready. He sent me out for my second interview with a twenty-seven-year-old guy named Ivan, a Hungarian former tennis pro who never made it on the tour. He had an aunt living in this country, so he'd come over, ostensibly to go to college, but had quit midway through and started doing everything under the sun to make a living, including stripping at bachelorette parties and teaching ballroom dancing. He also claimed to have been a bodybuilder for a while, which he said explained why the collar of his dress shirt was at least an inch too big for his neck.

Ivan wasn't alone in dressing badly. Though we were walking door-to-door out in the elements, the bosses insisted that we wear suits and ties. Most of the guys on the staff were too hard up to afford a real suit and too tasteless to buy a presentable one. Not a single one of them had the slightest idea how to tie a tie. As a result, they all looked like the epitome of the cheap salesman, rumpled and unctuous without a word in their mouths or a thought in their heads that hadn't been put there by management.

Ivan was six feet tall, and did have an athletic build, so I could believe he'd been a stripper if not a bodybuilder. He'd begun to lose his hair early, so he'd decided a few years back to shave his entire head. He had one black Hugo Boss suit that he'd bought back when he was actually making money. He made a point of telling me this and showing me the label. He said sometimes he kept his pen in the breast pocket of his jacket so that when he was trying to make a sale he could flash the client his label. He wore this suit every day, and though it was nicely cut, somehow he managed to make it look saggy and disheveled, partly because it gathered dust on the country dirt roads that we worked in our territory.

On my first day out with Ivan we gave a ride to a third salesman named Troy who was working part of our territory but didn't have a car. A lot of these guys didn't, so they often had to share rides and then get dropped off in the middle of nowhere with a promise that their partners would be back to get them in seven hours. We did this with Troy, and the first time we did it I thought Ivan was joking. We dropped him in his black suit with nothing but his bag of merchandise, or "merch," as they called it, on an eighty-five-degree humid sunny day at the corner of the highway and a dirt road that led deep into farmland. He'd eaten a convenience store Danish for breakfast and that was the only food he was going to see for the next seven hours.

As we left Troy, I made a comment about his condition, and Ivan said, "Don't worry about him. He'll be fine. He dropped seventeen books once in a trailer park. A trailer park. The guy's amazing."

"How does he stand it?" I asked.

"He's from the ghetto," said Ivan. "This is his only shot to make some real money. He doesn't have a choice. It's basically this or McDonald's, and at least here he has a chance at advancement."

That was the truth of the Red Bull jobs. Anybody who stuck it out in them was desperate. They clung to the hope that they, too, might get promoted to management if only they worked hard enough. It was certainly possible, but you'd have to put yourself through ten-, eleven- and twelve-hour humiliating days, six days a week even to have a shot at assistant management.

"He's one of our best salesmen. He's got some unorthodox sales techniques."

"What do you mean?"

"Well, you couldn't do it out here, because a lot of these people are totally racist [Troy was black], but in another territory we worked, a rich, liberal white territory, he did some crazy shit. One time, when I was out with him, a little kid answered the door, and Troy said, 'Go tell your mommy there's a nigger at the door.' So the kid went back into the house and you could hear him shouting 'Mom, there's a nigger at the door.' When the lady came to the door she was mortified, and she said, 'Oh my God, I am so, so sorry.' And Troy just said, 'Oh, it's okay. Here's what you do. I've got these great entertainment books that we're selling for a good cause . . .' And he launched right into his pitch, and she bought two books on the spot. Can you believe that shit?"

Actually, before long on the job I could. These guys were justified in doing just about anything to sell their merch, as far as I was concerned. They worked hard enough for it.

Clutch Advertising had a sales force of about twenty-five people, only four of whom were women, and although all three of the Red Bull companies I worked for were male dominated and ran on what you might politely call a masculine vibe, Clutch was especially macho. And while in certain respects Ivan was a fish out of water in this environment — being a foreigner, he was better educated, more cultured and spoke better English than the rest of the staff — he was in other respects a perfect fit. Like him, a lot of the people who excelled at the Red Bull companies had played competitive sports. Davis, the second in command at Clutch, had been a college basketball big shot who had never made it to the pros.

These guys all thought and spoke like coaches and star players. They had that single-minded combative edge that had always
disqualified me from ever taking sports seriously. Being the best,
beating the other guy, selling more, scoring higher, fucking better-
looking women. Those were the only things that mattered to them
in life, and they mattered a lot. Selling, for them, was just another
form of scoring or ranking or winning, and the office reflected
this attitude in every respect. It was a musky men's locker room
environment.

Every morning and every evening when the sales force gathered in the unfurnished room, there was rap music or some cock
rock band like AC/DC blaring on the boom box. On my first
morning at Borg Consulting, another Red Bull company at which
I was employed for a short time, I was especially dismayed to hear
the rap song "OPP" (which stands for Other People's Pussy)
blasting at seven-thirty a.m. None of the women on staff seemed
bothered in the least by the anthem or its purported implications.

Ivan, too, was a big one for rap music. It was part of how he'd
learned American slang, and he found it endlessly amusing to re-
cite lyrical snippets he'd heard on the radio, especially the misogy-
nistic ones. He was always blurting them impromptu and laughing
at himself while flooring it down the dirt roads of our territory in
his beat-up old uninsured, unregistered 1989 Ford Escort. Kicking up swarms of dust and shimmying the car sideways on the
loose-pebbled roads was one way to relieve the tedium of the long
afternoons. He especially loved the term "cluster fuck," which he
often said at random moments for effect, because in his thick accent, I had to admit, it had a certain humorous onomatopoeic
quality about it.

Like every other guy in the Red Bull companies, Ivan saw his
job as an extension of his dick. His masculinity depended on his

ability to perform, and every sale was like a seduction, like a pickup in a bar. It was, as the gurus always said, about taking control of the situation. Behind every door was a sale if you had the balls to make it. It was as simple as that. Everything about the business was sexual or an extension of male sexuality—conquest, confidence, capability. Making the sale was like getting the panties, and losing it was taking it up the ass. There was no middle ground. There were no excuses. Just fortune or failure.

Ivan talked about sex almost constantly, which wasn't hard to do when every sale or lost sale was a sexual metaphor. When we lost a sale, Ivan took it personally and usually had to make it up to his ego in some way. He would say, "You know, some guys can take that and not do anything. But I can't. I gotta have my own back if somebody gets in my face." On the job, though, he usually knew enough to keep it to himself, so often he'd save his "own back" for a malicious comment in the car. It seemed to relieve his mind.

One time we stopped at a guy's house, got out of the car and made it only halfway up the driveway before the guy said, "This is private property and you're not invited."

When we got back in the car Ivan hissed, "That guy probably chokes his wife and fucks her in the ass."

Then he cackled and went on to tell me about a woman he claimed to have picked up in a bar. He said that when they got back to her place and sat down with a drink she said, "Don't tell me when you're going to do it, but when you're ready to, just push me up against the wall, choke me and fuck me in the ass, *raw*."

That was when I realized how completely full of shit Ivan was. But then that's what made him such a good salesman. And he was a damned good salesman. He could sell to anyone. Once when we were out together he sold a coupon book to a woman who was walking her dog by the side of the road. He didn't even get out of the car. He just leaned out of the window and pitched her right there. It was amazing how congenial and sincere he could sound without seeming slimy in the least.

But then, slimy or not, some people just wouldn't give you an inch. One guy who had a guard dog that circled the car as we pulled up to the house, told us to get lost right away. "Don't even get out of the car," he said. This set Ivan going.

"Motherfucker," he said. "Call that dog over here."

He whistled to the dog as he turned the car around in the driveway. He sucked a wad of snot down from his nose into his throat as he tried to get the dog to come by his door, but the dog wouldn't come close enough. Ivan spit toward him but missed, saying, "When guys are like that, I like to spit on their dogs, a nice big loogie right in the face. It really pisses them off."

That was the scummiest side of Ivan, and in the car with me he let it out full blast in a hail of vitriol that never seemed to let up. He had an answer for everything.

After he told me the raw story I said, "Ivan, how many women have you slept with?"

"Seventy-four," he said without hesitation.

Again, probably a giant lie, but who knew?

Ivan also claimed to have an IQ of 180 and a nine-inch dick. But don't they all, at least to each other.

I asked him about what he liked in a woman and he said something that confirmed with startling precision what I'd heard from other men and had myself surmised from my experiences in the strip clubs.

"It's probably from watching a lot of porn when I was a kid," he said, "but I expect the pussy to be odorless and tasteless."

Just like a doll, I thought. Just like a plastic Barbie doll. Nothing you'd ever find in nature.

On our way back to the office that night—our time in the

field finished at eight p.m.—we talked this subject over with Troy. He said, "I'm fine with the pussy so long as it tastes like pussy. If it's skanky then we have a problem."

Then he launched into a speech about how he could have any one of the women at the office if he wanted her. No one challenged him on this. It was like the IQ, big-dick thing. You didn't mess with a man's line. It was just part of the gig. When he was done telling us about what a lady-killer he was, Troy said he had a joke for us.

"Why does the blonde have a bald pussy?" he asked.

"Why?" Ivan and I said in unison.

"Ever seen grass on a highway?" said Troy.

Each day in the field ended with another gathering back at the office for settle-ups. To settle-up with management, you logged the number of entertainment books (or applications, or VIP cards) you had sold for the day, took your cut of the proceeds, and gave the rest to the bosses. At Clutch each set of entertainment books (we sold them in sets of two) cost $40, $13 of which went to the salesman, $10 to the direct manager, and the rest to upper management and various clients for whom the books were also making money. So, if on a given day you sold six sets of books, you made a total of $240, $78 of which went directly into your pocket that very evening in the form of cold, hard cash. The other $162 went out the window and up the stairs.

Selling six sets was a respectable day's work. Selling ten was mighty fine, and for this privilege you got to ring the cast-metal bell, which was kept at the front of the rumpus room for end-of-day celebrations. When you rang the bell, you got high fives and congratulations all around from the managers and the rest of the sales force. Congratulations usually came in the form of a Red

Bull acronym—JUICE, which stood for Join Us In Creating Excitement. Everything good was JUICE, and every accomplishment was "JUICE by this" or "JUICE by that." If you rang the bell you were greeted with a chorus of "JUICE by Ned, JUICE by Ned." As I said, it was like being in a men's locker room postgame.

So even on a very, very good day—selling ten sets of books took a lot of hustle and didn't happen very often—you'd only make $130, and when you spread that over the eleven-hour day, you were only making $11.81 an hour pretax. On an average day when you sold maybe five books, you made $65. That made an hourly wage of $5.90, just barely above minimum wage, and that without benefits of any kind. You were employed as an independent contractor, which meant that you were expected to pay your own quarterly taxes. It also meant that the company didn't officially employ you, which in turn meant that they didn't have to pay you an hourly minimum wage, or offer you medical benefits or paid vacation. In short, you were a legal slave, hoping upon hope one day to earn your forty acres and a mule.

At the end of my first day, which was technically only my second interview, Ivan gave me a stellar recommendation, and Davis and Dano offered me a job on the spot. They wanted to know if I could start work the next day. The next day was Saturday, a normal workday at Clutch. I said I could. They were having an interoffice sales conference in the morning, and I didn't want to miss that show.

Dano was a savvy slave driver. He knew that in order to keep his crew making money for him, he had to motivate them enough to take the initiative but play on their insecurities enough to control them. To accomplish this he used a double technique. Push them from one end by exacerbating their greed and desperation to acquire the almighty dollar and the lifestyle that comes with it, and at the same time pull them from the other end by threatening their already piss-poor self-esteem. So, he would imply, if you succeed at this you'll be one of the big guys. You'll have everything that I have. If you fail, you'll be a quitter, a nobody, a loser. It was a very effective combination. Every morning he or Davis would give a speech on this order, publicly rewarding the high rollers from the previous day, and solidly rebuking the sore losers. That's what morning office culture was all about, keeping people's heads above water and kicking them in the ass so that they would go out for one more egregious day and trudge the territory with sloppy, gleaming grins on their faces.

Saturday was a special gathering of all the Clutch sales folk in the metropolitan area, probably about a hundred people in all, only 10 percent of whom were women. Ten percent at the most. We met at nine a.m. in a warehouse in a suburb near our office. For the first hour Ivan and I mingled with the rest of the reps. Ivan introduced me around as the new guy, and I got a lot of welcoming slaps on the shoulder and hearty handshakes from droves of execrably clad men. Every one of them looked like the black sheep son of some family, resentfully cleaned up for church because their dads had dragged them there under penalty of grounding. Most of them wore button-down shirts and ties, and some form of khakis, a nod to management dress codes, but every garment looked as if it had been slept in.

Whispering in my ear, Ivan gave me the lay of the land. He pointed at a pudgy middle-aged black guy in a suit, one of the very few older guys in the company. He had a thin, carefully trimmed, graying mustache, which, as Ivan told it, the other reps had long been telling him to shave.

"We tell him it makes him look cheap, but he won't shave it," said Ivan, "because, get this, his mother tells him that it makes his mouth look so good it could be a pussy."

I thought I had misheard. "His *mother* told him that?" I asked. "Yep."

The guy in question pushed his way toward us in the crowd. He was one of those people who gets right up in your face when he shakes hands.

"Hey, new guy," he said, grasping my hand, and spreading his best spittle-moistened salesman's smile all over me like a coating of snot.

"Hi," I said, looking away.

"Now that chick over there," resumed Ivan, pointing to a tall, skinny blonde in mules and a miniskirt, "she's eighteen and pregnant, and all she wants to do is fuck. My one goal for the day is to do her tonight."

He was living up to his nickname, RDK, which stood for Raw Dog King. Davis had crowned him this after a night of boozing it up together at a bar. At some point in the evening, Ivan had left the bar with his chick pick of the evening, and was seen fucking her between two cars in the parking lot.

"Yeah," said Davis about the incident, "he was raw doggin' her all night." I gathered that raw doggin' meant you didn't even bother to warm her up, or as they might have put it, lube her up with a little foreplay before you rammed it in her, probably without a condom. According to company lore this was standard practice for Ivan. On "dates" he was like a drive-through wrecking crew, hence the fast-food moniker Raw Dog King. It sounded like a hoagie shack by the side of the road, the kind that would give you dysentery for life.

As we meandered through the groups of guys, invariably we happened on a conversation about one of the few women in the room—which ones were fuckable and under what circumstances.

Troy was going to work on them. He slid away from us toward a couple of girls from one of the other offices. They seemed to be clinging to each other for comfort and support. Apparently, as one of the guys standing around with us was good enough to inform me, some of the girls from one of our sister offices had formed their own sales team and called themselves The Swallows. All the guys in my circle chortled at this.

"We can't figure out if they know what it means or not," said one of them.

God, I thought. These poor girls have no idea what they're dealing with, and now that I know, I wish I didn't.

Ivan's attention had drifted to other prey. He pointed out the ass of a very short girl standing about ten feet away on our left.

"Check that out," he said. "I'd do her. She used to be a figure skater. Nice tight little body."

The crowd was calming at Davis's command. He was indicating with his arms that we should form a circle against the walls of the warehouse and take a seat so that Dano could give his speech. Ivan and I were already against a wall, so we squatted. The figure skater was still standing. Ivan elbowed me, nodding toward her. "Now we have a good angle on her ass," he said.

As Dano stepped into the middle of the circle, in seconds the atmosphere in the warehouse changed from brothel barroom to prayer meeting. All eyes were on the man and the crowd went silent.

"Hey, you," yelled Dano.

"Hey, what," yelled the crowd.

These were stock responses. The bosses of all the Red Bull companies started their morning meetings off this way. Dano occasionally varied the script slightly at our office during morning awards ceremonies when the high roller from the day before happened to have been a woman. After the "Hey, you," "Hey, what" intro he'd say, "I got a guy."

The staff would repeat, "We got a guy."

"A highly motivated type a guy."

Again the staff would repeat, though this time jumping toward the ceiling with their hands in the air when they said the word "highly."

Then Dano again, "It's not a guy. It's a girl."

And the staff in response: "Holy sheep."

Dano loved this shit. You could tell he lived for it. He was like some high priest in a cult of free trade working himself into a froth for the faithful, justifying his greedy little enterprise with all the demagogic flair of a Jim Jones sans the Kool-Aid.

The script went something like this.

DANO: To get you excited about our company, we don't have to come up with an impressive benefit package, 401(k), retirement plans, stock options, whatever. What we have to do is get you guys to see that we've put together a formula for instant success and huge profit unlike anything you've seen before. And all you have to do is take advantage of it. It's as simple as that. All you gotta do is pay your dues, put in your time, and you'll be running your own office before you know it.

You get paid on every sale you make and the more sales you make the more money you make. If you work the system, and you work your asses off, I can guarantee that you're going to get somewhere, because in my twenty years in the business, I've never seen anybody fail. I've just seen people quit.

Everybody wants my job, and if they say they don't they're full of shit. Who wouldn't? I make a lot of money, I wear a $20,000 watch. The business is what gave me my net worth, my house with a pool, my cars, my vacations, my family. I've got a better-looking wife than I ever thought I'd get, and I got her because I've got a lot of money.

ALL: (*Big laugh and applause*)

DANO: You guys are saying to yourselves, "Dano is promoting good-looking wife. Time for prenup."

ALL: (*More laughter*)

DANO: Look. Bottom line. There are top guys, middle guys, new guys and losers. Obviously a top guy is there earlier than the manager. Obviously a top guy stays later than the manager. Obviously a top guy rings the bell every day. Obviously a top guy can train and motivate just about anybody. Obviously a top guy is here to win. You want to be that top guy, because that's what's going to get you the house, the cars and the wife. The top guy is the guy who's next in line for promotion. JUICE?

ALL: (*Shout*) JUICE.

DANO: This isn't about what you're selling or where you're selling it. It's about you. Do you have what it takes? (*Exits*)

ALL: (*Shout*) JUICE, JUICE, JUICE, JUICE.

At the end of Dano's speech we got our marching orders. Incentives for the day. If you sold up to five sets of books you would get the usual thirteen dollars per set. If you sold between five and ten sets of books you'd get fifteen dollars per set, and if you sold between ten and fifteen sets of books you'd get twenty dollars per set. We were setting out in teams of threes. The first team back to the office having sold all fifteen books would get an added bonus of three hundred dollars. The cut-off time, or DQ (disqualification) time, was 6:30 p.m.

Ivan had arranged it so that he and I would be riding with Tiffany, the pregnant eighteen-year-old that he was out to fuck by nightfall. The minute we got in the car Ivan started scheming about how we could win the three-hundred-dollar bonus. He pulled into the parking lot of a Wendy's to let Tiffany get something to eat.

He and I were standing by the car doing the math.

"What about if you go to an ATM, buy all fifteen books with your own money, then we'll get back to the office first, get twenty dollars per book and the bonus?" he said, his eyes widening.

"I'd only just break even," I said. "I'd shell out three hundred dollars and only get three hundred dollars back. We've actually got to sell them or it won't work."

"Fuck," said Ivan. "All right then. We've got to use Tiffany. She's got big tits and you've seen her walk. She's got an advantage."

I had to admit, she had a sashay that belied her age, but still, she was an eighteen-year-old unwed mother-to-be who lived on junk food and Diet Coke, and who worked on her feet all day because she had no other choice. Her baby's father, as I'd learned in the car, was in prison for dealing drugs. She had just about the shittiest prospects of anyone in the company, and all Ivan could think of was how he could pimp her to make a quick buck or get his dick off. He was merciless.

When Tiffany came back to the car Ivan told her outright what he'd planned. The idea, he told her, was to drop multiples in a single location and get back to the office as soon as possible. Businesses were often good places for dumping multiples, because the coupon books were a tax write-off for business owners and could be offered as employee or even client incentives. To make the best use of Tiffany, we'd have to target a male business, he explained, like a tool-and-die shop or a car dealership.

She was happy to play the role. She felt it was in her best interests to walk as little as possible.

"Besides," she sighed, exhaling on a cigarette she'd just lit, "I really need that bonus."

"You want it," Ivan said, winking at me in the rearview mirror.

"Yeah, I really want it," she said.

"Well, trust me," he said, peeking at me again and smirking at the double entendre, "you're gonna get it."

Tiffany lifted up her shirt just past the navel. She was wearing a white blouse over a tight white lycra tank top. She wanted to know if we thought she was showing too much to pull off the vixen maneuver. The poor-pregnant-girl routine would work against us, we decided.

"Nah, you're fine," said Ivan.

We set off, looking for a car dealership on the main drag. Ivan was pumping me for a workable scenario, something that Tiffany could run with, something that would help her dump the merch quickly.

"C'mon, you're the former writer," he said.

So I ventured the following: Tiffany is the only woman in an office full of guys—not far from the truth. They don't respect her—again, not a lie. It's her first week on the job and they want her to quit, so they've sent her out with more merch than she can possibly drop in a few hours. They've got an interoffice bet that she'll fail. They've sent her out with Ivan, who doesn't speak much English, because he's the only guy who'll have anything to do with her.

Ivan liked this. "Yeah, yeah, good, okay," he said.

"I'll wait in the car," I said, ashamed.

By then Ivan had found a car dealership, pulled up on a side street and parked the car out of sight. Tiffany was unbuttoning her blouse and adjusting her tits to maximum advantage. Due to the pregnancy, they were already fairly monstrous for her still slight frame. With the blouse totally unbuttoned, she was all business up front. When she got out of the car and started her cakewalk across the lot toward the showroom, legs striding, chest out, hips kicking back and forth under her miniskirt, her blouse trailing like a flag behind her in the breeze, suddenly I felt fairly sure she understood all too well the double meaning of "swallows." She knew what she was doing. It was pretty awful to see. Like Troy, she was using for what it was worth the very thing they used against her. Also like Troy, she was a pretty successful salesperson.

Ivan followed her into the showroom, walking a few paces behind to let her have her full effect. They were gone for about twenty minutes. I took this to be a good sign. But when they straggled back to the car, they hadn't made a sale. We tried another dealership and a body shop on the strip, but nothing doing, so we decided to hit some residential neighborhoods and do it the old-fashioned way, door-to-door.

This was where I got my first chance to pitch. It was a nice, generic upper-middle-class neighborhood with carefully sodded plots, groomed driveways and enviable cars. People were out mowing their lawns or playing with their kids, lots of dads doing their Saturday duties with the munchkins, throwing a baseball or wielding the hose. And there I was, the loathsome solicitor in his loafers, having to walk up to these people and give them the worst, most depressive sales pitch they'd probably ever heard.

It's very humbling to become the thing you hate. I felt like an insect loping into people's private lives in my snappy clothes. I couldn't bring myself to smile gregariously. Sheepish was the best I could do. On my first ten or so pitches, the first words out of my mouth were always "I'm sorry." Because I was. I was really sorry to be foisting my ratty little coupon books on anyone, especially in their homes.

"I'm sorry to bother you," I'd say or, "I hate to get in your way." It was the only thing in the entire pitch that I said wholeheartedly. The rest came out like the shit it was, and people mostly just shook their heads and closed their doors without saying a word.

day. When you were selling, or as Ivan called it, when you were "in the zone," you felt like a holy vessel of mammon, and it was unmistakably sexual. Every sale was a con, but a slightly different con, depending on the person who answered the door. You had to dance around their weak points, and punch it home when you saw the opening. Every sale made you more confident, and more confidence produced more sales, the coaches were right enough about that.

It happened to me one day when I was out with Ivan again, taking egg on my face, rejection after rejection, until I felt sure that I would never make a sale. Ivan had been making ceaseless fun of me all day, watching me pitch on the doorsteps as he sat smoking and smirking in the car.

"Take control, dude," he'd say. "Have a pair. Jesus."

At one house we drove up to an old woman who was pacing her front yard for a little exercise, a prime buyer, Ivan assured me. But before I could get past the first sentence she shut me down cold. "We're not interested."

I was still too fresh and embarrassed to know that you never stopped there, so I just said, "Oh, okay then. Thanks anyway."

As we drove off Ivan said, "Unbelievable. You just got bitch-slapped by a ninety-year-old lady."

And that's how it went for the rest of the afternoon, until around five o'clock, by which time Ivan was singing rap songs to goad me. "All right, here we go," he'd say as we pulled up at the next inevitable defeat. "Shake your ass. Watch yourself. Show me what you're workin' with."

Then finally, at what felt like the hundredth house I'd pitched that day, some guy who didn't look like the type just rolled over and handed me the forty bucks. I couldn't believe it. Neither could Ivan. And I have to admit it felt good to relieve someone of a little cash for once, even if it meant relinquishing a piece of my cherished moral superiority in the process.

The corruption of the sell caught me up very quickly after that, and in the space of a few hours I went from being the gawky virgin who pops his cherry in the cathouse to the slick postman who always rings twice. I made six more sales before quitting time, winning even Ivan's smug endorsement in the process. I proved my manhood, took control, showed my balls, whatever—the very thing I had failed to do repeatedly in the field, not only at Clutch, but at the other Red Bull firms I'd visited.

At Borg Consulting, I had spent my second day on the job out with another twenty-three-year-old guy who, in his high-octane, hormone-driven approach to the business, was very much like Ivan and Doug. He, too, saw himself retiring in his early thirties. He, too, sexualized everything into a zero-sum game. Like Ivan, he was confused and frustrated by my inability to show the requisite balls in pitching customers.

"You're a man," he'd say. "You gotta pitch like a man."

He was very clear on this point. Girls pitched differently. They flirted. They cajoled and smiled and eased their way into the sales underhandedly, which was exactly how I'd started out trying to do it. I'd tried initially to ask for the sale the way I asked for food in a restaurant as a woman, or the way I asked for help at a gas station—pleadingly. But coming from a man this was off-color. It didn't work. It bred contempt in both men and women. In this sense it was very much like trying to pick up a woman in a bar. As a guy, I had to shed my sympathy for myself and the victim, and the appearance of weakness and need. People see weakness in a woman and they want to help. They see weakness in a man and they want to stamp it out.

When I made my first sale that afternoon with Ivan, I

stepped over this divide. I got back the attitude I'd had in my interviews, and the more I saw it working in people's minds and on their faces, turning them over to my side, the more I used it to my advantage.

After I'd made two sales in a row I felt high. I'd broken the curse. I was on a roll. I'd stopped asking for the sale like a girl and started taking it like a man. I'd seduced two people and I could do it again. What's more, I didn't need the bosses' pitch. I could make up my own, and it would sound better and more spontaneous than anything the dolts at Clutch could devise. People knew bad bullshit when they heard it. Good bullshit was what I needed.

That was the chain of thought, and the chain of thought became an act, a performance, a man's performance supplanting a woman's: confidence, competence, control—not my former supplication, apology and need. Success lifted my spirits. Good spirits got my juices flowing, and my juices wrote their own evil script. I got creative, and creativity, however seedy and low it may be, is something that very few people see coming. I had learned as much from Ivan.

At the third house I bounded out of the car and across the lawn toward a woman who was working outside in her garden. I was in a good mood and she could tell. My smile was genuine, and she responded to it warmly.

"How ya doin'?" I asked.

"Not bad," she said. "How are you?"

This was a miracle already. None of my other greetings had evoked courtesy. Everyone else had cut through my crap right away: "What do you want?" or "What are you selling?" I had managed somehow to finesse those snags at the previous two houses and make the sale anyway, but now I didn't need to. This woman was relaxed. She was taking my lead. We were standing there like two people without agendas who had all the time in the world.

I asked her about her garden. She had an accent, so I asked her where she was from. It turned out that she was English, so I told her about having grown up there myself. We talked about this for a few more minutes, as she went back to her planting, kneeling in front of one of her flowerbeds and scooping the soil with a trowel. Finally, when there was a lull, she nodded at the coupon books in my hand and said, very politely, "So what do you have there?"

I looked down at them as if I'd forgotten they were there.

"Oh, well, I'm out here doing some market research," I said, "and these are the prototypes. I'm trying to get a sense of what people think of them. Can I show you a copy and maybe you'd give me your opinion?"

This was completely untrue, of course, but it would ease her into the pitch, which I planned to give at the end of our conversation, not the beginning. I had learned this lesson from my previous flops. When I made the pitch up front, most people put up a wall and denied me the sale before I'd even gotten a chance to show them the product. I'd learned this as a single guy, too. The in-your-face pitch was the salesman's equivalent of accosting a woman in a bar with a ten-ton come-on, and leading the charge with a cheesy pickup line. You'd be dead before you reached the end of your sentence. So, I reasoned, if I took the sale out of the equation at first and simply asked the customer for her opinion, she would let down her guard.

And I was right. She did.

"Sure, what is it?" she said.

I leaned over and leafed through the coupons, pointing out the best ones and asserting that the book, if used properly, would make up its forty-dollar value many times over. That part was true. The books actually were a good deal, but when you pitched like a wimp or a teleprompted Clutchhead, you'd never get the chance to point this out to anyone. On the other hand, I thought, if you did get the chance to point it out, people would be hard-pressed to deny it.

Once again I was right.

"So," I said, "what do you think? Is it a good value?"

"Yeah," she said. "It looks like it."

And there it was. Done. I was in control. I had her right where I wanted her. She'd admitted that the product was desirable. Now if I offered to sell it to her, she would, by her own admission, be passing up a deal if she didn't buy it.

"All right," I said. "Well, here's the thing. We'd really like people to try the books out, to see how they work, and maybe give us pointers on how to improve them. So we're offering these few prototypes for sale. Do you think you'd be interested in trying one out for us and letting us know what you think?"

And whaddya know, she would. She did. Out came the checkbook, and down in manly glory went another Ned score. Slam-dunk.

"Dude," said Ivan. "You're the man."

And for a few degraded hours I guess I was, God help me.

At the end of the day I gave my earned cash to Ivan. I didn't want anything to do with it. Besides, he needed it more than I did, and when it came to selling the male mystique, he had taught me practically everything I knew.

It's a little frightening, actually, how often I've thought back on those days with Ivan, heard those words "take control" or "show your balls" echoing in my mind in my everyday life as a woman. They are not idle words. They work. They work in a lot of situations that might otherwise control a person. They are Ned's lingering voice taking over, almost like an alternate personality getting the job done when I can't. They linger irritatingly, like Muzak heard at the supermarket, and they remind me that perhaps the strongest remaining male advantage is purely mental. Thinking makes it so.

The next morning Davis gave me the full star treatment in the morning rap session.

"I got a guy . . . a highly motivated type a guy . . . Mr. Ned Vincent. Yesterday he went out with Ivan and dropped seven times, put more than ninety dollars in his pocket. JUICE by that."

"JUICE," yelled the reps amid a round of applause.

I had been coached for this moment. Davis had told me what to say on cue when he singled me out for the high-roller speech. I was to credit my success to the system, working the system, working the so-called law of averages, which, according to company definitions, meant that one out of every ten people would buy the product pretty much no matter what you said to them—the idea being that if you pitched a hundred people in a day you were bound to sell ten books just by default. Whipping yourself on to the next house, house after house, was called working the law of averages. Sooner or later you'd make the sale. Telling the other reps that working the law of averages had worked for you on a big day was central to sustaining morale. Telling the truth, that is, saying that you had sold as many books as you had because you'd just gotten better and better at lying as the day wore on, wasn't company policy. It didn't engender office pride, even though, of course, learning to lie better was what everyone who did well was really doing. Not that the law of averages didn't work. It had to at some point. But very few of the people who sold ten books on any given day had really visited a hundred people. They cut corners, and those corners were the hard facts, rounded into S curves by the end of a good day's work.

I said what I was supposed to say, and everyone duly patted

me on the back and high-fived me until my palms were stinging and I wanted to garrote Ned with his own tie. Doug, the ex-marine who was usually the high roller, approached me suspiciously that morning, wondering if I was onto his secrets.

"Good job, man. What was working for you?"

He was wearing a shapeless powder blue suit with a white windowpane check.

"I made people think that I was giving them something, rather than taking something from them," I answered.

He was stopped by this for a second, as if I'd quoted him a price in a foreign currency. You could see the calculation pass over his face and then the flicker of recognition. He'd decided that this was a useful remark even though you could tell he didn't quite know what it meant. He socked it away in his little ferret brain for future use, probably in some seminar he'd be giving before long at a Sheraton in Cleveland.

He changed the subject, fixing me with his opaque eyes.

"Yo, man, I'm taking you out today, and we're gonna be on the golf course by four o'clock."

The bosses were behind this, I suspected, wooing me through him because they couldn't be bothered. He was going to show me the life of a high roller, the fruits of the promised income in the form of a niblick and a cigar.

I couldn't face this prospect, striding the fairways with this slate-eyed scrapper telling me his boot camp stories and correcting my swing.

But the day didn't go as expected. We stopped for gas on the way to our territory, and he tried to push off a few books while we were there, pitching other people who were filling their tanks.

Nobody bought.

We weren't going to make it home before ten at this rate, let alone to the golf course, unless we sold to every soused rake and divorcé in the clubhouse. I couldn't face that, either.

In the car Doug told me stories about his time in the field, all of them again about sex. He said he'd walked up to a house once and heard a couple fighting loudly inside. He could hear it all the way up the walk. "You fucking bitch" this and "you fucking cunt" that. When he rang the doorbell, the door flew open right away and the lady of the house was standing there naked. The husband was in the background near the stairs watching Doug look at his wife, or as Doug told it, watching him try not to look at his wife. Doug made his pitch looking down at the floor or directly into the woman's eyes.

"She's pretty good looking, isn't she?" the guy said to Doug.

"Sir," said Doug, "I really wasn't looking."

This was classic territorial guy stuff, like the men on the street who didn't look into my eyes when they thought I was a guy. You didn't look another man in the eyes and you didn't look too long at his woman. You looked long enough to register your envy in his eyes maybe, but no longer. A guy wanted to know that you thought his woman was hot, and even that you wanted her, but more than that would cross the line and you'd be in trouble. Doug knew this instinctively, as any guy would.

By this time Doug had already made whatever panicked pitch he was going to make. The woman had reached for her checkbook, mostly out of spite, Doug figured—piss off her husband with a needless purchase. As she bent over to write the check on the hall table, the guy smacked her on the ass and looked at Doug.

"She likes that—don't you?" he said.

Of course, all of this was probably a lie, just more guy talk. Projected fantasy. What door-to-door salesman doesn't want to find a naked lady at home?

At around noon Doug pulled into a brand-new subdivision

nestled into a crook of land behind the major thoroughfare. He was clearly poaching on another rep's territory, but that was one of his shortcuts. He'd buy his own books (even at a loss sometimes, I suspected), poach, whatever it took to better himself in the bosses' eyes and get to assistant management. It was all he had to live for. Money was all that seemed to matter to him, and without a college education or any prospect of one, self-made schemes like this one were his only road to riches. He swallowed everything Dano said. Without cash there would be no house, no boat, no hot wife, no kids, no sense of himself as a provider and therefore no sense of himself as a man.

Once he'd parked curbside, Doug told me to circle around the houses counterclockwise. He would go the other way, and we'd meet in the middle. I started on my route, but we were mostly making "no home" lists—writing down the numbers of all the houses where no one was home, so that we could circle back that evening around cocktail hour and maybe clean up. I did about ten houses and only two people were home, neither of whom was interested in coupons.

It was a sweltering day. My beard was melting on my face and I was wearing a big sweathole in the back of my shirt under my blazer. After the tenth house I gave up and sat at the end of someone's driveway in the shade of a baby tree—the sub was so new it barely had sod—a surreal touch that lent an extra dose of existential despair to the whole proceeding; as if this wasn't earth at all and you were dead and didn't know it and the afterlife was this hellish little plod around suburbia for all eternity. I waited for Doug, who had gone all the way to the end of the serpentine cul-de-sac, to make his way back into sight. Hanging out under a tree was something I'm sure a lot of the salesmen did on certain days. Ivan had said sometimes he just sat in his car by the side of a deserted road and smoked cigarettes, hiding from the heat and humiliation. It was enough to make anyone as bitter as he was, and I could see how some of the older reps who were trying to support families on this work would sit there consumed by self-loathing and impotence.

Doug came back after about an hour or so, having dropped only one book in that time. He'd lost face in front of the new guy. The shine of the morning had worn off him. His pestering sparkle was gone and his eyes were a little fiercer than before, almost substantive, with a pinprick of resentment at their centers.

I wondered, given all the potency metaphors and bravado that the male salesmen brought to the turf, whether accepting this kind of defeat wasn't easier for a woman. Winning or conquering wasn't part of our cultural definition. It wasn't tied to our genitals. There was a residual sexism in this for women, a benign twist on being thought useless in the world of work for so many centuries. If we did it people would say, "pretty good for a girl," and if we failed we were still commended for trying. But a guy, he was a useless clod if he couldn't perform, and he said that to himself at least as harshly as anyone else did. Sitting under a tree in the middle of a workday, glooming over the little or nothing you had to show for yourself, was about as emasculating as it got.

I could quit with impunity, so I did. I did what hundreds of desperate people had done before me. I said to myself that it just wasn't worth it. I didn't want to walk around in the heat anymore. I didn't have anything left to say to Doug, nor did he to me. It was just going to be more splitting up and walking around. Ned's butch apotheosis had come and gone.

I asked Doug to give me a ride back to the office, and he did with very little protest. I walked in, dumped my merch in the empty conference room and left. The bosses weren't there, but they were used to people quitting, so they weren't going to make a fuss or need to know why. They knew why. That's why they had an ongoing ad in the paper.

I decided not to reveal myself to Clutch management. They didn't have time for or interest in anything that wasn't about profit. What were they going to say? "Yeah, but how many books did you sell today and how did you do it?"

To them each of us was just another pair of grubby hands potentially pulling in their cash. Gender didn't seem to have any deeper implication for them. They—unlike the reps, who used it stereotypically to their advantage in the field—weren't particularly interested in or, as far as I could tell, even conscious of its dictates.

During one of my interviews at Borg I had explicitly asked the boss, Diane, what she thought about the differences between men and women in the business—how well they fared comparatively, what they used to their advantage and what held them back.

All she said was, "I don't see gender. I really don't."

And she meant it. She believed it to be true, and certainly in hiring practice and company decorum it was true, since the staff at Borg, unlike the staff at Clutch, was pretty evenly split down the middle, half men, half women, and each of us was expected to live up to the same expectations. At Borg nobody exclaimed "holy sheep" when a woman kicked ass in the field.

But it was unlikely that Diane was blind to people's sex when she dealt with them as people one-to-one, that is, unless she was employing some highly sophisticated brand of self-hypnosis that eludes the rest of us. In my dealings with her as Ned, I did not observe that to be the case.

I thought she treated me like a guy, and I say this with some confidence because I met and worked with her late in my career as Ned, and had come to recognize the signs pretty well by then — the supplely controlling smile, the slightly coddling gaze, both of which said, "You're a man and I'm a woman and this is how we talk to each other."

This, of course, wasn't the only way that women interacted with Ned, but it was one of them, one of what was usually only a handful of ways. Sometimes, as on my dates, they were suspicious or superior. Sometimes they were distant, protected but polite, the way the women in the bars had sometimes been when I'd approached to buy them a drink. Other times they were consciously flirtatious, touching my sleeve or my collar for emphasis.

Men were no different. They, too, assessed you for *what*, not *who*, you were, and spoke to you accordingly, by rote, like they were addressing a set of characteristics, not a person. It was as if people had five or ten scripts in their minds, each labeled for a type, and all of them geared toward one sex or the other. When they saw you, they'd choose whichever script fit you best, and work from it unconsciously. For guys there was the buddy bonding script, and the "Hey, you're not gay, are you?" script, and not a whole lot else.

In all my experience passing back and forth between male and female — often going out in public as both a man and a woman in one day — I rarely if ever interacted in any significant way with anyone (even store clerks) who didn't treat me and the people around me in a gender-coded way, or freeze uncomfortably when they were uncertain whether I was a man or a woman.

It was the freezing that always struck me most. People will literally stand paralyzed for a moment, sometimes in mild, sometimes in utter panic when they don't know what sex you are. You can see the confusion registering, or with polite people, being suppressed, and then you can see the adjustment being made either for male or female or for an extremely uncomfortable and robotic neutral ground between the two. If they don't know what sex you are, they literally don't know how to treat you. They don't know which code to opt for, which language to speak, which specific words and gestures to use, how close they can come to you physically, whether or not they should smile and how. In this we are no different than dogs—with the notable exception, of course, that no dog has ever been mistaken about anyone's sex.

So prevalent was this gender-coded behavior that I came to ask myself whether it isn't almost as impossible for any of us to treat each other gender neutrally as it is to conceptualize language without grammar. Linguist Noam Chomsky is famous for positing that all languages share certain grammatical principles in common, and that children are born with a knowledge of those grammatical principles intact. This inborn knowledge, he argued, explains the success and speed with which children learn language. In Chomsky's terms, then, the human brain is hard-wired to think grammatically, or, more generally, to slot information and stimuli into certain categories of thought. That is how it functions and how we, in turn, are able to think. In this sense, I wonder, could there be a preprogrammed and possibly inescapable grammar of gender burned on our brains? And is every encounter pre-scripted as a result?

To my mind, the Red Bull environments were unmistakably sexed even in their more subtle incarnations at places like Borg.

Diane did "see gender," and she treated her employees like sexed beings, often flirting with the men as a means of exerting control, and bonding superficially with the women for the same reason. As in everyday life, not every interaction was loaded, and not every interaction was loaded in the same way. But there were gender-coded patterns of behavior happening most of the time, currents running underneath the words and gestures, and if you were looking for them, as I was, standing inside someone else's suit, you couldn't mistake their intent. They told you what you were and how to behave.

With their mad-dash modus operandi and quasi-cultish environments, the Red Bull companies were hardly representative of average American office culture or corporate environments. For one thing, we were rarely in the office. For another, we lived mostly off the grid when it came to getting paid and paying taxes, and even reporting for work. Almost everything in these places was an exaggeration of what you'd find in large, respected, well-known and established companies of long standing—the kinds of places I worked in my early career before becoming a writer, and my only point of comparison. The Red Bull companies had a culture all their own, though that culture was always seeking to spread itself farther and wider, and was doing so, not only across the country but the world, promoting new young managers, opening new offices, and hiring more young minions to shout JUICE on every continent.

Everything Red Bull was exaggerated. The trash talk, the pace, the motivational hype. But then I suppose that's *Glengarry Glen Ross* for you, a foreshortened view to sharpen the focus. There I saw things rough, much the way I'd seen them in the strip clubs.

Would I have seen them quite so unadulteratedly at a white-shoe law firm or a blue-chip company? I doubt it. For one thing, no one could blast the song "Other People's Pussy" in the boardroom at such places, or prostitute the female employees at power lunches as brazenly as we used Tiffany to sell coupons, and get away with it for long, even in jest.

Yet somehow I don't have a great deal of trouble imagining

highly paid male professionals talking just as dirty as we did when they're alone together in someone's office, or whooping it up over cocktails after work, or, as some executives have been known to do, taking a long lunch at the titty bar. Nor do I have trouble imagining that in more insidious ways women are still objectified and used to gain strategic advantage in the upper echelons of white-collar America. Sexual harassment law has pushed a lot of blatant sexism and boys' club culture under the table, but most of us don't kid ourselves that it isn't there. Nor would it be fair to assume that simply because, of necessity, I took jobs that didn't require advanced degrees, working people of all income levels and educational backgrounds don't bring sexually charged and gender-coded ideas and behaviors to the office. They must. They can hardly help it.

And neither can "we," always the supposed exceptions to the rule in our own eyes. We operate in most ways, but especially at work, within the lines that are drawn for us, and gender roles are no exception. Our expectations for ourselves as men and women are largely those of our parents or caregivers, who, as numerous psychological experiments have shown, are more than likely to have done things as crudely conditioning and silly as dressing us in blue and giving us trucks to play with if we were boys or, if we were girls, dressing us in pink and giving us dolls instead.

Selling door-to-door as Ned helped me to live more of an average man's life for a spell. I got to be one of the slick boys in sales, to see the target girls across the room, and myself in them. I got to feel the workplace pressures of manhood, and understand first-hand that they are still as tied as they ever were to male virility and, hence, self-esteem. I saw the women around me working by a different motivation — disproving still the ever-implied assumption of their inferiority, and deflecting persistent sexual objectification. I remembered having been motivated similarly myself.

I saw the clashing styles of the male and female salespeople who tried to teach me to be a man. I grew a pair of balls for a while, and felt the high that well-wielded genitals can induce. And perhaps most important, for the one and only time in my life as Ned, I felt empowered as a man, though I attribute this feeling far more to the clothes I wore than to the circumstances in which I wore them. My jacket and tie had a surprisingly powerful effect both on me and on people's perceptions of me.

Thinking back on the experience and how absurd it is that a man's attire can so thoroughly "make" him, I am reminded of a passage in the Jerzy Kosinski novel *Cockpit,* which I came across after completing my work experience as Ned. In the novel, the main character pulls a stunt very much like my own, and gets a similar reaction from the public. He has a military uniform custom made for him by a tailor, though he cobbles it together from various designs (using, for example, the lapels of a British uniform, the pockets of a Swedish uniform and the collar of a Brazilian uniform) so as to make it unrecognizable as any country's actual uniform. Then he wears it in public wherever he goes for the next few weeks.

When he returns, uniform-clad for the first time, to the hotel where he has been staying, the concierge is so blinded by the uniform that he doesn't recognize the man himself until he gives his name. Thereafter the concierge insists on treating the man with exaggerated courtesy. These reactions persist with nearly everyone the man meets while in uniform. The parking attendant brings his car around without being asked, ignoring six other waiting customers in the process. In restaurants with long lines, he is seated immediately. Airlines give him preferential seating on fully booked flights. And perhaps most outrageously, his word is taken as true without question, even when he goes out of his way to tell whopping lies.

Kosinski writes: "Confronted with my camouflage, it is the witness who deceives himself, allowing his eyes to give my new character credibility and authenticity. I do not fool him; he either accepts or rejects my altered truth."

My experience was much the same, though not as grandiose. A suit, or a jacket and tie, is a uniform—quite literally in fact, since the first men's suits were derived from military dress. My business attire gave me credibility, respectability, license. It was a disguise for my disguise and in it I, the impersonator, was invisible, though not by any means invulnerable.

I soared briefly. Then I got dropped on my ass and didn't get up. I was one of the quitters, I guess. Not a top guy.

The only contact I had with anyone at Clutch after I left was with Ivan. We spoke briefly on the phone a few days later and he told me that the only thing the bosses had had to say about my disappearance was, "Yeah, well, he wasn't that impressive."

7 | Self

The poet and translator Robert Bly ignited the modern men's movement in the United States in 1990 with the publication of his book *Iron John*. In it Bly identified what he saw as a crisis of identity in American manhood caused largely by the prevalence of broken relationships between fathers and sons, the disappearance of male initiation rituals and a dearth of male role models for young boys. Using myth and fairy tale as his guides, especially the Grimm brothers' story "Iron John," from which the book takes its title, Bly encouraged men to reconnect with the buried Wild Man inside them as a means of healing their bereft and wounded souls.

Men, he argued, had gone through a painful evolution in recent decades, moving from one broken model to the next. First there was the fifties man who was supposed to "like football, be aggressive, stick up for the United States, never cry, and always provide." But he was callous and brutal, isolated and dangerous. Then came the sixties man beset by guilt and horror over the Vietnam War and encouraged by the early feminist movement to get in touch with his feminine side. Bly praised this new gentle, thoughtful man for leaving behind the crusty stoicism of his father's generation, but lamented his eventual deterioration into the seventies man, or what Bly called the soft man, a man without backbone or force, an unhappy man, more compassionate than the fifties man, but out of touch with vital, fierce parts of his masculinity.

In Bly's reading of the Grimm tale "Iron John," passive, fearful men must have the courage to reclaim their essential manhood by literally dredging up this lost fierceness and vitality from inside them, just as the young men in the Grimm story dredge up hairy, muddy Iron John from the bottom of a swamp. Iron John, or the symbolic Wild Man, scary, unkempt and ugly as he may seem, is, said Bly, the key to men's self-actualization and freedom, the way forward in men's lives.

Iron John became a national bestseller, and though Bly and others had been leading private men's workshops throughout the 1980s, the book brought this work and its stated purpose to public consciousness. New men's workshops and organizations have since sprung up across the country and the world.

When I started this project I had heard of Bly and *Iron John* and the men's movement, but I had no idea what men did or talked about at these secret meetings. Women aren't allowed to attend them, and the men who attend are generally secretive about what goes on.

Like the monastery, this was another shuttered male world that I thought might offer me valuable insights into male experience and men's struggles to redefine themselves in the postfeminist age. But unlike the monks, the men who joined these groups were facing their problems, talking about them openly and pointedly examining their masculinity, both as they and the culture defined it. It was the perfect place to end Ned's journey.

I chose an intimate group of about twenty-five to thirty guys that met once a month. I had to travel about an hour and a half each way by car to get to the meetings, which were held in a rented rehearsal room in a community center. The room itself was the size of a small dance studio, bare except for a piano in the corner and mirrors on two of the walls. We sat in folding chairs arranged in a circle in the center of the room.

There, just sitting and listening, I thought I was going to coast through the end of Ned's odyssey in a cozy therapeutic setting. Little did I know that this last leg of the trek would push me to the breaking point.

I went to my first meeting in mid-July, the worst time of year for Ned to try to pass at close quarters in a poorly air-conditioned, brightly lit room. I was dabbing my face constantly with a handkerchief to avoid beard slippage. Add to that the special notice I got for being the new guy, and you can imagine why I was sweating profusely from the moment I walked in. I had been hoping to sneak in and sit at the back unnoticed, but the group hadn't seen a newcomer in some time, so Gabriel, one of the group's longest-standing members, introduced me around the room.

Gabriel was sweet. Heartbreaking, really. The minute you met him you could see that his sense of self was in pieces all over the floor, like a motorcycle someone had taken apart in a garage years before and hadn't been able to put back together again. He was handsome in an earnest, outdoorsy sort of way, midforties but still dirty blond and trim in his jeans, long-sleeved T-shirts and Birkenstocks. He was harmless and well-meaning, but a little off-putting at first in his eagerness to bond with me as a brother. On my second visit he insisted on hugging me hello and good-bye.

I'm not generally a big one for therapy groups, especially cultish ones that circulate mimeographed booklets full of toothless mantras and aphorisms, or airy poetry that's supposed to sound deep but usually isn't. This group was a classic of that genre, at least in its literature. It had its own mimeographed booklet, which one of the founding members had assembled, and it was full of quoted snippets from men's-movement gurus like Bly, Joseph Campbell and Michael Meade, as well as a few scattered gems from Yeats, Eliot, Emerson and other dead poets of note. But to me, in this context, even the masters sounded flaccid and ill used.

The rest of the booklet consisted mostly of questions that were supposed to function as loose guidelines for discussion on that meeting's assigned theme, questions like: What are my un-met emotional needs? How much is my masculinity defined by other people or society's expectations of me? Do I respect other men?

There were seven themes or stages of growth in all, instead of the usual twelve that recur in addiction recovery meetings. Like a twelve-step group, we rotated through them from week to week. When we'd finished stage seven, we'd begin again the next time at stage one.

Call me unevolved, but I didn't want to hug anybody there just because it was part of the program. I don't do "program." I don't like "program," even though I know people who participate in them, and have changed their lives immensely for the better as a result. I wanted to hug people when I felt something for them, when I was ready. Besides, I saw myself as the enemy in this group and I thought it best to keep it that way.

But hugging was central to the therapy there. Most men don't tend to share much physical affection with their male friends, so here the guys made a point of hugging each other long and hard at every possible opportunity as a way of offsetting what the world had long deprived them of, and what they in turn had been socialized to disallow themselves.

It wasn't at all uncommon at the beginning and end of these meetings to see pairs of guys engaging in prolonged hugs. Sometimes they'd be crying, sometimes they'd just be shoring each other up with reassuring words.

Even as someone who has seen and never been startled by the sight of a lot of gay men hugging each other long and tenderly in public, it took me a while to get used to seeing these straight men hugging this way. They were really holding each other, taking care, and this just isn't something you see very often in the outside world. Ned hadn't seen it in his. And when you saw these guys doing it, it made you realize how badly they needed this surrogate brotherly/fatherly love, and how much they needed it to be expressed physically.

These men had been making do all their lives with traditional nods of silent understanding. But that wasn't enough anymore. The monks, or someone among them, perhaps influenced by the men's movement, had been savvy enough to figure this out. But it's not the kind of thing you can force, especially when you're trying to reverse a lifetime's worth of programming. These guys were here because they wanted to be, and though during my time with them there was always a part of me that remained uncomfortable with groupthink self-help, in this case I had to admire the effort. I knew enough men who could have used similar help, if only they could have opened a pinhole in their defenses. Who was I to scorn this medicine, even if its bywords weren't to my liking?

The meetings always started out the same way, the way that most AA and other twelve-step meetings begin, with one of the members reading from the designated portion of the booklet, then giving a five- to ten-minute speech to the group on the topic of the evening. Usually this was a fairly rambling affair, full of expressed discomfort with the whole endeavor. None of these guys was particularly eager to get up in front of a room full of other men and tell them how he felt. As one of the guys said, it was a feat for him to realize that he even *had* feelings. Learning to identify and express them, especially in the presence of other men, was asking a lot.

It didn't really matter what they said. It was a miracle that they were talking at all.

To me this was amazing, the idea that a person could be incapable of expressing his emotions. Identifying and expressing my emotions had usually come fairly easily to me. It had never occurred to me that some people not only didn't do it, but didn't have the slightest notion how to do it. This, I now realize, is a highly privileged, largely feminine point of view, and one whose value and comparative rarity Ned has since made me appreciate. To my mind—and it was clear from what these guys were saying, to their minds as well—living your whole life without connecting to your emotions could be as detrimental to the spirit as starvation is to the body. And though hearing about this handicap came as something of a revelation to me when I heard these men talking about it so candidly, it shouldn't have, since it was only a confirmation of what I'd found at the monastery and elsewhere in the world as Ned. A lot of men were chronically caught incommunicado.

After this initial outpouring to the group, the speaker would step down and the group would split up into smaller discussion circles of threes or fours. These smaller discussion groups, which lasted nearly an hour, functioned like cocounseling workshops. These were usually the dark heart of the meetings, the intimate times when breakthroughs could be made. For me, they were usually just times to learn more about the core issues, the specifically gender-related problems these guys shared in common and hashed out together. I often sat aloof taking mental notes.

It was in one of these small discussion groups that I had my first conversation with Paul. It happened several months after I'd started going to the meetings. I'd met him very briefly once before, early on, but he intimidated me, and so I kept the contact to a brief hello, terrified that he would see through Ned immediately. I had heard about him from the other members, about his problems with rage, but also about his perceptiveness and intelligence. I thought I should be very careful around him. I said to myself, if anyone will sniff you out, he will, and it won't be pretty when he does.

I was afraid of him. He was a powerful-looking man, probably in his late fifties. No taller than five feet nine, but heavy, with solid arms, large hands and a sizable paunch, which he wore like a sumo, as if it would be an asset in a fight, not a liability. He probably couldn't move very fast, but he looked as if he could crush you with a single blow. He had the bloated, toughened face of an Irish boxer or a corrupt old-world cop, and his whole head, woolly with his russet graying hair, looked like a wad of scar tissue.

Even though he scared me a little, as the godfather of the group and the leader of its biannual retreats, Paul was fascinating to me, too. As much as I wanted to avoid him for fear of being found out, I also wanted to know his story, to pick him apart. I saw him as a self-styled neopagan guru with a ragtag pack of foundlings whimpering at his heels. I couldn't help thinking of it that way at first, and disliking Paul for the petty tyranny he seemed to exercise over these men. It wasn't hard to dominate this group. These were mostly broken people, and as much as Paul may indeed have been out to help his fellow men, his brothers, as they called each other, he was, I thought, probably also in it for the bimonthly adulation. Plus, one weekend a year he got to go into the woods with drums and hatchets and play Colonel Kurtz, spouting his aphoristic horrors to his followers and roasting offal on the fire, or some such. I didn't know what they did on those weekends, but I was going to find out.

To me, he seemed dangerous on some level. Volatile, at least.

And what I was doing was invasive to his pet project, or could be. The rage it could provoke in him might be considerable. It would press all his buttons. As he told it, one of the defining conflicts of his psyche was his hatred for his mother, whom he said had been psychotic (she was dead now) and had tried to kill him. He said he had the scars to prove physical abuse at her hands.

I imagined that Paul had transformed his abiding hatred for this woman into a pervasive and virulent misogyny. His response to me, if he found me out, especially if he found me out in the woods with all of (what I supposed to be) his sharpened instruments at hand, could, I thought, easily turn nasty. I could see it happening, all the matriphobic ire finding its focal point in me, the treacherous female, nosing her way in where she didn't belong, listening to their secrets and invading their sacred space.

Of course, none of this was fair. I didn't even know the man yet.

But Paul was emblematic for me from the start. This was the end of Ned's journey and Paul was his last trial, the last person to deceive and perhaps confront. I wanted to make it easy for myself to dislike him, because it was going to make me feel a lot less guilty about spying on him. Posting him out there somewhere as my nemesis in effigy made him neatly detestable in my mind. Besides, the way he presented himself on a first or second meeting didn't help his cause. He seemed gruff and egocentric, even a little belligerent when he spoke, spitting his words like a preemptive strike.

The first time I heard him address the group he speechified with self-important authority. He condescended, almost angrily, as if he were a principal lecturing truants.

He said, "Someone said about me recently, 'Paul thinks he's the center of the universe,' and I say if you're not the center of the universe there's something wrong. You are the center of your universe, because if you're not, who is?"

He went on to talk about the need for each man to respect other men's egos. This made the feminist in me bristle at first. Haven't we had enough of men's egos, I thought? But then I remembered my first night out in drag in the East Village and my perception that respecting one another's egos was exactly what men were often doing with their eyes and body language, slipping past one another's protected zones with minimal engagement. It wasn't about pride so much as protection.

As if reading my thoughts, Paul said, "When you look another man in the eye it means one of two things. What?"

He waited for a reply. I was ready with the answer.

"I want to fuck you or I want to kill you," I said.

Everyone turned to look at me.

"Exactly," said Paul. "I want to fuck you or I want to kill you."

This much I knew and understood. I'd experienced it myself. But in Paul's rendering, there was more to it. He was making a larger point, a point that was central to the purpose and methodology of the men's movement, but I didn't find that out until much later, until I'd heard more of these men's stories and learned what they were trying to accomplish at these meetings. At the time it just made me think that Paul was a petty tough guy, showing his homemade troops how to piss in all four corners of the room.

But then Paul and I met again in one of the small discussion groups. We were sitting two feet from each other, face-to-face, and he wasn't an abstraction anymore. Nor, I soon discovered, was he the bully I'd taken him for.

I sat quietly for the first half hour, just as I usually did, listening to what the other guys were saying. He was listening, too. And as I listened and watched the way he listened, I began to see that there was much more to him than the illusion of certainty he'd presented at the front of the room. He wasn't just a windbag who loved the sound of his own voice. Actually, he was the only man in the group who really listened. He listened intently, instead of just waiting for his turn to speak.

Most of the other guys tended to talk at and past each other, rarely to or with each other. They listened, it seemed, mostly for things that reinforced their own experience or point of view about themselves. They'd nod when something resonated, but then, as soon as the speaker finished, they'd often just launch into their own story, relevant or not. This ships-passing-in-the-night approach didn't seem to bother most of the guys. Probably because they were so unused to talking this frankly about their feelings, a mere airing was good enough. They weren't practiced at the art of give and take.

But Paul was. He actually responded to what you said. He'd ask a follow-up question, probe you a bit to make you examine your thoughts. He'd interact. This, coupled with his intelligence and depth, stood out markedly in this company. It almost made me want to participate.

And that's what happened that night. Paul drew me in and drew me out.

He turned his chair around, as he often did in meetings, and he folded his arms on the chair's backrest, propping his chin on one fist. He looked me right in the eye and wouldn't look away. I'd been silent all evening, but there was no denying that look.

It said, "So what's your story?"

"I'm in a very bad mood," I said. "I don't think I'm going to say anything helpful."

"Anger isn't helpful?" he prompted, fixing me more intently.

A good point. This came up often in the group—the idea that anger was not an unproductive emotion if followed to its source. The way these guys told it, anger was the one emotion they had in abundance, the one emotion that the world had allowed them to have in abundance, so by implication it contained everything else—sorrow, pain, need, shame. You name it. It was a feeling they knew well, and it was the place where most of their other feelings hid. Nobody here was going to judge you for letting it speak.

This was refreshing, actually, and, I thought, particularly masculine. I, and most of the women I knew, had been sublimating anger for as long as we could remember. It was the one emotion we weren't quite allowed, or didn't allow ourselves. Eschewing it was part of being nice and attractive. You didn't want to be thought of as a bitch, so you put it all underground or turned it on yourself.

With these guys, I liked taking it in the face for a change, hearing anger spoken out loud in no uncertain terms.

I heard people venting spleen without apology in harsh and cutting words. They'd say things like, "I hate my sister," or they'd tell you in detail about how they'd fantasized about ripping their wife into tiny pieces. At one of the yearly retreats, for example, one guy had found it very therapeutic to pretend that he was chopping up his wife with an ax—this after he'd come home from a business trip to find that she'd left him and taken the kids with her. Paul said he got a wedding invitation from this guy a few years later. On it the guy had scrawled a personal note saying that his second marriage would have been unthinkable without the healing he'd experienced on that retreat.

Many of the guys in the group were not afraid to admit that they had murderous rage inside them. Some people said it outright. "I'm homicidal." Some said they knew there was a potential rapist in them—not that any of these fantasized crimes ever came to pass or would. They were just talking, saying the worst things, letting out the worst thoughts, not always violent, but ugly, uncharitable thoughts, the kind of thoughts that, if most of us were honest, we'd admit we've had, too, in some form or another. I respected their frankness.

Of course, if you heard all of these wife-mangling stories out of context you'd misunderstand what was really going on. It would sound like motivational misogyny, or some sick rallying cry for the thwarted. But it was more complicated than that. The anger came from legitimate feelings, and the more time I spent with these guys, the more the underlying causes for these feelings took shape and actually vetted things I'd undergone or perceived as Ned. Many of them seemed linked to common male experience.

Sometimes, as with Paul, the anger and hostility these guys felt toward the women in their lives sprang from an unsurprising Freudian source. Their wives and girlfriends were often versions of their mothers. They remembered their mothers as being suffocating, omnipresent influences on whom they had felt humiliatingly dependent, and from whom they were still desperately trying to get free. One guy in the group talked openly about this, and in his comments about his wife you can hear the humor and pathos of his struggle.

"If I put on her underwear, I would drown. I couldn't live in her underwear. She's pretty big. And she really shouldn't try to live in mine. She doesn't have the balls. She's a woman. She doesn't have balls. I try to detach, but the truth is that when I think I'm going to die, my wife's life flashes in front of my eyes instead of my own. There's still a little kid in me that still needs mommy very badly. I admit that. I even referred to her a few weeks ago as my mother instead of my wife."

This push and pull with mommy, and hence with women in general, became even more tangled and ferocious when you factored in dads. Aside from having had, and sometimes still having, difficulties with their mothers, a lot of these guys had terribly strained and loaded relationships with their fathers. True to form, as I had also discovered in the monastery, the breakdown between father and son had happened largely as a result of the two men's culturally conditioned inabilities to communicate with each other. It was a curse that fathers had been handing down to sons for generations: emotional remove, hypercritical expectation, silent judgment, abandonment. This had left populations of sons without role models, teachers or guides to lead them through the tangled, confusing and often painful process of becoming a man.

In groups with other men, these guys were trying to find the love that their fathers had been unable to give them, or possibly the love that the entire culture had conspired to keep men from giving each other. Again, like the monks, they had a profound need for other men's love. Love alone wasn't enough. They needed a man's affection and respect, a man's approval, and a man's shared perspective on their feelings. Having a mother's or a woman's love just wasn't and could never be the same. It couldn't fill the hole.

As Bly wrote in *Iron John*, "Only men can initiate men, as only women can initiate women. Women can change the embryo to a boy, but only men can change the boy to a man. Initiators say that boys need a second birth, this time a birth from men."

This was the crucial and remarkable difference between the way these guys felt about their mothers and fathers. They placed blame on both parties, but they actively mourned their fathers. They were seeking to reclaim and make peace with them. As for their mothers, it was mostly good riddance.

In the context of this longing for male love, sometimes female love was all the more repugnant and enraging to them, only serving to emphasize what was missing.

As I packed for the retreat I grew increasingly anxious about making the trip. What if they found me out? What would they do? Was this a crazy idea? I was going up into the woods alone with a bunch of guys who thought I was a man and who had serious rage issues about women. They'd even talked about tearing women to pieces or chopping them up with axes. These were psychodramatic exaggerations, yes, but so what? Anything could happen in the woods, right? Look what happened to Teena Brandon. She passed as a guy in rural Nebraska, and then when her so-called friends found out she was a woman two of them raped and murdered her. And what about Matthew Shepard? For the crime of being gay and being in the wrong bar at the wrong time, he was beaten senseless and left for dead hanging like a scarecrow from a fence in a Wyoming pasture. Whether I had reason to or not, I was starting to get scared.

And on top of all this there was the guilt. It was gaining on me too. Despite the intimate encounter Paul and I had just had, all my initial fears about him resurfaced. They got worse, in fact. Now that we'd bonded in some way I thought it likely that he'd be much angrier about the lie if he ever found it out. He'd shown me affection and concern. He'd been especially pleased to learn that I was coming to the retreat. I thought I'd actually heard tenderness in his voice.

I tempered some of these worries by taking a few precautions. I made sure that my girlfriend knew where I'd be and with whom. She knew Paul's address and full name. I sent e-mails to friends giving them the same information. In case something awful happened, I figured the detectives would know where to start.

The lodge was in a wooded area on a small lake. The leaves were in full color and from a distance the trees along the shoreline were like a quilt draped over the hills. When we arrived, the air was cool but humid, the day's rain having turned to fog. The property was elevated and secluded enough to be out of cell phone range, but not more than a few miles from the nearest village. This assuaged some of my fears about what I'd do in an emergency, but it would still be a long run down the dirt road in my underwear if it came to that, and somehow I didn't think the sight of tits and tighty whiteys would inspire much sympathy in the locals. Only one other structure shared the lakefront, and it was far enough away to be out of earshot.

The main floor of our dwelling had a large communal dining room with five or six round tables, each of which seated six or seven. There was also one long rectangular table that could accommodate about fifteen or twenty. There was an industrial kitchen just off the dining room, worked by several amenable cooks for hire—food service was included in the price of the trip.

Also on the main floor, leading off the dining room, was a large living room. Its main feature was an imposing floor-to-ceiling fieldstone fireplace in which a well-tended fire was always burning. On its mantel Paul had placed the group's talismans, one of which was—lamentably enough—a large, crudely carved wooden penis. The rest of the room was filled with armchairs and sofas and a few folding metal chairs. Over the weekend, we conducted most of our talks and seminars in this room.

The sleeping quarters were upstairs. Ten bedrooms in all, each of which could sleep four men in two sets of wooden bunk beds. As it happened, one of my bunk mates didn't show, so I had only two roommates to deal with instead of three. Still, I can assure you that, given the way these guys snored and farted in their sleep, two roommates was quite enough. Through the walls, I could hear the guys in the next room roaring like wildebeest all night long.

Thirty-three men in all attended the retreat. Make that thirty-two men and one woman. It was a full house.

I had planned on sleeping in my clothes and not showering, leaving my beard untouched and making good cover of filth if need be. It was only going to be two days, and if I got covered in mud during that time, so much the better for disguise.

I chose one of the bottom bunks, and I was able to disrobe there inside my sleeping bag. Once the lights had been turned out, I stripped down to my T-shirt and underwear, stashing my flannel shirt and jeans in the corner of my bunk, to be put on again in the same way at first light.

The first night, we arrived in the early evening and had dinner. The festivities began thereafter with an initiation ritual. This involved all thirty-three of us standing together in the main dining room in as tight a mass as we could manage. Paul encouraged this by laying a rope around us on the floor and tightening its circumference as much as possible around our feet.

When we were packed together, Paul stood in front of us and told us what to do. This was a given throughout the weekend. Paul told us what to do and we did it.

The ritual we were about to undergo was called smudging, a Native American custom. It consisted of lighting a bowl full of incense—mostly sage from the smell of it—holding the bowl in front of each man and fanning him with the smoke, up and down his body, both front and back, with what looked to be a fully feathered and preserved eagle or hawk's wing.

The idea, as Paul explained, was for each man, one by one, when he felt moved to do so, to step outside the circle, walk over to the smudger, raise his arms and receive the smoke as it wafted around him.

Per Paul's instructions, some of the guys had suspended a tarp from the ceiling, draping it over each side of a rope so that it hung down in an A frame and formed a tunnel. After you had been smudged you were supposed to walk through the tunnel to what Paul had called an unknown beyond that awaited you in the next room.

Paul went first, of course, because, as he explained somewhat archly, in the wild the alphas always get first dibs on the meat. He had an impish look in his eye, but he took this very seriously all the same. He stood in front of the smudger with his eyes closed. He had one hand over his heart and one hand over his prick, as if he were saying a priapic pledge of allegiance, which I guess in a way he was.

I was one of the last to go through. When I stood in front of him, the smudger looked me in the eye and nodded gravely as he fanned me. I nodded back with my best square jaw and turned to enter the tunnel of unknowing. At the end of it I encountered two obstacles, which Paul had said represented the obstacles one faces along the way to masculine enlightenment. The first obstacle was a bench they had placed in the doorway. You had to step over it. The other was a low lintel, which you had to duck under in order to enter the next room. Ducking under had the effect of bringing you into the living room at half height.

The action itself was pretty silly, but I understood its symbolism well enough. Coming into a room at half height put you in a disadvantaged posture, one that I could imagine inspired considerable discomfort among these guys, especially when other guys were present.

Some part of them was always thinking in terms of conflict and defense, especially around each other. As a guy, you had to be at your full height and in possession of your faculties when in close proximity to other men. I had learned this, too, as Ned.

It was complicated, because on one level everything was easy and brotherly, full of those inclusive hey-buddy handshakes I had felt early on in my term as Ned, and had felt here in the group as well. But all of this camaraderie depended on a strict observance of the rules. The boundaries were strong between men, and as I had learned at the monastery, you had to navigate them appropriately or risk a strong negative reaction. I could see why it was hard for these guys to let down their emotional defenses with each other.

For me, as a woman with other women, the contact was always fluid. The company of other women doesn't generally make women tense. We don't have our guard up in the same way. We operate under different rules. Our territories, such as they are, are not hard and fast. We hug and touch and break the barriers of one another's space in ways that men find startling among themselves. Our hugs may be superficial, and they may not always be sincere, but they are not threatening. We may also be competitive and undermining at times, but even at our worst, the most we are likely to do is hurt one another's feelings. As a result, you don't often hear women talk about being afraid of other women. But these guys talked about fear all the time, as if exposing yourself to another man was like putting yourself under his knife.

When I emerged from under the low lintel, Paul was standing there in the light, close enough to touch, with his arms wide open for a hug. Again a symbolic act. You'd come up from below expecting a sucker punch, and instead, you'd get a long-lost father's hug. I folded myself into Paul's chest defensively, worried that he would feel my bra beneath my flannel shirt, or the stickiness of my beard.

"Welcome, Ned," he said, exhaling deeply and crushing me against him.

Unexpectedly, I felt him soften in the embrace. It wasn't a bear hug. He didn't slap me on the back or grunt encouragement. He held me. Really held me, and unlike Gabriel's early proselytizing hugs, which had felt faintly shallow and cloying, Paul's hug was real and generous. Here was the guy I'd been demonizing, fearing, disliking, and he was taking me in as a son. My guilt ratcheted up a notch.

Paul often played the father figure in the group, and he played it expertly. The guys looked up to him. A lot. But their respect had an edge to it, too. Earlier in the evening, while constructing the tunnel and obstacles, Paul had shouted encouragement to two of the younger guys.

"Looks great," he'd said.

"Hey," quipped one of them under his breath. "Praise from Caesar."

He'd meant it affectionately, but it was a jab, too. He was right on the nose. Caesar indeed. Little Caesar. The emperor in a shoebox bloated with his own importance. I'd thought of him that way, too, complete with the desire to betray him. But after our therapeutic talk in the previous week's meeting, and now after this hug, I felt ashamed of my former judgments. Like everyone else here, Paul was full of wounds, and he didn't share them easily.

I had seen him earlier in the evening, sitting off by himself at one of the tables in the dining room, working up the next day's lesson plan. He had been leafing through some books of poetry and inserting bookmarks in the places he wanted to read from later. Then at one point, very deliberately, he put the books down, stacked them in a small pile, crossed his arms around them, and rested his head on them. He sat like that for a while before I realized that he was crying.

I had wanted to approach him then, to put my palm on the back of his neck and show him that someone was paying attention. But I still sensed a volatility in him that made me worry he might swing around and belt me, like a bear surprised at his meal. Besides, my move would have been feminine, or at least have come from a nurturing place, and that stuff got a complicated reception in these parts where mothers were birds of prey.

Fanned out in the room behind Paul, all the other guys who had gone through the tunnel before me were standing in a semicircular receiving line, each waiting for a hug from me. I hugged them all in turn, bristling, just as many of them did, at the forced physical intimacy with a stranger, but mostly for fear of being found out.

That was the end of the initiation ritual, and I have to admit that I found the whole thing a little ridiculous. I knew what they were trying to do and I respected the attempt. Bly's preaching was full of paeans to rites and rituals, myth and symbolism. The loss of them was crucial, he'd claimed, to the breakdown of modern masculinity. But to my mind these insipid parlor games were no replacement. Either offer a genuine obstacle, a real trial that would test the limits of a person's character and sense of self, or leave it alone. But don't have them walk through a pup tent smelling like a cookout and expect them to find salvation at the other end.

The next morning after breakfast, we all gathered in front of the fire in the living room and Paul handed out large pieces of sketch paper, one to each of us. He distributed crayons, pens and markers as well. Then he asked us all to draw a picture of our inner hero. This had been the advertised theme of the weekend: Are you a hero? And if so what kind?

This had made me cringe when I'd first seen it written on the retreat literature. They can't be serious, I'd thought. But, of course, I knew they were. Heroes and archetypes were straight out of Bly's bible.

"What does your hero look like?" Paul asked.

To get us in the right frame of mind, he mentioned John

Wayne, Batman, the Lone Ranger and Achilles as examples of archetypal heroes. Was our hero like them, he asked, or something different? What was his quest, his mission? What was his Achilles' heel?

Gabriel began scribbling furiously with a black crayon. He'd been coming to these retreats for years, so I guessed he was familiar with the procedure. His hero was right under the surface.

Looking over his shoulder I could see that he'd taken the Batman thing to heart, though he appeared to have hit on some messianic theme as well and was drawing a big cross on Batman's chest. Later, he would describe the character as Batman-Jesus.

I, on the other hand, was blocked. My sheet was blank. The freakish Joan of Arc doll that I'd so loved in childhood sprang to mind, and I had to stifle a laugh. Somehow I didn't think a cross-dressing peasant warrior woman would go over well in this crowd, or do much for my cover. So I drew an atomic bomb instead.

When all the guys had finished sketching and scribbling notes on their drawings, Paul asked some of us to share, and while several of the sketches were as absurd as Gabriel's, some of them were actually quite revealing and unexpectedly reflective of Ned's experience.

Before this retreat I hadn't had an opportunity to find out how many of Ned's feelings about his masculinity and his place in the world were real or imagined, a genuine part of masculine experience or just the product of my female eyes filtering that experience.

A guy named Corey was the first to share his drawing. I had just met him the previous evening. I had never seen him at the regular bimonthly sessions. He said he didn't go to those anymore, but he always made it to the retreats. They seemed to do something important for him. In a way he was the prototypical men's movement guy. He was a real education in hidden male fragility. To look at him you'd think this guy had the world on a string, at least romantically. He carried himself like the accomplished athlete that he was, and he had a sculpted, perfect body whose every muscle was visible, practically even beneath his clothing. He reminded me of guys I'd seen in high school and college who always had legions of girls around them, all clamoring to be their next conquest. I used to look at guys like that and think: "What must it be like to be that guy, a god among men?"

I got my answer.

When we arrived at the lodge, we had all been assigned to subtherapy groups of four or five. In these we were expected to convene over the course of the weekend to explore more intimately the things we'd discussed in the workshops. Corey and I were in the same group, and we hit it off right away. There was a Ping-Pong table in a small room behind the living room fireplace, and we'd played a couple of games together. He was likable and easy, not the kind of guy you'd think was haunted by self-loathing and doubt. But he was.

He shared his drawing eagerly. He'd called it "Solo Warrior," and it was a picture of a guy who looked like a cross between Lancelot and Grizzly Adams. He was carrying a shield and a sword, and he'd been wandering in the forest for a very long time. He was out there, Corey explained, because he was an outcast, barred from entering the villages he came upon.

"Why can't he enter the villages?" asked Paul.

"Because he's not good enough yet," said Corey. "He needs to perfect himself before he can join civilization."

"And what's his Achilles' heel?"

Corey paused. "He's needy. He should be able to live alone bravely without help, but he can't. He wants love. He needs it."

"And it's that very need that makes him too imperfect to enter the village?" asked Paul.

"Yeah," said Corey.

Later, in our small group, Corey talked more about himself. Sharing intimate therapeutic time with him and the rest of these guys shattered for me another of the stereotypes I'd always harbored about men, the idea that they don't talk about their relationships, especially not with each other. I'd always assumed that they weren't nearly as concerned as women are with the minutiae of intimacy. But after listening to these guys I thought it was probably truer to say that most guys had simply never had the opportunity or license to explore the subject.

In our group we spent the bulk of the time talking about their relationships past and present. All of them were in relationships, and all of them felt concerned about and insecure in them. Especially Corey. He had a beautiful girlfriend, he said, but it sounded as if he couldn't enjoy his time with her because he was constantly afraid of losing her to another guy, specifically another guy who made more money, a guy of higher social status. Guys were always buzzing around her, he said, and this drove him crazy, partly because she indulged their attentions.

Here he was, the outwardly powerful masculine ideal, an outcast in his own life, excruciatingly insecure in his position, compelled to make a brave show of it on the outside, forbidden to show weakness, yet plagued by it nonetheless.

Thinking back on it, I wondered now how much I and every other girl in school had invested in worshipping guys like him from a distance, and how much sustaining our admiration, acting the part, had cost them. I suppose Corey symbolized a lot of what I thought I was going to find in manhood or had envied in it, so much of what I and the culture at large had projected onto it: privilege, confidence, power. And learning the truth about this pose, both firsthand as Ned, and secondhand through Corey's and these other guys' confessions, learning the truth about the burden of holding up that illusion of impregnability, taught me an unforgettable lesson about the hidden pain of masculinity and my own sex's symbiotic role in it.

We needed men not to be needy, and so they weren't. But, of course, ultimately we did need and want them to be needy, to express their feelings and be vulnerable. And they needed that, too. They needed permission to be weak, and even to fail sometimes. But somewhere in there the signals usually got crossed or lost altogether, which often left both men and women feeling unfulfilled, resentful and alone.

Corey wasn't the only physically imposing guy I met in the men's group, and he wasn't the only guy who had issues about it, not just issues about vulnerability, romantic or otherwise, but specifically about body image.

Most of us who grew up on women's studies knew intimately the struggles that we and most of our women friends had been through on this front: body as battleground. Mutilation, objectification, violation. These were key words in the feminist vocabulary, and still are, and that vocabulary was built on verifiable female experience. We saw ourselves in it because most of us had been on crash diets in our teens, obsessed about our noses, breast and ass sizes, our leg hair, our pubic hair and our menstrual flow. Many of us had known or been anorexics or bulimics. Most of us couldn't think of a single female friend who hadn't been through a war with her own body. The truth of the claim was obvious.

But likewise most of us didn't know, or didn't think we knew, any guys who had the same problems. They ate what they wanted. They weren't ashamed of their fat—most of them had none—or their body hair or the way their jeans fit. We resented their insouciance. To us, body issues were a woman's problem imposed by the culture of fashion, by men's rapacious eyes and of course, by the insidious product of the two: the beauty myth.

Before I took on Ned, it had never occurred to me to consider whether or not men, too, had body image problems, except maybe about hair loss and penis size. Even as Ned I thought that most of the discomfort and inadequacy I felt about being a small guy had to do with being a woman trying to pass as a man. That and my own internalized "feminine" neuroses. But as with so many other things about male experience, I had my eyes opened in the group, and my assumptions challenged.

At my first men's meeting I met a guy named Toby. He was built like an English bulldog, with wide lats, burly shoulders and a tiny waist. Even his face, compact as his jarhead haircut, had that pushed-in pugnacious quality about it that made you assume, without a politically correct second thought, that he was stubborn and stupid.

Painfully insecure in my own "male" body, and certain in my residual feminist knowledge that there couldn't be any negative emotion attached to being the strong man, I made the mistake of calling attention to his brawn by saying with obvious envy: "How does it feel to be in *that* body?"

I had hit a sore spot. Toby said nothing at first. Then leaning over his lap with his fingers interlaced, his powerful forearms resting on his thighs and his head bent low over his knees, he sighed and said, "Objectified."

It wasn't a word I'd ever heard a man use about himself.

"Every time I come into a room or a restaurant," Toby continued, "especially with other guys, I can see the fear on their faces, like they think I'm going to hurt them. They assume I'm violent because of the way I look."

He had a point. Was this really any less insulting than presuming every blonde to be a bimbo?

You could tell he fought against this prejudice every day, sitting there carefully, deliberately translating the hurt into language, while people stood there expecting him to lash out like a dumb brute.

He told us that he felt trapped by the judgments people made about him from afar. He said he was a soft, emotive, thoughtful guy in the body of a boxer, and why did everyone think it was okay to look at him like that, like an ape at the dinner table?

He was stuck just as fast as everyone else in the role the culture had assigned to him. He didn't come to the retreat, and it was too bad. I would have liked to have seen his drawings.

Other guys at the retreat shared their drawings, and a pattern started to emerge. Two guys had drawn their heroes as Atlas, holding the world on his shoulders. One of them was a family man. He said he was going through a rough time in his marriage. He was really feeling the burden of being the safety net, the breadwinner and the Mr. Fix-It of his household.

"I'm tired," he said.

When Paul asked him to explain more about the significance of Atlas he said, "I guess I think that if I hold it all together, if I take care of everything and everyone, that eventually I'll be loved. But the price is my life. I'm trying to do the impossible. So I guess I'm really Sisyphus, too."

It was an insightful combination, and perhaps the perfect depiction of modern man at his most beset and wasted, taking the world on his shoulders and rolling it uphill. Being the man in charge brought with it a whole host of burdens and anxieties that seldom if ever occurred to me or the feminists I knew. We saw it from our side, and from there it seemed pretty damned good to be in power, make decisions, have choices, to escape the homemaker's gulag. For ambitious women, having a career was a lot better than changing your millionth diaper or staring at the yellow wallpaper. When you're feeling trapped and disenfranchised, it doesn't register that being the working stiff in the gray flannel suit isn't any picnic either.

The other guy who had drawn his hero as Atlas emphasized this aspect. Beside his Atlas, in the margins of his picture, he had also drawn Hercules, the more expected hero. When Paul asked him what that meant he said, "Well, you know Hercules is going for the golden apples, and Atlas is envious. He says, 'I've got a real job.'"

You couldn't put it more succinctly. To these guys, going to work and supporting the family was a man's job. Still. And it was hard. There was no vacation in it, and you weren't going to get many women to see or admit that. Worst of all, holding up the world in this way wasn't just painful and tiring, it was also one of the most vulnerable poses a man could assume. And this is almost certainly something that would never occur to a woman.

"See," said the guy, "Atlas can't protect himself in that position. Anybody could just walk right up to him and kick him in the balls."

There it was again—the fear of conflict in vulnerability, the assumption that even your most basic job in life made you weak to enemies and contained within it the invitation to attack. And all of this was built into the mission of a man's life, his sense of his own masculinity.

As always, women were an integral part of that conflict. To these guys being Atlas didn't literally mean supporting the world. It meant supporting their little piece of it. Being Atlas was about being the guy who takes care of all the pesky logistical (and often fiscal) hassles so that daily life can run smoothly. It meant worrying so that the wife and kids didn't have to. And that alone was burden enough for any man. He could have been a carpenter, as one of the Atlas guys was, or a corporate mogul. It didn't matter. It was still the same feeling.

The guys felt profoundly responsible for the women in their lives, to give sustenance primarily, but more importantly—and yes, in this sense, chivalry is most emphatically not dead—to "take the pain so that she wouldn't have to." The drive among these guys to save and protect women—and this drive was truly visceral—astounded me. Something impelled them inexorably to shoulder women as their burden, and it was that drive and its cultural impositions that they came to resent. Then, of course, ultimately they came to resent the women themselves.

Another of these guys expressed the same feelings about his inner hero when he drew himself as what he called "the wounded man." His job was to save women, to take the blows and the bullets in her stead. Still another guy drew himself as "the saver." The guy who could build fires and fight fires and carry women out of them.

Yeah, in part, it was Victimography 101. But it was also a very real part of these guys' sense of themselves as men, and a fair complaint. Ask some of the breadwinner guys you know what they think about it and if they're honest they're likely to say: "I work my ass off to support my family and yeah, I'd like a little credit for it."

Both sides have their gripes.

Many women worked and still work tirelessly as homemakers and child rearers to support their families, too. But a whole generation or two or three has given voice to those complaints and offered the alternative—enshrined it even in law. And a lot of enlightenment has come along with those voices and those laws. We knew better, for example, than to let Hillary Rodham Clinton get away with a snide remark about staying home and baking cookies, because we know that homemaking is hard work. We also know that she, like every other female member of Congress, owes her Senate seat to the feminist movement and the employment equity it forced. But do we know enough to call somebody on a cheap jab at the company man, whom we all too often presume to be nothing more than the continual beneficiary of inveterate male privilege? Do we understand his hardships?

What's more, do we know, as feminist poet Adrienne Rich wrote, that "our [women's] blight has been our sinecure"? Being the second sex imprisoned us, but it came with at least one sizable benefit. We didn't have to carry the world on our shoulders.

The feeling is officially mutual. Women thought they held up the world and made it go, and for that service deserved a vacation. Men, it turns out, think the same thing. And we're both right. But it took being Ned, especially being Ned among these retreatants, who drew the same pictures again and again, to really see this clearly from the inside out.

The most jarring expression of the man's burden came from a guy who drew himself as the wolverine's claw. "It's the meanest animal on earth," he said. "His message is *'Go Away.'* He fights his male rivals and enemies to the death, especially his father.

And what was his Achilles' heel? Pussy, of course. "The fight," he said, "is about pussy." Protecting it. Possessing it. Needing it. That was his whole life right there.

This guy was angrier than any guy I met in those meetings. He just stewed wherever he sat, as if the demons were so strong in him that he was afraid to move.

The rage and the pain were consuming and they were colored by the imposition of a masculine role, a role whose blatant symbolism Paul had had us draw on paper and thereby expose as the crude crayon scrawling that it was.

That was the lesson in the exercise. Drawing your hero wasn't quite as dumb as it sounded. You weren't reinforcing an idiotic image of yourself as the man god. You were drawing your cartoon self and exposing it as such, then tearing it apart for good measure. You were learning to stop being a straitjacketed man, bouncing off other men's manhood, and trying instead to be a person who could respond to the world without scripts of conflict or defense already written in your head.

It was different for every guy, and that is what Paul had really meant that first night when he'd spoken so assertively about the ego. Each man's journey of self-discovery was his own. He had to do it himself, to know and to actualize himself from the inside out or be lost altogether. It was his alienation from himself, his capitulation to "masculinity," that had led him into despair in the first place. Respecting his own and another man's ego wasn't about walking around puffed up and pugnacious, every man a king among kings. It was about treading lightly around the other man's singular vulnerability, being present and available for contact, but not intrusive. It meant that it might be possible to look another man in the eye without intending to fuck or kill him.

The spirit dance happened on Saturday night. It was the pinnacle of the weekend, or it was supposed to be. It was the time when you were meant to enact and thereby resolve or dispel all the buried conflicts you had unearthed over the previous day and a half.

This was where the weapons came in. This was where guys like the bereft businessman chopped up their wives, and where guys like Corey could playact the humiliations of their relationships and achieve at least a partial catharsis in the process. Over a Ping-Pong game late Saturday afternoon Corey had told me what he was planning for the dance.

"I think I'd like to have some of you guys pretend to be those other guys who are always hanging around my girlfriend. Maybe you could pretend to flirt with her and insult me and then I can work through this."

I said I'd be glad to help.

I in turn told him what I was envisioning and asked him if he might help me. I asked Corey if he'd be willing to cut me.

Yes, you read it right. I asked him to cut me.

Even now just seeing those words on the page is hard. Explaining them is harder still.

Why, you may ask, after having spent the past few weeks worrying about whether these guys might attack me, would I then of all things turn around and invite one of them to cut me?

The answer is complicated.

By this point in the weekend, and in Ned's unraveling life, I was drowning in guilt and Paul was the focus of that guilt, partly because we had become closer, but mostly because he was the founder of the group. It was his baby, and in deceiving the group I felt that I was deceiving him the most. I suppose I would have asked him to cut me if part of me hadn't still been afraid that he might take me up on it. Corey was a safe substitute. Obviously there was a very skewed logic at work here, but I thought that if I paid some penalty, some physically painful penalty for lying to Paul and everyone else, then everything would be paid for, not just everything there in the group, but everything throughout the project.

The idea of undergoing pain at these men's hands had possessed me by then subconsciously, and it surfaced all at once in my conversation with Corey. Punishment was the thing I thought I needed to enact in the spirit dance. My ritual, my pseudohero's trial, was expiation. I suppose in a way it should come as no surprise that my envisioned penance took the form it did, since I had just spent three weeks in a monastery surrounded by icons of the tortured Christ. Like I said, once a Catholic always a Catholic.

The only history I had as a man was one of deceit, and with these guys it went deeper than anything before. Their safe space was carefully carved out, and I had found my way into it through a lie. I knew their secrets, albeit secrets that would remain anonymous in my telling of them and, with luck, bring perhaps some women and men closer to an understanding of one another's struggles. But, and this was something I had addressed directly with the monks since leaving the abbey, how do you reconcile genuine interpersonal connection and potentially valuable insights into human behavior with false pretenses?

At the time I couldn't reconcile them. Not without some grisly form of absolution, or so I thought.

Even as I was asking Corey to cut me I didn't realize how wacko this scenario had gotten in my mind, or how crazy it would sound coming out of my mouth.

"What?" Corey asked. "You want me to cut you for real?"

"Yeah," I said. "I want you to take a knife and cut me slowly in stripes on my arms and legs until I tell you to stop."

"Why would you want me to do that?"

"Because it's what I need to do. It's my conflict. I can't explain it any better than that. Isn't that what this thing is for?"

"Well, yeah," he said, still incredulous, "but man, you don't wanna do that. I've felt a lot of physical pain in my life and believe me it doesn't do anything for you. It's just pain."

"Where did all this pain come from?" I asked, trying then to steer the conversation away from the alarming request.

"Injuries, mostly from sports. I've had a lot of injuries. Man, pain is just pain, that's all. You don't need that."

The two of us were like a travesty of man versus woman,

standing there talking about pain in such opposing terms. He, a typically athletic guy whose relationship to the physical world had been smash-bang probably since junior high. Me, a typical female looking to turn abuse on herself.

Corey reminded me of guys I'd dated in college, football players especially, who had talked about the aggression and need for violent physical contact that the testosterone infusions of puberty had engendered in them. I thought, too, about the guys on MTV's reality program *Jackass*, or the teenage skateboarders you see on street corners, throwing themselves headlong into scrapes with concrete, testing the boundaries of physical space without fear.

Then I thought about self-mutilators—people who cut and burn themselves ritually—and how 70-some percent of them are women. Pain for them, and now apparently for me, was like a bath, a relief, a penalty paid and a release ensuing. I'd never cut myself before, or binged on cigarette burns, or anything like that. But now it seemed like the only way to free myself from the guilt. Talking about it this way with Corey, I guessed I was showing my colors. He thought I was really weird—as well he should have—a guy with a really odd relationship to pain.

I thought in this context about the guys who spoke about saving women, taking the pain so they wouldn't have to. Pain was something they took out of duty or in necessary conflict. Most often it was the by-product of something else entirely. But most women weren't expected to face pain to prove themselves. It was in us, part of our monthly cycle, our first fuck, our physical design to give birth, but it wasn't part of our outward cultural definition, never a mandatory rite of passage. Everybody has a relationship to pain. Too often women's is intimate and self-inflicted, and in extreme form, that is what mine became.

Though I didn't know it then, my time as Ned was ending prematurely. I had planned to go to the men's meetings for another few months, but what began as a fantastical notion of bloodletting in the woods became in the coming weeks a dangerous obsession with purgative torture. Asking Corey to cut me was just the start of that devolution.

I was losing it and Ned was coming with me.

But losing it, or at least going mildly ape was something guys had done before at retreats. That's part of what the retreats were for. Loss of control was something that Paul and the other retreat organizers had anticipated. They had taken steps to prevent serious injury. Giving sharp weapons to rage junkies was a disaster they knew enough to avoid.

Finding this out the way I did was rather funny in the end. The night of the spirit dance I painted my face black with charcoal from the fire. It was another form of cover and my own boyish jab at spooking it up for the dance, where all the ghosts and demons were meant to surface.

The men had cleared the dining room for the festivities and set up an array of African and other drums in the corners so that various members of the group could provide the soundtrack for the evening. The room was aglow. They had lit candles all around and turned out the overhead lights. It was then that I saw all the weapons and implements lying on the long dining table, which had been pushed up against the windows out of the way.

There are moments when the power of fantasy is brought up humiliatingly short by real life, and this was one of them. Big time. As I looked the table over I realized that all the spears and knives and other weapons I'd seen gleaming so beautifully menacing in my mind's eye were in fact made of plastic. Yes, plastic. They were toys. Toy Viking and conquistador helmets and breastplates and machine guns that went *rat-tat-tat* when you pulled their triggers. I couldn't believe it.

I had to laugh at myself. Here was the ultimate clash of consciousness, a bunch of boys playing war, and me wanting a butchering at their hands. I felt like a twisted babysitter. I had come to the retreat worried about what might happen to me, but with the possible exception of Paul and the wolverine guy, I was the most dangerous person there. The other guys were pussycats to a one.

As we assembled I saw that people were half dressed in various costumes. One of my group mates was wearing his commando pajamas, a kind of camouflage sweat suit he'd been wearing all weekend. Corey was wearing a short bathrobe, the top half of which he soon dribbled over the belt and let hang from his waist. He danced topless that way for much of the evening, as did many of the other guys. Gabriel had donned a tragic thespian mask and was scampering around the room in a crouch, cowering periodically behind chairs and other people like a dog trying to dodge a beating. One of the middle-aged guys was wearing nothing but off-white long-john bottoms. His cock and balls wiggled and dangled as he skipped around in circles to the sound of the drums, his pecs drooping and withered, a look of awkward concentration on his face.

My commando-pajamaed group mate picked up one of the plastic axes and spent a good ten minutes mock wanking with it between his legs, running an open fist furiously along the shaft, arching his back and falling to his knees in ecstasy at the climax.

He said later, "I wanted to get in touch with my balls and my orgasm — my cum."

How original.

Corey eventually joined a small group of guys writhing together on the floor, half wrestling, grunting and groaning and throwing themselves around. Nobody dared throw anyone else around in this group. They were having a hard time letting go, and most of them would have been too scared of what such a gesture might unleash. At any given time five to ten different guys were off squatting in one of the corners, watching uncomfortably. Paul would go over periodically to shoo them out and they would move away reluctantly into the dance, only to peel off ashamedly into another corner to hide. The whole thing would have worked a lot better if we'd all gotten stoned beforehand or taken other hallucinogens, as native cultures often did and still do in such rituals. The whole idea was to get out of yourself and have a vision, but nobody here was going to do that sober, including me.

I sat cross-legged in one of the corners with a pair of bongos I'd picked up off the long table. As long as I was engaged in music making I figured I could remain outside the circle and watch. But before long it became clear that there would be no collective zenith in the dance, no fever pitch reached and passed. People grew tired and disappointed by revelation's failure to show.

Yet for me, revelation was showing even then. It already had at the Ping-Pong table with Corey, though I would understand it only later when I caught up with it. My conflict was happening to me without prompting and when I got home I would have it all out.

The spirit dance ended without fanfare. It wound down with a final group shout at the end, something we always did to cap off our biweekly meetings, gathering in a tight circle, joining hands, raising our hands and letting loose. At those times I could always hear my own voice higher than the rest, reedy and incongruent, beside but never quite joining the struck note.

The retreat finished the way the spirit dance had, uneventfully, with a quiet, mostly reflective breakfast on Sunday morning and a thankful parting of ways thereafter. I said nothing about myself to anyone.

I came back from the retreat with a host of accumulated feelings in tow. No one found me out and, of course, no one cut me. But the malaise inside me was still there and growing.

I was coming close to the end of a year and a half spent masquerading as a man. The men's retreat was the culmination of that masquerade, and in certain ways the hardest part to pull off. I had gone to the woods with these guys not knowing what the retreat leaders were going to ask us to do. I had envisioned all sorts of things, none of which, thankfully, came to pass. Yet somehow this didn't relieve the pressure in my mind, and I continued to imagine scenarios in which I would elicit some violent reaction from Paul or someone else.

Once the retreat was over I knew that I had accomplished the last big task. Some part of me knew I didn't have to hold Ned together anymore, or the girded mind-set that made him possible. And once I knew that, all the guilt about being an impostor, the anxiety of getting caught at it and the by then extreme discomfort of contravening my own gender identity came rushing in. I didn't have the resources or the reasons anymore to stop it.

I could use the term "crack-up" to characterize what happened next, but it doesn't really describe what it felt like. "Nervous breakdown" is another handy term of art, but it too does little more than brand the experience as some filmable catastrophe that makes for good TV. The reality was not nearly so dramatic. There was no earthquake. The floor of my house didn't open and swallow the furniture.

It was all very quiet, as if I had gone out one day to do errands and come home to a summer house where all the chairs and tables had been covered with sheets.

I did not become paranoid or hysterical or make a scene in public. I didn't feel overwrought or afraid. I felt nothing, and that was scarier. There was no break with reality. None whatsoever. I heard no voices. I saw nothing that wasn't there. If anything, the opposite was true. The everyday unremarkable scenery became so heavy, so imaginationless, that I felt as if I were wearing my surroundings like a cement suit.

I simply quit, or some part of me did, and then left the rest of me to work out the particulars, which in my case meant checking myself into a hospital.

The event itself had been so subtle, or perhaps my notion of what mental collapse is really like had been so overblown, that I wasn't even aware that it had happened. I knew something had happened. I knew that I had taken steps to prevent or mitigate some impending disaster, but once in the hospital I found myself bewildered by my fellow patients and my presence among them. Absurdly so at times.

Over institutional pancakes one morning I asked one of them what he was "in for," and he told me he'd had a nervous breakdown after his wife left him for another man.

"Oh, really," I said. "What is a nervous breakdown like anyway? I've always wanted to know."

It seemed at the time as though I had checked myself into a locked psychiatric ward for no particular reason at all. I didn't associate my condition with anything that had happened over the previous year and a half. I thought my antidepressant medication had simply stopped working, and accordingly I had tripped into the nearest hole. That was my official line: "I'm having my medication adjusted." A euphemism at last. As if checking yourself into the bin was no different or more involved a procedure than irrigating your ears.

The truth was I had been what the experts called "passively suicidal." I was walking around in a trance looking for Pauls in everyone I met, Pauls, that is, who happened to be carrying real knives on their persons and were practiced at using them. Given that such people are all too easy to find in New York City, my therapist thought it wise to suggest that I take myself off the streets, and the waking part of me agreed.

It wasn't until I sat in the day room of the mental ward talking to various social workers and med students and distracted psychiatrists that I connected this episode in any meaningful way with Paul or Ned, or even came to realize that Ned was over.

Sure, Paul was someone associated with Ned, he was the focus of my guilt, that much I knew going in, but he was not the only or even the most prevalent cause of Ned's demise.

The deeper cause was in Ned, inherent to him, and had been there from the start. First of all, Ned was an impostor and impostors who aren't sociopaths eventually implode. Assuming another identity is no simple affair, even when it doesn't involve a sex change. It takes constant effort, vigilance and energy. A lot of energy. It's exhausting at the best of times. You are always afraid that someone knows you are not who you say you are, or will know immediately if you make even the slightest false step. You are outside yourself in two senses. First because you are always watching yourself from beside or above, trying to get the performance right and see the pitfalls coming, but also because you are always trying to inhabit the persona of someone who doesn't exist, even on paper. You don't have the benefit of a script or character treatment that can tell you how this person thinks, or what his childhood was like, or what he likes to do. He has no history and no substance, and being him is like being an adult thrown back into the worst of someone else's awkward adolescence.

But there was more to it than that. Ned was also a man, albeit a Potemkin man, all facade and no substance, but I was still very much a woman peering through his windows, and the cognitive dissonance this set up was simply untenable in the long term, like holding two mutually exclusive ideas in my mind while trying to juggle and ride a bicycle at the same time.

Being him was a bit like being a zebra who is trying to pass himself off as a giraffe. Trying to be a man when you are a woman is not just being a horse of a different color, or a person who has traded in her old trappings for new ones: new clothes, new makeup and new hair. Through Ned I learned the hard way that my gender has roots in my brain, possibly biochemical ones, living very close to the core of my self-image. Inseparably close. Far, far closer than my race or class or religion or nationality, so close in fact as to be incomparable with these categories, though it is so often grouped with them in theory.

When I plucked out, one by one, my set of gendered characteristics, and slotted in Ned's, unknowingly I drove the slim end of a wedge into my sense of self, and as I lived as Ned, growing into his life and conjured place in the world, a fault line opened in my mind, precipitating small and then increasingly larger seismic events in my subconscious until the stratum finally gave.

I left the hospital after only four days, not because I was cured, far from it, but because listening to my roommate talk all night about the Swedish troll people, or about how DJs on the radio were calling her a whore, wasn't helping me to get better.

It took me a solid two months of meticulous care and home rest to get myself out of that state. Several times during that period I reached for Paul's number but didn't use it. I could never quite trust my motivations for wanting to see him and tell him about me, so I put off any meeting and concentrated instead on purging myself of Ned.

Ned had built up in my system over time. This allowed me to convey him more convincingly as the project went on, but it was also what made me buckle eventually under his weight. It was to be expected. As one rare (rare because insightful) psychiatrist would later put it to me when I declared that my breakdown would surely impeach me as a narrator, and hence impugn the whole project: "On the contrary, having done what you did, I would have thought you were crazy if you hadn't had a breakdown."

In an odd way I think that what happened to me as Ned is what happened in some form or another to most of the guys in the men's group, though I experienced the alienation more intensely because I was a woman. Square peg, round hole and all that. My effort was disastrous of necessity. But for these men, living in their man's box wasn't a particularly good fit either, and learning this in spades may have been Ned's best lesson in the toxicity of gender roles. Those roles had proved to be ungainly, suffocating, torpor-inducing or even nearly fatal to a lot more people than I'd thought, and for the simple reason that, man or woman, they didn't let you be yourself. Sooner or later that conflict would show, even if you weren't trying to cross the boundaries of sex.

Manhood is a leaden mythology riding on the shoulders of every man.

True enough. But what to do about it? I can hardly write those words and defend them. Men's liberation isn't a platform you can run on, even if it is the last frontier of new age rehabilitation: the oppressor as oppressed. In our age we feel no political sympathy for "man," because he has been the conqueror, the rapist, the warmonger, the plutocrat, the collective nightmare sitting on our chest. Right? Right. "Boo hoo," we say in the face of his complaint. "The tyrant weeps." When the bellowing image of the Great Oz turns out to be the befuddled homunculus pulling levers behind a curtain, we are understandably lacking in sympathy.

Yet as Paul, who has spent years in the men's movement trying to defend it to angry feminists, once put it to me, "It is women who are paying the highest price for men's dysfunction. We are not in opposition to them at all." And he's right. Men's healing is in women's interest, though for women that healing will mean accepting on some level not only that men are—here is the dreaded word—victims of the patriarchy, too, but (and this will be the hardest part to swallow) that women have been codeterminers in the system, at times as invested and active as men themselves in making and keeping men in their role. From the feminist point of view this sounds at best like an abdication of responsibility, an easy out for the inventor, and at worst an infuriating instance of blaming the true victim. But from Paul's point of view it means that men and women are finally agreeing on something: the system sucks.

All of this is why the men's movement has remained a largely clandestine affair, relegated to retreats in the woods. Being a victim is far less practicable politically when the victimizer is also you, and the rending yoke is self-imposed. Can anybody really march the streets crying *j'accuse* and mea culpa in the same breath? Can you be "The Man" and the rebel at the same time?

Not in our revolution, pal.

It's hard to position a movement when the territory is so intimate. Men, after all, can't exactly gather on the White House lawn and demonstrate for their right to cry in public or claim their lost fathers' love. These, it would seem, are matters for the therapist's couch. Private matters.

But, of course, men's private lives are ours as well. Paul was right about that. Whether or not you're a feminist has little bearing on the matter. If men are really still in power, then it benefits us all considerably to heal the dyspeptic at the wheel. And if they're not, they're still members of our families and they still make up half the breeding population of the planet. We can hardly exist, much less live or change without them. And as the feminists might say, it doesn't get much more personal or political than that.

I don't really know what it's like to be a man. I never could. But I know approximately. I know some of what it is like to be treated as one. And that, in the end, was what this experiment was all about. Not being but being received.

I know that a lot of my discomfort came precisely from being a woman all along, remaining one even in my disguise. But I also know that another respectable portion of my distress came, as it did to the men I met in group and elsewhere, from the way the world greeted me in that disguise, a disguise that was almost as much of a put-on for my men friends as it was for me. That, maybe, was the last twist of my adventure. I passed in a man's world not because my mask was so real, but because the world of men was a masked ball. Only in my men's group did I see these masks removed and scrutinized. Only then did I know that my disguise was the one thing I had in common with every guy in the room.

In the end I decided not to tell Paul about me. I wasn't afraid of him anymore, but I worried that the embarrassment he would probably feel for not having sussed me out somewhere along the line might put him on the spot in a way that by now seemed unfair and unnecessary. This was an aspect of my previous disclosures that I hadn't fully appreciated at the time but now saw all too clearly. I had expected people to be shocked or bewildered, even angry, but not embarrassed. Yet embarrassment was I think at bottom what most people felt when I told them that Ned was really Norah. I had learned a lot about the chemistry of male/female interactions by talking through the transition with people, but I had done so somewhat at their expense. I had done it unknowingly then, but now I knew enough to know better. I wasn't going to make Paul squirm, and that, I feared, was most of what telling him would have done.

I never said good-bye to the guys for the same reason. I just stopped going to the meetings. I was tempted, however, to go back as myself. I wanted to tell them that I had heard what they had to say, that what they said had helped to buttress my own discoveries about manhood and helped me to see my own life as a man in sharper relief. Their honesty had made that possible and I was grateful to them for it. Most of all I wanted to wish them well, to tell them that I thought they were doing important work and that maybe, before long, a few more people would know it.

8 | Journey's End

It was hard being a guy. Really hard. And there were a lot of reasons for this, most of which, when I recount them, make me sound like a tired and prototypical angry young man.

It's not exactly a pose I relish. I used to hate that character, the guy in the play or the novel who drones on and on about his rotten deal in life and everyone else's responsibility for it. I always found him tedious and unsympathetic. But after living as a guy for even just a small slice of a lifetime, I can really relate to that screed and give you one of my own. In fact, that's the only way I can truthfully characterize my life as a guy. I didn't like it.

I didn't like how wooden I felt and had to make myself in order to pass as a believable guy. I had to do a lot of crossing out when I crossed from woman to man. I hadn't anticipated this when I'd started as Ned. I had thought that by being a guy I would get to do all the things I didn't get to do as a woman, things I'd always envied about boyhood when I was a child: the perceived freedoms of being unafraid in the world, stamping around loudly with my legs apart. But when it actually came to the business of being Ned I rarely felt free at all. Far from busting loose, I found myself clamping down instead.

I curtailed everything: my laugh, my word choice, my gestures, my expressions. Spontaneity went out the window, replaced by terseness, dissimulation and control. I hardened and denied to the point almost of ossification.

I couldn't be myself, and after a while, this really got me down. I spent so much time worrying about being found out, even after I knew that nobody would question the drag, that I began to feel as stiff and scripted as a sandwich board. And it wasn't being found out as a woman that I was really worried about. It was being found out as less than a real man, and I suspect that this is something a lot of men endure their whole lives, this constant scrutiny and self-scrutiny.

Somebody is always evaluating your manhood. Whether it's other men, other women, even children. And everybody is always on the lookout for your weakness or your inadequacy, as if it's some kind of plague they're terrified of catching, or, more importantly, of other men catching. If you don't make the right move, put your eyes in the right place at any given moment, in the eyes of the culture at large that threatens the whole structure. Consequently, somebody has always got to be there kicking you under the table, redirecting, making or keeping you a real man.

And that, I learned very quickly, is the straitjacket of the male role, and one that is no less constrictive than its feminine counterpart. You're not allowed to be a complete human being. Instead you get to be a coached jumble of stoic poses. You get to be what's expected of you.

The worst of this scrutiny came from being perceived as an effeminate guy. Other guys, it turned out, were hypervigilant about the rules of manhood, and they were disconcerted, sometimes deeply so, by my failure to observe those rules. They could be obtuse as hell about all kinds of other signals, especially emotional ones, but boy were they attuned to the masculinity quotient. So much so that it really does justify the term homophobia—and I've certainly never been a fan of that word. But it felt to me as if most men were genuinely afraid, almost desperately afraid sometimes of the spectral fag in their midst. It's hard to explain it otherwise. Only fear could make them spy that much on another man's signals, especially when so much else in masculine interaction goes unremarked.

Of course, being seen as an effeminate man taught me a lot about the relativity of gender. I'd been considered a masculine woman all my life. That's part of what made this project possible. But I figured that when I went out as a guy some imbalance would correct itself and I'd be just a regular Joe, well within the acceptable gender spectrum. But suddenly, as a man, people were seeing my femininity bursting out all over the place, and they did not receive it well. Not even the women really. They, too, wanted me to be more manly and buff, and sometimes they made their fag assumptions, too, even while they were dating me. Hence the phrase "my gay boyfriend."

Women were hard to please in this respect. They wanted me to be in control, baroquely big and strong both in spirit and in body, but also tender and vulnerable at the same time, subservient to their whims and bunny soft. They wanted someone to lean on and hold on to, to look up to and collapse beside, but someone who knew his reduced place in the postfeminist world nonetheless. They held their presumed moral and sexual superiority over me and at times tried to manipulate me with it.

But standing in the pit of the male psyche was no better. There I saw men at their worst, too. I saw how degraded and awful a relentless, humiliating sex drive could make you and how inhuman it could make your incessant thoughts about women become. I'll never truly know what that drive feels like on the brain when testosterone is fueling it, but I saw how by turns brutish and powerless a man can feel in the company of women and how bitter and often puerile he can be in the company of men. I know how much baser that drive could become in the circle jerk, where the expectations of manhood again exert their noxious influence, egging you on to cover the need and insecurity with crudity or pretend potency.

My buddies encouraged me to talk shit and I encouraged them to do the same. We let out all the hateful air in our balloons like mad monologists with a cogent form of Tourette's. We said all the things we didn't mean and did mean and couldn't say in mixed company, and a kind of catharsis happened then much like it did in the men's group meetings, but without the therapeutic self-consciousness. The company of your brothers can make you worse and better. Better because it lets you drain away some of the rage, but worse because it keeps you from talking about the pain underneath, because this ritual of male bonding itself is just another part of the manhood that's kicking you.

That's how it was when I was being manly with men. The dialogue was ugly and as a woman in the middle of it I felt soiled and frightened just hearing it. I was shocked because at its worst it was so much worse than I thought it would be, so foreign and relentless were the obsessions with fucking and competing and hazing the weak guy. It was all there almost all the time and it made me think that many men are far worse than most women know, but then also far better, because I knew where so much of it was coming from and how hard it was to overcome. I knew they were tied in a thousand knots and tapping out their distress in stilted code.

That is probably the part I hated the most. As a guy you get about a three-note emotional range. That's it, at least as far as the outside world is concerned. Women get octaves, chromatic scales of tears and joys and anxieties and despairs and erotic flamboyance, and now after black bra feminism, we even get vitriol, too. We get to be bitches, at least some of the time, and people write proud books about it. But guys get little more than bravado and rage. Forget doubt. Forget hurt. They take punches. They take care of business. And their intestines liquefy under the stress.

I know mine did.

Yes, it's true guys get good stuff, too. Sometimes they still get a special respect and deference and a license to brag. I found this in the workplace. I got the power to exaggerate, to believe in my "nine-inch dick" and my "180 IQ," illusory or not. It didn't matter. I had the spit to say "Try me" even when I didn't have any idea what I was doing. I had at times the billy club confidence of pure stupid unwarranted self-belief that I have seen in more guys than I can count. I always used to wonder how they did it. Now I know. They did it because a tough front is all you have when there's nothing behind it but the weakness that you're not allowed to show. It's the biggest gift you get, compensation for all the rest, as if the culture were telling you, "We're going to cut out your heart, but we'll give you legs and a VIP pass to make up for it."

Even when Ned was at his best, getting the full benefits of manhood, wearing a jacket and tie, strutting down office hallways, full of a sense of his own importance, even then I disliked his life. Even then the swagger was false, and not because I was a woman, but because the good feeling was coming from outside me. Even positive feedback was still feedback, still a cultural expectation purporting to make me who I was, to make me acceptable as a real man in a way that I had not been in the monastery.

And that hurt personally. There was still someone telling me how to be, saying "Attaboy. Now you've got it." There was still someone hanging over my shoulder taking notes, and even though hearing encouragement was always better than being demeaned as a fag, or a brute, or a failure, it was still insulting all the same, because it told me that just being me wasn't enough.

This was not just my complaint, not just a woman's mismatch with a man's part in the world, though that certainly heightened the contrast. It was the complaint of every guy in my men's group, and a problem if not always a complaint for almost every guy I met, though some of them were too shut down to express, much less see, how much damage "manhood" was doing to them.

In that sense my experience wasn't unique. Being a guy was just like that much of the time, a series of unrealistic, limiting, infuriating and depressing expectations constantly coming over the wire, and you just a dummy trying to act on the instructions. White manhood in America isn't the standard anymore by which women and all other minorities are being measured and found wanting, or at least it doesn't feel that way from the inside. It's just another set of marching orders, another stereotype to inhabit.

Learning this surprised me. At the beginning of the project I remember thinking that living as a man and having access to a man's world would be like gaining admission to the big auditorium for the main event after having spent my life watching the proceedings from a video monitor on the lawn outside. I expected everything to be big and out in the open, the real deal live and three feet from my face, instead of seen through a glass darkly. To be sure, there was a time in America when this would have been so, when boardrooms and a thousand other places were for men only, and worming my way into them would have gotten me the royal treatment and given me the very feeling of exclusivity and enlargement that I was anticipating.

But for me getting into the so called boys' club in the early years of the new millennium felt much more like joining a subculture than a country club. Walking around in the world as a man and interacting with other men as one of them seemed in certain ways a lot like how it feels to interact with other gay people in the straight world. When certain men shook Ned's hand and called him buddy it felt as if they were recognizing him as one of their own in much the same way that gay people, when we meet each other, often give each other some sign of inclusion that says: "You're one of my people."

Being with the guys on bowling night as Ned was in a way like going to a gay bar as myself to be with my own kind. That is a lot of the reason why walking into that bowling alley for the first time on men's league night was as jarring to me as walking into a gay bar would be to any one of my bowling buddies. I was in the wrong secret club, that is, until Jim, taking me for an insider, a regular guy, shook my hand for the first time and let me know without needing to say it that I was among friends, that there would be no judgments here, that—if I had a mind to—I could swear and fart and drink my beer and talk about strippers with as much impunity as I can be a raging queer in my local lesbian bar.

Making this removed comforting contact with men and feeling the relief it gave me as my life as a man went on was not a sign of having joined the overclass, for whom superiority is assumed and bucking up unnecessary. It was more like joining a union. It was the counterpart to and the refuge from my excruciating dates, which were often alienating and grating enough to make me wonder whether getting men and women together amicably on a permanent basis wasn't at times like brokering Middle East peace.

I believe we *are* that different in agenda, in expression, in outlook, in nature, so much so that I can't help almost believing, after having been Ned, that we live in parallel worlds, that there is at bottom really no such thing as that mystical unifying creature we call a human being, but only male human beings and female human beings, as separate as sects.

In the end, the biggest surprise in Ned was how powerfully psychological he turned out to be. The key to his success was not in his clothing or his beard or anything else physical that I did to make him seem real. It was in my mental projection of him, a projection that became over time undetectable even to me. People didn't see him with their eyes. They saw him in their mind's eye. They saw what I wanted them to see, at least at first, while I still had control over the image. Then later they saw what they expected to see and what I had become without knowing it: the mind-set of Ned.

I know this to be true because in several situations late in the bowling season, for example, or late in my stay at the monastery, I stopped wearing my beard, my glasses, and even at times my binding, yet no one questioned my disguise. No one stopped seeing Ned. They were just as surprised as everyone else when I finally told them the truth.

Even in the thick of the project when I went out into the world as myself, during the off periods when I was writing or taking a break from full-time Ned, people almost invariably mistook me for a man even when I was wearing a tight white T-shirt without a bra. Yet after I had finished the project, detoxed from Ned for several months and reclaimed my mental femininity, people everywhere addressed me as "ma'am" even in the dead of winter when I was wearing a black watch cap and a man's navy peacoat.

Knowing as I do now that my gendered state of mind could have such a powerful effect on other people's perceptions of me, it is no wonder that that state of mind warped my own perceptions as strongly as it did.

But, of course, getting inside men's heads and out of my own was what this project was all about. Part of the purpose of writing a book like this is to learn something about the infiltrated group and then ideally to put that knowledge to good use. Inevitably then I have to ask myself whether or not my experience as Ned has changed the way I see and interact with men.

Unexpectedly, the answer to that question is both yes and no. Yes, in the sense that I have an inescapable empathy for men that could not help but come of living among them. I know in some sense how it feels to be on their end of things and to receive some of the blows and prejudices the world inflicts on them. I understand them better, of course, than I once did, and I like to think that in my more mindful moments I act on that understanding in helpful ways.

Though such an occasion has not yet arisen since I ended the project, I hope that the next time I see a man in emotional distress I will curb my instinct to smother him with care, unless invited to do so. Instead I hope that I will remember my more intimate moments with Jim and perhaps draw on what I learned from Paul and the guys in the men's group about the respectful space a man often needs around him when he is vulnerable or in tears. It may be possible now to interpret the silences of the men around me as something more than voids or standoffs, and to feel more comfortable being present and available to them without always needing our exchange to be explicit or neatly resolvable in my language.

Often I am merely a witness, processing other people's interactions with more sympathy and insight. But usually I am in no position to intervene. Recently, for example, I saw a man and a young boy sitting at a nearby table in a restaurant. It was a Saturday afternoon and you could tell that this was a father and son having one of their two days a month together per the rules of some barely contested custody agreement. You could also tell that the father was bored, and probably only dragging the kid around because the mother had insisted on it, wanting a day to herself. The father was ignoring the kid, even chatting aimlessly with someone on his cell phone for much of the meal, as if he was just killing time on a street corner waiting for a bus. The boy sat slumped in his seat staring at his eggs and into space with the defeated expression of someone who has grown accustomed to being discounted. Yet you could also see the pain and desperation in his eyes. You could see him registering the effect of yet another nonchalant rejection from the one person whose slightest encouragement would have meant the world. Here was the making and unmaking of yet another fatherless man, whose life and sense of himself would be forever altered by experiences like these. There was nothing I could do except catch the boy's eye and smile apologetically, knowing, of course, that a woman's compassion was useless at times like these.

That same day I saw another father tossing a football back and forth with his young son in the park. On the completion of one pass the father ran after the boy and tackled him lightly on the grass. They both fell laughing to the ground, half wrestling, half embracing. It was the kind of scene I would have thought infuriatingly trite and manipulative in a commercial, but which now seemed newly touching, a passing moment in a boy's life that could make all the difference.

At times like these I see men's lives in a new way, and this is invaluable. But as for the question of whether or not I interact with men differently on a daily basis after having lived as Ned, that is another matter altogether. I thought for certain that I would interact differently. Very differently. That I would not be able to help it. But much to my surprise, I have not found that to be so.

Day-to-day I am very much the way I was: a woman again, living as I must, on my side of the divide between the sexes' parallel worlds. Men are likewise now, as they were before, living on their side of that divide. They are mostly inaccessible to me now, and I think this remoteness has a lot to do with the pervasive psychological component of Ned that both made and broke the project. As Ned wore on I found it increasingly difficult and then impossible to keep my male and female personae intact simultaneously. I have said already that it was like trying to sustain two mutually exclusive ideas in my mind at the same time, and that this cognitive dissonance essentially shut down my brain. To bring myself back from that blackout I had to learn to be my gendered self again and to exclude or even unlearn Ned. I could not live in both worlds at once, so I chose the side to which habit and upbringing have accustomed me, and to which my brain in all likelihood predisposes me.

I say I "chose," but I use this word in only a limited sense, because I am not sure how much meaningful choice we can exercise in these matters. I think I chose to be Ned somewhat the way a gay person can choose to get married. I put on the trappings, adopted the behaviors and even hypnotized myself into the mentality. But by going through the motions of manhood I did not substantively change my bedrock gender identity any more than one can change one's sexual preference by adopting a heterosexual lifestyle. Rather than choosing to become a woman again, it is probably truer to say that I reverted to form. I stopped faking it. I came back to myself, and in doing so I forfeited, as I had to, my insider status in the other camp.

Of course, on some level what a woman wants and needs from manhood is bound to be far different from what a man does, and that must account for a fair amount of my trouble in my male role. But it does not account for all of it. If it did, there would be no men's movement to speak of, or at least not one with the same agenda, an agenda that has not sought to redeem or exonerate the patriarchy, but in many ways to indict it further from the inside out. Something is genuinely out of joint in "manhood," and though perhaps I saw that disjointedness more clearly or felt it more painfully because I was not born into it, there is no denying the very real dysfunction in many men's lives. I saw too many men decrying it or suffering visibly in silence under its influence to chalk it all up to my estrogened perspective.

A lot of men are in pain. That's evident. Too many of them are living emotionally without fathers or subsisting in dire conflict with the fathers they have, and this has injured and even crippled both parties far more than most of them are able to say, which is why so many of us don't know the half of it.

Boys have the sensitivity routinely mocked and shamed and beaten out of them, and the treatment leaves scars for life. Yet we women wonder why, as men, they do not respond to us with more feeling. Actually, we do more than that. We blame and disdain them for their heartlessness. And we aren't the only ones. Men are at the center of their own conflict. They as much as anyone toughen each other in turn and often find no fault in it, since to do so would be to display an emotional facility that most were long ago denied or forbidden to express.

Healing is a vacant word in this context, limp, mealymouthed and reeking of self-pity. It inspires contempt, or it will in the men who need it most. Yet healing is what is called for, especially among men, where it will be hardest to inspire. Men have their shared experience going for them, their brotherhood, the presumption of goodwill that Ned felt in strange men's handshakes. And that's a start. But overcoming all the rest of it, the territorial reflex, the blocked emotional responses and the all-consuming rage, this will take more trusting vulnerability than most men grant to anyone. It will be like bulldozers learning the ballet.

Maybe it will happen. Slowly, fitfully, tentatively. I hope it does. Men haven't had their movement yet. Not really. Not intimately. And they're due for it, as are the women who live with, fight with, take care of and love them.

I, meanwhile, am staying right where I am: fortunate, proud, free and glad in every way to be a woman.

Acknowledgments

I would like to thank my agent, Eric Simonoff, who became a big shot when I wasn't looking, yet still deigned to represent me thereafter. Your patience, counseling and hard work were indispensable. I would also like to thank Viking's publisher, Clare Ferraro, for her vision, generosity and stewardship. I offer a million thanks to my editor, Molly Stern, both for seeing and realizing this book's potential. I offer a million more to my publicist extraordinaire, Carolyn Coleburn, for bucking me up under the weight of Eeyore and all else negative and morose in the media. I am indebted also to Viking Assistant Editor Alessandra Lusardi, whose tireless and mostly thankless hard work behind the scenes has made everything go smoothly. Special thanks are also due Viking's sales and marketing departments for their encouragement, skill and contagious enthusiasm. I bow forever before the brilliant Bruce Nichols for his editorial help and sensitive encouragement in the midst of my worst despair and self-loathing. I send love and gratitude to my dear, dear friend Claire Berlinski for reading everything first and then again and again, being honest, unfailingly supportive and always insightful. I am indebted to Ryan McWilliams for teaching me how to make and maintain a beard. Without you, Ryan, this book truly could not have been written. Thank you Kate Wilson for your expertise and coaching. I am grateful to Gary Mailman for his wise counsel, John Gallagher for his helpful and gracious first reading of the manuscript, to Scott Steimle for his humor, tolerance and friendship, to Donald Moss for helping to slay the demons, to Chris Parks, Laurie Sales and Kurt Uy for being my intrepid partners in crime, to the monks for their hospitality, wisdom and grace, and finally to everyone else who participated in this project unwittingly and shared their reactions, insights and forgiveness so willingly. Finally—though "thanks" doesn't even begin to cover it—I would nonetheless like to thank my parents and my brothers for their love, support, tireless understanding and life-giving belief in who I am. I owe you everything.